Engaging Learners with Comp
Learning Difficulties and Disal

CW00816469

Children and young people with Complex Learning Difficulties and Disabilities (CLDD) have co-existing and overlapping conditions which can manifest in complex learning patterns, extreme behaviours and a range of socio-medical needs which are new and unfamiliar to many educators. Their combination of issues and layered needs – mental health, relationship, behavioural, physical, medical, sensory, communication and cognitive – mean they often disengage from learning and challenge even our most experienced teachers.

This book provides school practitioners and leaders with an approach and resources to engage this often disenfranchized group of children in learning. The Engagement for Learning Framework has been developed and trialled by over 100 educational settings (both special and mainstream) with learners from early years to post-16. It gives practitioners from a range of disciplines a shared means of assessing, recording and developing personalized learning pathways and demonstrating progression for these children. The focus on inquiry means that however complex a young person's needs, educators will be able to apply the approach.

This practical and engaging book provides literature, tools and case study examples outlining who children and young people with CLDD are, why their engagement for learning is important and how the Engagement for Learning Framework can be used effectively by teachers and other professionals to ensure the best possible outcomes for these children.

Barry Carpenter, OBE, is Honorary Professor at the Universities of Worcester (UK), Limerick (Ireland), Hamburg (Germany) and Flinders (Australia).

Jo Egerton is a Schools Research Consultant and educational writer.

Beverley Cockbill is Training Co-ordinator and TEACCH Practitioner in complex learning needs for Chadsgrove Teaching School, Bromsgrove.

Tamara Bloom is a Chartered Educational Psychologist working in both local authority and charity sectors.

Jodie Fotheringham is a Lead Teacher at Tor View Community Special School in Lancashire.

Hollie Rawson is an Occupational Therapist, currently working in mental health rehabilitation.

Jane Thistlethwaite is a Complex Needs Consultant, specializing in autism and sensory/ vision impairment, and Director of Positive Path International in New Zealand.

Engaging Learners with Complex Learning Difficulties and Disabilities

A resource book for teachers
and teaching assistants

Barry Carpenter, Jo Egerton,
Beverley Cockbill, Tamara Bloom,
Jodie Fotheringham, Hollie Rawson
and Jane Thistlethwaite

Routledge
Taylor & Francis Group

LONDON AND NEW YORK

First published 2015
by Routledge
2 Park Square, Milton Park, Abingdon, Oxon OX14 4RN

and by Routledge
711 Third Avenue, New York, NY 10017

Routledge is an imprint of the Taylor & Francis Group, an informa business

© 2015 Barry Carpenter, Jo Egerton, Beverley Cockbill, Tamara Bloom, Jodie Fotheringham, Hollie Rawson and Jane Thistlethwaite

The right of Barry Carpenter, Jo Egerton, Beverley Cockbill, Tamara Bloom, Jodie Fotheringham, Hollie Rawson and Jane Thistlethwaite to be identified as the authors of this work has been asserted by them in accordance with sections 77 and 78 of the Copyright, Designs and Patents Act 1988.

All rights reserved. No part of this book may be reprinted or reproduced or utilised in any form or by any electronic, mechanical, or other means, now known or hereafter invented, including photocopying and recording, or in any information storage or retrieval system, without permission in writing from the publishers.

Trademark notice: Product or corporate names may be trademarks or registered trademarks, and are used only for identification and explanation without intent to infringe.

British Library Cataloguing in Publication Data
A catalogue record for this book is available from the British Library

Library of Congress Cataloging in Publication Data
Carpenter, Barry.
  Engaging learners with complex learning difficulties and disabilities : a resource book for teachers and teaching assistants / Barry Carpenter, Jo Egerton, Beverley Cockbill, Tamara Bloom, Jodie Fotheringham, Hollie Rawson and Jane Thistlethwaite.
    pages cm
  Includes bibliographical references and index.
  1. Learning disabled children—Education—Handbooks, manuals, etc.
  2. Learning disabled children—Education—Handbooks, manuals, etc.
  3. Learning disabilities—Handbooks, manuals, etc.   I. Title.
  LC4704.C37 2015
  371.9—dc23   2014033806

ISBN: 978-0-415-81272-6 (hbk)
ISBN: 978-0-415-81274-0 (pbk)
ISBN: 978-1-315-72535-2 (ebk)

Typeset in Galliard
by Keystroke, Station Road, Codsall, Wolverhampton

Contents

Figures

Tables

Contributors

Tamara Bloom is a Chartered Educational Psychologist working in both local authority and charity sectors, where she supports schools to meet the educational needs of children with a wide range of social, emotional, behavioural and learning difficulties. Tamara holds a Ph.D. in developing an appropriate learning environment for children with profound autism and a Professional Doctorate (D.Ed.Psy.) in which she examined the secondary school experiences of children with autism attending both mainstream and specialist schools. She was also a researcher for the Complex Learning Difficulties and Disabilities (CLDD) Project where her areas of specialism were autism, sensory impairment and pre-term birth. Tamara has lectured on special educational needs within higher education settings and assisted in the development of multi-media training resources for educators working with children with severe, profound and complex learning needs. Tamara has also worked directly with children with severe and CLDD for over ten years.

Barry Carpenter, OBE, is Honorary Professor at the Universities of Worcester (UK), Limerick (Ireland), Hamburg (Germany) and Flinders (Australia). In a career spanning more than 30 years, Barry has held the leadership positions of Academic Director, Chief Executive, Principal, Headteacher, Inspector of Schools and Director of the Centre for Special Education at Westminster College, Oxford. In 2009, he was appointed by the Secretary of State for Education as Director of the Children with Complex Learning Difficulties and Disabilities (CLDD) Research Project. Since completing that research, Barry has overseen the development of a national project developing on-line Training Materials for Teachers of Learners with Severe, Profound and Complex Learning Disabilities, and from 2012–2013 he acted as Lead SEN Consultant to the South Australian Department of Education and Children's Services. The author of over 150 articles on a variety of topics in special educational needs, he won the prestigious Times award for his co-edited book *Enabling Access* (Fulton, 1996). With Jo Egerton and Dr Carolyn Blackburn, he prepared the first British and European text on the education of children with Fetal Alcohol Spectrum Disorder, and subsequently edited *Fetal Alcohol Spectrum Disorders: Interdisciplinary perspectives*. In his role as co-founder of the National Forum for Neuroscience in Special Education, he hosted the first UK conference on the education of children born premature. Barry lectures nationally and internationally. Most recently he has given lectures in Russia, Australia, Germany, Ireland, Turkey and Norway. He has been awarded Fellowships of the Royal Societies of Arts and Medicine, and in 2001 was created OBE by the Queen for services to children with special needs.

Barry has three children – one a teacher, one an occupational therapist and a daughter who has Down's syndrome and now has a home of her own.

Beverley Cockbill is Training Co-ordinator and TEACCH Practitioner in complex learning needs for Chadsgrove Teaching School, Bromsgrove, and has worked in the field of special educational needs for 13 years. In addition to 'School to School' support, Bev is currently supporting care homes for adults on the autistic spectrum using TEACCH approaches and the Complex Learning Difficulties and Disabilities (CLDD) engagement for learning tools. Previously, she worked for SSAT (The Schools Network) Ltd as Training Co-ordinator for complex learning needs and as a Researcher on the Department for Education-funded Complex Learning Difficulties and Disabilities (CLDD) Research Project. In addition, Bev has been an Assistant Teacher and Structured Teaching Advisor/Trainer within a residential school offering 38/42-week education and 52-week care to children aged 6–19 years with severe and complex learning disabilities and autistic spectrum disorder. Bev lectures and delivers training for children with CLDD in schools across the UK and internationally, most recently in Australia and New Zealand. She has published articles, and contributed to the Teaching Agency's 'Training Materials for Teachers of Learners with Severe, Profound and Complex Learning Difficulties'.

Jo Egerton is a Schools Research Consultant and writer. Previously she worked as lead research coach on the Research Charter Mark Award for schools at SSAT (The Schools Network) Ltd. She was lead researcher and co-ordinator on the Department for Education/SSAT's Complex Learning Difficulties and Disabilities (CLDD) Research Project, and Research Consultant on the Teaching Agency project 'Facing the Challenge and Shaping the Future for Primary and Secondary Aged Students with Foetal Alcohol Spectrum Disorders' research project. She was a contributor and editorial team member for the Teaching Agency's 'Training Materials for Teachers of Learners with Severe, Profound and Complex Learning Difficulties' (2011–2012). She has co-authored and co-edited a number of books, most recently *Fetal Alcohol Spectrum Disorders: Interdisciplinary perspectives* (Routledge 2013), *Educating Children and Young People with Fetal Alcohol Spectrum Disorders* and *Creating Meaningful Inquiry in Inclusive Classrooms* (both Routledge 2012). She has presented on special education topics in the UK and internationally. Jo worked in special education and residential care settings for 12 years as a researcher, teacher and key worker. She has a PGCE and a Masters in Learning Disability Studies.

Jodie Fotheringham graduated from the University of Liverpool with a degree in Psychology in 2006 and obtained her teaching qualification in 2012. She began working in Sunfield Residential School as a Psychology Assistant and throughout this time she provided behavioural intervention, psychological and educational assessments and trained extensively in intensive interaction, the TEACCH approach with colleagues from North Carolina, and Sherborne Developmental Movement.

Jodie then began to work in RSA Academy secondary school in Tipton completing educational assessments and working to provide counselling and behavioural interventions throughout the school. She worked extensively as a researcher on the Department for Education-funded Complex Learning Difficulties and Disabilities (CLDD) Research Project. This project allowed Jodie to travel to a large range of educational settings throughout the UK and abroad and complete individual consultancy work for schools on their SEN provisions and behaviour management. After completion of this project Jodie worked for 3 months supporting special schools in New Zealand and Australia. Jodie has presented at several conferences including travelling to Mito, Japan in 2008 and has several publications through the CLDD Project. She also worked on the Teaching Agency's 'Training Materials for Teachers of Learners with Severe, Profound and Complex Learning Difficulties'. She currently works as a Lead Teacher at Tor View Community Special School in Lancashire and leads on curriculum in a unit for young people with Autism and Challenging Behaviours.

Hollie Rawson is an Occupational Therapist, currently working in mental health rehabilitation. She has a varied background in learning disability and special educational needs. She has worked in learning disability support as a respite sessional worker, as a teaching assistant in a school for children and young people with severe and profound autism, and within school family services. With a vested interest in family support through personal experience, Hollie has also been involved in qualitative research projects looking at adult sibling experiences and family support through the transition from education to adult provision, and has published a number of articles and chapters which focus on this. She worked as researcher on the Complex Learning Difficulties and Disabilities (CLDD) Research Project, and contributed to the 'Training Materials for Teachers of Learners with Severe, Profound and Complex Learning Difficulties'. Within her current role, although a move away from education, Hollie is able to build on her Psychology degree and combine her interests of sensory integration, complex needs and collaborative working to support people with mental health problems to develop skills and independence through engagement in meaningful occupations.

Dame Philippa Russell, DBE, is Chair of the Government's Standing Commission on Carers (since 2007) and a member of the Cross-Government Programme Board for the Carers Strategy and of the Ministerial Advisory Group on the Mental Health Strategy. She is a member of the Programme Board for the Think Local, Act Personal Partnership (TLAP) and of the TLAP National Co-Production Advisory Group, representing carers' interests. Philippa was formerly a Commissioner with the Disability Rights Commission and Director of the Council for Disabled Children. She is an Honorary Fellow of the Royal College of Paediatrics and Child Health and of the Royal College of Psychiatrists and a Fellow of the Royal Society of Arts, and, in 1990, she was awarded the Rose Fitzgerald Kennedy Centenary International Award for women who have contributed to the field of learning disability. In 2005, she was awarded the RADAR (Royal Association of Disability and Rehabilitation) Lifetime Achievement Award for the furtherance of the human and civil rights of disabled people. Philippa is the parent of a son with a learning disability and has wide contacts with voluntary and user organizations with an interest in disabled children, young people and their families.

Jane Thistlethwaite is a Complex Needs Consultant, specializing in autism and sensory/vision impairment, and Director of Positive Path International in New Zealand. She brings to her consultancy work her life experience as a vision impaired person, and the first to graduate from a New Zealand teachers' college as such. She is an experienced classroom teacher in special needs, mainstream schools and at tertiary level, and a student and practitioner of both institutional and inclusive education philosophies. Jane contributes to international research on children with Complex Learning Difficulties and Disabilities (CLDD), and was vision impairment advisor to the DfE-funded Complex Learning Difficulties and Disabilities (CLDD) Research Project (2009–2011). She has presented lectures at conferences and universities in the UK, the USA, Australia and New Zealand. Jane regularly provides student and teacher support and education both throughout New Zealand and internationally on student engagement strategies, assessing and developing programmes for learners with autism and sensory problems. Jane has an M.Ed. Special Education Autism (Children) from the University of Birmingham, UK, Postgraduate Diplomas in Education of Students with Vision Impairment, a Bachelor of Education and a Higher Diploma of Teaching.

Sue Williamson is Chief Executive of SSAT (The Schools Network) Ltd. Sue's early career began with various posts at Rounds Manor School in Northamptonshire, Sponne School in Towcester and Herschel Grammar School in Slough before becoming headteacher of Monks' Dyke School in Lincolnshire. Under her headship, examination results went from 15 per cent to 56 per cent GCSEs 5 A*–C. Sue joined SSAT in 2002 as Director of Affiliation with responsibility for membership, innovation and the national conference. She developed SSAT's suite of leadership programmes working with outstanding headteachers. She later worked with Professor David Hargreaves on the personalizing learning agenda, and introduced iNet, working with schools in Australia, China, Mauritius, the Netherlands, Northern Ireland, Wales and the USA. She became Chief Executive in November 2011.

Foreword

Dame Philippa Russell

I was delighted to have been invited to write the Foreword to *Engaging Learners with Complex Learning Difficulties and Disabilities*. The past decade has seen a welcome and growing awareness of the increasing numbers of children in our schools (and pre-school facilities) who have complex and multiple difficulties. These children challenge schools, families and the wide range of community services which they may hope to access. Many lack an immediately comprehensible diagnosis, and families and schools can be bewildered by these children who do not fit neatly into an understandable category. Most importantly, the children and young people present challenges to themselves! As my grandson, Dylan, now age seven, said to me the other day, after a difficult day at school with an autistic spectrum disorder: 'It's very difficult to be me sometimes because I don't really understand myself. I don't always know who I really am!'

The number of children who need help understanding themselves and 'don't know who they really are' (together with the families and schools who struggle to support them) is growing. We have a generation of what the Nuffield Council on Bioethics (2006) describes as 'the new survivors', that is to say children who are triumphs of new technology but whose lives once back home in the community are frequently subject to disappointment and challenges.

Twenty-first century education (like its health and social care counterparts) is increasingly described as 'personalised and person-centred'. The personalization agenda acknowledges the importance of whole school systems – and whole family support – but also acknowledges the growing number of children who do not fit into convenient categories of need and who require a differentiated approach in order to succeed. As David Hargreaves writes:

> If students are to engage in deeper learning, they will need new forms of enriched support.
>
> (Hargreaves 2006: 8)

> Personalised learning demands that schools transform their responses to the learner from the largely standardised to the profoundly personalised.
>
> (Hargreaves, in Carpenter 2010: 5)

This book offers that rich resource not only to teachers but to the 'whole schools', 'whole families' and 'whole communities' within which children and young people can grow and hopefully flourish. I am particularly pleased to see that we are also offered practical guidance and resources around mental health. There is a lively debate about '*health and well-being'* across all public services, but the broader parameters of children's own health and *emotional* well-being and their capacity to learn has been less well explored in the context of special educational needs and disability. As one teacher – a SENCO in a primary school – said to me the other day:

> We have to ask ourselves, 'For what are we educating these challenging children?'. Do we just want to make them fit in and not disrupt the other children's learning? Do we see them as purely educational problems, or as citizens of the future? Do we care about them and their families as they get older and all too often the rejection begins?

The answer is of course as challenging as the question itself. As Professor Michael Rutter has commented, we also have the bigger challenge of ensuring against the odds that these children will develop into competent, confident and caring citizens. Therefore we need to understand how these children learn, and to work collaboratively across schools, families and a wide range of professionals in order to enable the children themselves to be resilient in managing the complexities of their everyday lives. As Professor Rutter (1985: 607) writes: 'Resilience seems to involve several related elements. Firstly a sense of self-esteem and confidence; secondly, a belief in one's own self-efficacy and ability to deal with change and adaptation and thirdly a repertoire of social problem solving approaches.'

Reflecting on how we develop a repertoire of problem solving techniques, Liz Barraclough writes about her experience of being a parent to Eleanor (a young lady with very complex needs). Eleanor's story, like the stories of a group of other children whose parents have become 'family leaders', reminds us of the importance of families as 'co-producers' of good outcomes for children with complex learning difficulties. Liz describes how she:

> discovered that if you take a chance, you will find allies in some very unexpected places. In the 21st century, parenting can be a very isolated job but it does not have to be. The proverb 'it takes a village to raise a child' is never truer than when your child is disabled. People around you feel helpless when you have that initial diagnosis. You need to find ways of giving them the chance to help.
>
> (Barraclough and Sanderson 2014: 3–4)

Liz and her daughter Eleanor found what she called 'creative solutions', stressing the importance of: 'A welcoming and "can do" ethos at the school and an emphasis on maximising individual achievements what every level they might be' (ibid.: 5).

But a welcoming and 'can do' ethos requires a positive and confident school and, as Liz quickly discovered, we need to develop a 'whole school team – including families' to ensure that children like Eleanor get the education they deserve – and that schools feel confident that they have the repertoire of skills necessary to make this happen.

Not only does this book offer a wide repertoire of problem solving approaches for working with children within and outside educational settings, it similarly supports and reinforces the abilities of schools in partnership with families and others to make children like my grandson Dylan intelligible to himself and thereby to succeed. The report of the Nuffield Council on Bioethics (2006: 4) talks about 'partnerships of care', with all relevant professionals, parents and services working in the 'best interests' of the child. The new SEN and Disability Code of Practice reinforces the principles of partnership and integration with similar ambitions for all children to achieve 'happy and fulfilled lives . . . through an increased focus on life outcomes' (Department for Education/Department of Health 2014: 11). This book picks up that challenge of better outcomes and happy and fulfilled lives on behalf of Dylan, of Eleanor and of all the other children for whom education should be 'the springboard to life'.

Dame Philippa Russell, DBE
Chair, Standing Commission on Carers, UK

References

Barraclough, L. and Sanderson, H. (2014) *Eleanor's Story: One of a series of stories from family leaders who have used person centred planning*, Stockport: Helen Sanderson Associates.

Carpenter, B. (2010) *Children with Complex Learning Difficulties and Disabilities: Who are they and how do we teach them*, London: SSAT.

Department for Education/Department of Health (2014) *Special Educational Needs and Disability Code of Practice: 0 to 25 years*, London: Department for Education.

Hargreaves, D. (2006) *A New Shape for Schooling?*, London: SSAT.

Nuffield Council on Bioethics (2006) *Critical Care Decisions in Fetal and Neonatal Medicine: Ethical issues*, London: Nuffield Council on Bioethics.

Rutter, M. (1985) 'Resilience in the face of adversity: protective factors and resistance to psychiatric disorder', *British Journal of Psychiatry*, 147: 598–611.

Preface

Sue Williamson

The children with Complex Learning Difficulties and Disabilities (CLDD) Project is a ground-breaking and inspirational piece of research that is totally integrated with practice. The population of children with complex learning difficulties is increasing in special and mainstream schools, and teachers need to develop the pedagogical skills to meet the learning needs of these children. Professor Barry Carpenter, then Academic Director at SSAT, who is that rare combination of academic and practitioner, led the CLDD Project. A dedicated research team and a network of multidisciplinary experts from health, psychology, therapies and neuroscience supported him.

The CLDD Project is at the heart of SSAT's work – we believe that every child can succeed and that children need to be fully engaged in their learning. SSAT is also committed to the development of the teaching profession. The CLDD Project recognised that teachers need the pedagogical tools to teach children with complex learning needs as new challenges emerge. SSAT has always had a network of special schools and recognised their importance in the system. SSAT shares Professor Carpenter's view that their role should be 'ground-breaking, innovative and creative'.

The CLDD Project highlighted four key themes:

- the importance of dialogue with neuroscience;
- the value of transdisciplinary approaches;
- student engagement in the context of personalised learning; and
- partnership with families.

All four themes emphasise the need for teachers to update their knowledge and skills, as well as to work with all stakeholders. Special schools and their staff have an opportunity to train and develop professionals from mainstream schools and share their experiences of how children with different complex learning needs learn. The CLDD Project has generated guidance and resources which support the remodelling of pedagogy.

The CLDD Project identified the key features now enshrined in the revised SEN Code of Practice and the Children's and Families Act 2014: integrated work across a range of professions that promotes choice and diversity for children and young people with disability as well as their families.

SSAT is proud to be associated with this innovative research that provides tangible and specific approaches for schools, teachers and other professions to support our most vulnerable students.

Acknowledgements

The authors would like to extend heartfelt gratitude to all the children and adults who have contributed to the Complex Learning Difficulties and Disabilities (CLDD) Research Project, both 2009–2011 (listed in Appendix I) and since, including the Department for Education/Department for Children, Schools and Families for their support of the project (2009–2011). Other schools contributing to this book are listed in the text. We wish it was possible to name everyone, and we hope those whom we have not been able to name will also accept our thanks, if anonymously. Additional thanks to all those who contributed in many different ways to the case studies within this book.

Major thanks go to: the children, young people and families involved for their invaluable contributions, without which the project would not have been possible; the school headteachers and educators in (alphabetically) Australia, England, Ireland, New Zealand, Northern Ireland, Scotland, USA and Wales who have given their time, energy, support and insight into their practice. Also to Dr Carolyn Blackburn, Early Childhood Lecturer and Educational Researcher, Birmingham City University, for her contribution in capturing Early Years practice; David Braybrook, for his work on Quality Assurance; Lorraine Petersen (Educational Consultant, then CEO of nasen) as Chair of the Project Steering Board. And also to Dr Phyllis Jones, Associate Professor, University of South Florida (USA); Jane Thistlethwaite, Sensory Impairment Advisor/Director of Positive Path International (New Zealand); Dr Barry Coughlan, Clinical Psychologist, University of Limerick (Ireland); and Professor Michael Brown, Edinburgh Napier University (Scotland) for their work in the international partner schools.

The project benefited enormously from the professional wisdom of all members of the Project Advisory Group (alphabetically): Dr Carolyn Blackburn; Professor Michael Brown; David Braybrook, Independent Educational Consultant; Dr Patricia Champion, founder of The Champion Early Intervention Centre, New Zealand; Dr Barry Coughlan; Ann Fergusson, Senior Lecturer, University of Northampton; Anne Fowlie, Independent Educational Consultant; Paul Hutchins, Consultant Paediatrician, The Children's Hospital, Sydney, Australia; Dr Phyllis Jones; Jane Thistlethwaite.

For valued advice on and contributions to specific CLDD resources, we would like to thank: Dr Carolyn Blackburn; Dr Patricia Champion, Teresa Owen, Chadsgrove School, Bromsgrove; Dr Rona Tutt, National Association of Headteachers; Lynne Peters, Dyscovery Centre, University of Wales; Lindsey Rousseau, National Sensory Impairment Partnership; Paul Simpson, British Association of Teachers for the Deaf; and Gavin Filmer, Graphic Designer.

We would like to thank the CLDD Project Steering Board for their strategic advice, including Lorraine Petersen (Chair) and members (alphabetically): Rosemary Adams, Headteacher, Baskerville School, Birmingham; Hardip Begol, Department for Education; David Braybrook; Lesley Campbell, Mencap; Janet Dunn, Headteacher, Meath School (I CAN), Ottershaw; Susan Fleisher, CEO, National Organisation on Fetal Alcohol Syndrome UK (NOFAS-UK); Sharon Godden, parent; Melissa Hancock, Youth Sport Trust; Professor Amanda Kirby, The Dyscovery Centre, University of Wales; Dr Jane McCarthy, Consultant Psychiatrist, Estia; Michele Moore, formerly of the Teaching Agency; Helen Norris, Head of Specialist Support and Disability Services, Bromley; Christine Osborne, Independent Consultant/former advisor at the Children's Society; Dr Melanie Peter, Anglia Ruskin University; Dr Matthew Rayner, Headteacher, Stephen Hawking School, London; Dame Philippa Russell, Chair, Government's Standing Commission on Carers; Phil Snell, Department for Education; David Stewart, Headteacher, Oak Field School and Specialist Sports College, Nottingham; Janet Thompson HMI, Ofsted; Dr Rona Tutt.

We would also like to acknowledge the partnership and support of Hardip Begol and Phil Snell, Department for Education; Sue Williamson, CEO of SSAT (The Schools Network) Ltd; and also Ben Pearson, Pauline Holbrook and Wendy Skyte, all formerly of SSAT, during the CLDD Research Project; Ann Fergusson and the University of Northampton for their support in gaining research and ethics approval; David Behan, Director-General, and the Department of Health representatives, who interacted with the project in its formative stages.

Finally we would like to thank Alison Foyle and Sarah Tuckwell at Routledge Education, whose support and patience in the writing of books has to be unsurpassed!

Chapter 1

The Engagement for Learning Framework

An introduction

We are guilty of many errors and many faults, but our worst crime is abandoning the children, neglecting the fountain of life. Many of the things we need can wait. The child cannot. Right now is the time his bones are being formed, his blood is being made, and his senses are being developed. To him we cannot answer 'Tomorrow', his name is today.

> (Gabriela Mistral, 1889–1957; Chilean poet, educator, diplomat, and feminist; winner of the Nobel Prize in Literature, 1945)

The approach to engaging children and young people with complex learning needs described in this book emerged through the Department for Education[1]-funded Complex Learning Difficulties and Disabilities (CLDD) Research Project (Carpenter et al. 2011) following Salt Review recommendations (Department for Children, Schools and Families (DCSF) 2010).

The Engagement for Learning Framework is a resource for educators – all professionals who support children's education including teachers, teaching assistants and therapists. It enables them to explore and identify effective teaching and learning strategies for children with CLDD, as well as to record, measure and demonstrate learning outcomes in a meaningful way.

The impetus for the project emerged from teachers. The Department for Education (DfE)/Department for Children, Schools and Families (DCSF) listened to their repeated concerns about a new generation of children with learning difficulties whose complex learning needs they felt poorly equipped to manage. To address this issue, they commissioned under tender the then Specialist Schools and Academies Trust,[2] a schools networking organization, to investigate ways to improve learning outcomes for this group of children through developing evidence-based pathways to personalized learning.

These children with CLDD now coming through the school system are not only those who are traditionally considered to have the most complex needs, such as children in special schools at the profound end of the learning disability spectrum, but also a new population of children in mainstream schools whose difficulties were not being acknowledged or recognized. Chapter 2 describes this new population, which includes children whose needs challenge the creativity and resourcefulness of even the most experienced and talented teachers. As one teacher commented: 'I find it really hard, because I've never taught a child like this ever, not in mainstream settings, not here. We've tried everything. Nothing works consistently' (Teacher Interview, CLDD Project (Blackburn and Carpenter 2012: 41)).

These children's difficulties may arise from premature birth, advanced medical interventions in infancy, parental substance and alcohol abuse (e.g. Fetal Alcohol Spectrum Disorders (FASD)), or rare chromosomal disorders, for example. The group also includes children who have co-existing and co-occurring diagnoses, such as dyslexia and attention deficit hyperactivity disorder (ADHD), tuberous sclerosis and autistic spectrum disorders (ASD). Some children have compounding conditions such as sensory perceptual issues or mental health problems which exacerbate the difficulties of their primary diagnosis, and some require regular invasive procedures, such as supported nutrition, assisted ventilation and rescue medication.

The research

To address the needs of this group of children, Professor Barry Carpenter convened a core research team, as well as practitioner researchers – teachers, teaching assistants, therapists and psychologists – from 96 schools, and over 200 children as participants. They were supported by a multidisciplinary team of researchers and advisors with specialisms across education, health, psychology, therapies and neuroscience.

In Phase 1 of the project (November to July 2010), the research team worked together with 12 special schools and staff, 60 children, and their families, to develop an effective teaching and learning resource for the children with complex needs in their classrooms. Each of the schools was designated good or outstanding, and held Government-recognized special educational needs (SEN) specialisms in 'cognition and learning', 'communication and interaction', 'emotional and behavioural difficulties' and/or 'physical disabilities'.

The project built on and synthesized existing national and international expertise in the field, as well as drawing upon practitioner experience to develop and trial modified and new approaches for these children. Between September and December 2010, the resources were trialled in 50 further special schools in the UK and 15 internationally (five in New Zealand; one each in Wales and Northern Ireland; and two each in Australia, Ireland, Scotland and the USA). In Phase 3 of the project (January to March 2011), the resources were trialled in 12 mainstream schools – six primary and six secondary – and two early years settings.[3] There was also a transition group of six schools.

The Engagement for Learning Framework

The outcome of the project was the CLDD Engagement for Learning Framework – developed with schools and for schools to support educators of children with CLDD. The key components (available to download online at http://complexld.ssatrust.org.uk) include:

- CLDD Briefing Packs: a series of information sheets on conditions which commonly co-exist within the profile of CLDD; these give information on effective educational strategies associated with particular disabilities.
- The Engagement Profile and Scale: an observation and assessment resource focusing on children's engagement for learning.
- The Inquiry Framework for Learning: a framework of starter questions towards learning solutions in 12 areas including communication, emotional well-being, motor skills, etc.

The engagement for learning ethos

Attention, or engagement, is the most important predictor of successful learning outcomes for a child, even above IQ (Wolke 2013). Multiple studies over several decades have clearly demonstrated that without engagement there is no meaningful learning (see Chapter 3).

It is important to emphasize here that we are talking about engagement *for learning*. The engagement for learning tools support educational outcomes. This book is not about giving children what they like to 'keep them quiet', but about how educators can work with children to construct the 'learning readiness' that has eluded them. It is about making knowledge, understanding and skills desirable to them so that they thirst to learn, and become engaged *learners*. Ultimately, it is about extending their post-school life chances.

Educators often think about children's engagement in learning as though it is a quality over which they have no control – as if learners are either engaged or not engaged through their own inclination or disinclination. However, the reality is much more complex, and children's engagement in learning is very much in the gift of educators, as described in Chapters 4 and 5.

Engagement can be understood as an 'umbrella' which covers a group of related ideas. To be able to direct children's engagement for learning, educators need to break engagement down into manageable components that allow them to focus on, engineer and develop different aspects of learning. The Engagement Profile and Scale use seven 'indicators' of engagement for learning (see Figure 1.1).

When educators commit to these indicators in facilitating and adjusting children's learning experiences, the outcomes can be transformative. Chapter 3 looks at such outcomes for children from the CLDD Project.[4]

Even the most hard-to-reach learners have some interest, whether at school or outside, that captures their attention. As educators, we often know a lot about what children cannot

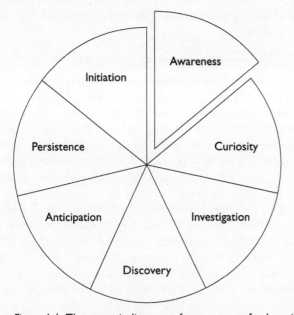

Figure 1.1 The seven indicators of engagement for learning

do, but very little about what they can, and do, do. For children with complex learning needs it is crucial that educators have a grasp of what engages their interest and why, and explore how this can be used to increase the learning impact of what educators deliver each day in the classroom. Other children may be prevented from engaging by distractions in their environment, and will need reasonable adjustments made to this and to educator's expectations to enable them to learn.

Multiple perspectives

Children with CLDD often have learning needs beyond the experience not only of educators but also the resources they are using. The educators who took part in the CLDD Project had often reached the edge of their considerable experience in trying to engage these children with unique learning needs. Meeting their needs required a shift in perspective that would take both learner and educator beyond the straightforward learner-learning task relationship. Chapters 6 to 8 introduce these processes.

Chapters 6 and 7 again focus on deepening perspectives to engage complex learners, but this time emphasizing the immeasurable gains brought by talking with families, and through multi- and trans-disciplinary discussions and practice.

Families – whether this is a birth or other relationship – have insights that we as educators cannot have. Parents have often researched their child's condition from a very young age, have been the constant presence through illness, hospital appointments or justice system involvement, and have out-of-school insights into what engages their son or daughter. Siblings have yet other perspectives on their brother's or sister's interests, responses and talents which may provide the missing key to successful learning experiences. Chapter 6 describes the inside view from families on their son's/daughter's complex learning needs, their impact, their ideas and their hopes. This family-focused approach has influenced the Government Green Paper on SEN, *Support and Aspirations* (DfE 2011), and the family-centred approach advocated in the new Code of Practice (DfE 2014), moving us on from the traditional parent partnership models.

Chapter 7 looks at the impact that colleagues from other disciplines had on the learning experiences of children involved in the CLDD Project. Occupational therapists, speech therapists and music therapists collaborated with teachers to orchestrate massive steps forward in children's engagement that were not seen when each worked individually. Even minor adjustments to children's learning environments made in consultation with occupational therapists, for example, meant that children who had not been able to do so previously were able to focus on learning or to communicate effectively with their educators and peers. Using the Engagement for Learning Framework, professionals from multiple professional backgrounds are able to share a common language which transcends their disciplinary boundaries and supports a collaborative focus on learner need. In so doing, they have opened up pathways to achievement, attainment and progress for children with CLDD.

In Chapter 8, the impact of emotional well-being and mental health problems on children's engagement is discussed. Among the children who took part in the CLDD Project, mental health difficulties or problems had the highest incidence of any of the other co-occurring, co-existing or compounding conditions. They had a massive impact on children's ability to engage in learning, but often were not being addressed through lack of school or regional resources. These issues must be addressed in order that children can learn (Dossetor et al. 2011).

For children whose learning pathways cannot be accommodated within educational approaches that often prescribe our teaching, educators need to move beyond the familiar and routine. Chapter 9 considers how schools can take engagement for learning initiatives forward using inquiry approaches, and, in Chapter 10, the schools themselves describe the processes and practicalities of implementing the Engagement for Learning Framework.

To meet the needs of this new generation of children with CLDD in this twenty-first century, schools are developing, as one headteacher described, a 'finding out culture'. Educators are beginning to see themselves as innovators, opening new lines of inquiry and following new leads into learning for children. The engagement for learning approach offers the resources to construct personalized learning pathways, the flexibility to adjust and optimize them, and an effective means to evidence children's progress. It has provided many educators, children and their families, both in special and mainstream education, with a way forward. As one CLDD Project mainstream teacher stated: 'Instead of failing all the time, [these children] can succeed.'

Notes

1 Previously Department for Children, Schools and Families (DCSF)-funded.
2 Now SSAT (The Schools Network) Ltd, London.
3 The project methods are described in greater detail at http://complexld.ssatrust.org.uk.
4 All children's names in this book, unless agreed otherwise, are pseudonyms to protect their identities.

References

Blackburn, C. and Carpenter, B. (2012) 'Engaging young children with complex learning difficulties and disabilities in early years settings', *Early Years Educator*, 14(2): 39–44.
Carpenter, B., Egerton, J., Brooks, T., Cockbill, B., Fotheringham, J. and Rawson, H. (2011) 'The complex learning difficulties and disabilities research project: developing meaningful pathways to personalised learning' (project report), London: SSAT.
DCSF (Department for Children, Schools and Families) (2010) *Salt Review: Independent review of teacher supply for pupils with severe, profound and multiple learning difficulties (SLD and PMLD)*, Annesley: DCSF Publications.
DfE (Department for Education) (2011) *Support and Aspiration: A new approach to special educational needs and disability*, London: DfE.
DfE (Department for Education) (2014) *Special Educational Needs (SEN) Code of Practice for 0 to 25 years: Statutory guidance for organisations which work with and support children and young people with special educational needs or disabilities*, London: DfE.
Dossetor, D., White D. and Whatson, L. (eds) (2011) *Mental Health of Children and Adolescents with Intellectual and Developmental Disabilities: A framework for professional practice*, Melbourne: IP Communications.
Wolke, D. (2013) 'The preterm phenotype: implications for learning'. Presentation to the National Forum for Neuroscience in Special Education Annual Conference, 'The learning and neurodevelopmental needs of children born pre-term – a conference to bridge thinking and understanding between education and neuroscience across the school years', Institute of Education, London (31 January).

Chapter 2

New generation children
The complex learning challenge

Many major educational initiatives in recent years have been committed to raising the quality of learning opportunities for all children in this twenty-first century. Indeed, the transformation agenda seeks to ensure that every child is a learner. However, often such exhortations fail to include those children whose educational opportunities may be limited or disadvantaged due to a disability which gives rise to difficulties in learning. Equality of educational opportunity, based on a child's rights as a citizen in their society, is a fundamental principle (Equality Act 2010; UN Convention on the Rights of Persons with Disabilities, article 24) if we are to fulfill their entitlement to a high-quality education that is rich with personalization, choice, diversity and technological opportunity.

In the twenty-first century, children with CLDD are presenting with new profiles of learning needs that the teaching profession struggle to meet through existing teaching styles or curriculum frameworks. We need to be honest about this – for the sake of our professional practice, and, even more so, for the sake of the children. As it stands, we are 'pedagogically bereft' (Carpenter 2011). This is not through professional negligence, but, as society has improved both in its medical skill and moral code, a 'new generation' of children with CLDD has emerged, whose brain functioning is different to that which educators of children with disabilities have previously known (Goswami 2008a).

This is a phenomenon facing many countries – it is a global challenge. For and with these children, we must navigate their routes to learning. With the tools of personalization (Hargreaves 2006), we must innovate a responsive pedagogy: one that will transform the life chances of children who otherwise will become disenfranchised from the universal education system, and will be ill-equipped to enjoy active citizenship in twenty-first-century society.

The global challenge

Children with CLDD are a global challenge requiring global resolution. Dr Michael Guralnick (2005a,b), President of the International Society on Early Intervention, has set out the scale of the challenge facing educationalists: 'Worldwide, 780 million young children are affected by biological, environmental and psychosocial conditions that can limit their cognitive development' (Guralnick 2005b: 313).

Professionals in all phases of the education system need to listen to colleagues working with young children in early childhood education. They are the first to identify shifts in the child population and can alert other sectors to prepare themselves for the necessary changes in curriculum and pedagogy.

It is only through an international sharing of our global wisdom, knowledge and understanding that we have any likelihood of evolving a framework of education that is meaningful and relevant, and that can truly address the significant learning needs of these children. For the very best of current research and practice in relation to various 'new' and emerging complex disabilities, we can turn to different countries as well as our own for guidance and inspiration: as well as to Marlow et al. (2005) and Johnson et al. (2011) in the UK, we can also turn to New Zealand (e.g. Champion 2005; Woodward et al. 2004) on prematurely born children; to Scotland (e.g. Brown 2009) on the medical management/ education delivery interface of these children; to Australia (e.g. Dossetor et al. 2011), Austria (e.g. Pretis and Dimova 2008) and Ireland (e.g. Coughlan 2007), as well as to Rae (2013) and Rose et al. (2009) in the UK on the burgeoning mental health problems plaguing adolescents in many developed countries (e.g. Australia, UK, Japan); to North America on chromosomal abnormalities such as fragile-X syndrome (e.g. Bailey and Skinner 2007; Bailey et al. 2000, 2008); to Australia (e.g. Elliott 2013; Elliott et al. 2012; O'Leary et al. 2007; Peadon et al. 2008) on the dramatic immediate and long-term effects of alcohol, and other drugs, on the learning brain; to Canada (e.g. Conry 1996) on educational provision for children with Fetal Alcohol Spectrum Disorders (FASD).

The challenge of poverty

There is, of course, the ongoing and almost intangible challenge of poverty. Blackburn et al. (2010) reported that there were now 950,000 families in the UK with a disabled child, and suggested that this may be an underestimate of 250,000. Blackburn attributed the increase in numbers from 700,000 in 2005 (McCluskey and McNamara 2005) in part to: 'not simply an accident of birth, but a confluence of intergenerational poverty and modern medical progress' (Ramesh 2010).

In itself, poverty can so limit a child's life chances that it impairs their developmental progress to the extent that they find themselves 'disabled'. Northern (2004) reported words from the World Health Organization: 'Poverty, violence and stress will condemn an increasing number of children and young people to life with a troubled mind.'

This is a perpetual challenge that we, as a global community of educators, must seek to fight. Let us not forget the liberation from the shackles of poverty that education can bring. For, while we must acknowledge the devastating impact of poverty, we must work in the hope that we can, through education, deliver some children from the bleakness of that existence.

For almost 40 years in the USA, the Head Start programme has served disadvantaged children in low-income families throughout the nation, with the overt goal of increasing children's readiness for school. The programme has been critically examined over those 40 years. Despite mixed reviews, often dependent on the political and economic climate, the latest longitudinal analysis by Barnett and Hustedt (2005) indicates generally positive evidence regarding Head Start's long-term benefits. Every $1 spent on children in the early years saved the state $7 later by reducing the intervention necessary on crime, welfare, mental health and job prospects.

The Head Start programme in the USA was the inspiration for our Sure Start programme in the UK. Similar universal childcare programmes helped the Nordic nations abolish child poverty by catching potential problems early. Within the Head Start programme, Webster-Stratton and Reid (2004) reported their work into early childhood conduct disorders.

Their sample of socio-economically disadvantaged preschoolers were at higher risk of developing oppositional behaviour disorders and attentional hyperactivity disorders, as well as experiencing language and learning delays.

Their programme has developed a range of interventions targeted at training teachers and parents to enhance children's social competences, reduce aggression and strengthen early literacy. In so doing, they aim to prevent some of the secondary risk factors such as school failure, peer rejection and conduct disorders. There is a particular emphasis on 'emotional literacy' and helping children to learn words to express their feelings and understand other people's feelings. Such skills as effective problem-solving, anger management, making and keeping friends, and communicating with others are taught during 'circle time' using child-sized puppets.

What is the potential for culturally sensitive, universal application of such programmes? This is just one example of how, as a global educational community, we could pool our resources for the common good.

Vulnerable children

Later in this chapter, a definition of CLDD will be given, but these children are not a homogenous group. In reflecting on this child population and associating them with teaching approaches and curriculum concepts widely employed in the special needs sector (Carpenter et al. 2002), we are left with a sense of an overriding, unifying factor across these children – their 'vulnerability'. This vulnerability is manifested in complex learning patterns, extreme behaviour difficulties and a range of socio-medical needs which are new and unfamiliar to many schools.

There are children in our twenty-first-century society whose causal base of CLDD emanates from some new medical or social phenomena – for example: assisted conception or premature birth; maternal drug or alcohol abuse during pregnancy; or medical advances. However, research shows that not only do biomedical and psychological factors give rise to CLDD, but also the interwoven experiences of poverty and educational disadvantage (Hirsch 2007) (see Figure 2.1).

Children can fall anywhere on the continuum of vulnerability due to disadvantage, economic or social deprivation or disability. Indeed, some children will find themselves disabled, living in situations of extreme social deprivation, and thus hugely disadvantaged

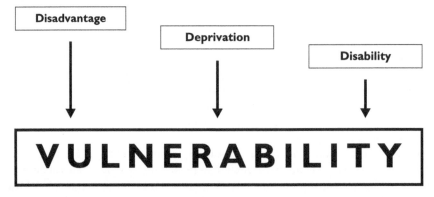

Figure 2.1 The continuum of vulnerability

compared to their peers in their own or other countries. Poverty can increase the risk of a child having impairment; indeed, it is a sad fact that in the developing world, iodine deficiency is the greatest cause of intellectual disability (Fujiura 2004). Poverty can create a life of risk for a child whereby they face on a daily basis physical illness, abuse, malnourishment or emotional starvation. Thus 'the challenge to our *global* society is to loosen and break the stranglehold of poverty on the development of our children' (Mittler 2000: 47 [my italics]).

While education may not be able to overturn poverty in our societies, it can build resilient children. Pretis and Dimova (2008: 154) describe 'resilience mechanisms' as those that have a 'general protecting or buffering effect between the child and their circumstances'. Many international studies (Bong and Skaalvik 2003; Mittler 1995) have shown that where a child experienced educational success, their self-efficacy was raised, enabling them to develop a level of emotional resilience which, in turn, raised their opportunities in life. This is at the heart of educational transformation; the capacity to transform a child's life for the better.

Towards defining CLDD

As a first step towards focusing our collective energies on resolving unmet need, both in our children and in our special-educational-needs-teaching workforce, we need to shape a definition of CLDD. This term has become widely used in education, and is the current focus of initiatives by major UK Government agencies such as the Office for Standards in Education (Ofsted) (Visser 2009). Generally, it is used to refer to that group of 'new learners' in our schools, but it is a loose, unfocused and all-embracing term. A helpful starting point is Porter and Ashdown's description (2002: 5):

> This is a wide and varied group of learners. They include children who do not simply require a differentiated curriculum or teaching at a slower pace, but who, at times, require further adaptation to teaching if they are to make progress.

A less accessible, but nevertheless indicative, definition of people with complex needs is that given by Dee et al. (2002: 4) who note: 'a complex aggregation of difficulties in more than one area of [their] lives.'

There is a range of words used in the literature, all of which indicate that when describing children with CLDD, we mean those children in whom two or more disabling conditions 'co-exist' (Visser 2009), 'overlap' (Dittrich and Tutt 2008) or 'co-occur' (Rose et al. 2009). The medical field would use the term, 'co-morbidity' to describe this phenomenon. In practice, this could mean children with Down's syndrome and mental health needs, with Noonan's syndrome and physical disability, with cerebral palsy and vision/hearing impairments (due to premature birth) or with ASD and ADHD.

The latter combination is an ideal example of a further dilemma facing teachers. Where two (or more) conditions do co-exist in one child, the styles of teaching intervention recommended to support the child's learning may not always be totally compatible. Have we truly thought through the resolution of the pedagogical demands of, for example, ASD and ADHD when working with the child? There are powerful literature bases and clear guidance on how to educate a child with either of these disabilities, but how does that look when the conditions co-exist? What is the pedagogical interface? Are there tensions?

Which aspects of which approach take precedence? What are the criteria to inform our professional judgements in resolving such issues?

What is clear, particularly in relation to the group of learners we describe as having 'complex needs', is that 'we must together seek to build an inclusive curriculum . . . around adaptation, modification and design . . . that will be relevant to all learners' (Carpenter et al. 2002: 2). Through the work of the DfE/DCSF-funded project on CLDD, the SSAT research team (cf. Carpenter et al. 2011) developed, through a series of school-focused trials, a definition of CLDD:

> Children and young people with Complex Learning Difficulties and Disabilities (CLDD) have conditions that co-exist. These conditions overlap and interlock creating a complex profile. The co-occurring and compounding nature of complex learning difficulties requires a personalized learning pathway that recognizes children and young people's unique and changing learning patterns. Children and young people with CLDD present with a range of issues and combination of layered needs; for example, mental health, relationship, behavioural, physical, medical, sensory, communication and cognitive. They need informed specific support and strategies which may include transdisciplinary input to engage effectively in the learning process and to participate actively in classroom activities and the wider community. Their attainments may be inconsistent, presenting an atypical or uneven profile. In the school setting, learners may be working at any educational level, including the National Curriculum and P scales. This specifically applies to England but might be relevant to the curriculum context of other countries.
>
> (Carpenter et al. 2011: 23)

The contribution of the international school community

Such is the complicated challenge of resolving the many concerns surrounding children with CLDD that it has become an international issue. The joint contributions of all countries will bring us closer to a deep and enriched understanding of how we resolve unmet need in this group of children. In considering who these children are and what their numbers are, we can already chart a pattern of international knowledge and understanding that can be maximized and utilized to develop practice that is evidence-based, inquiry-focused and research informed (see Figure 2.2).

Very premature and low-birth-weight births

The EPICure study suggests that 80 per cent of children born at less than 26 weeks gestation now survive due to medical advances, with 69 per cent having learning disabilities (Marlow et al. 2005). This may account in part for the increasing prevalence of children with disabilities noted above (Blackburn et al. 2010; Ramesh 2010; Wolke 2011).

The need for intensive, very early intervention with these children is crucial (as documented by a trans-European study (Soriano 2005)). However, again, do we actually have the intervention strategies that will truly maximize the learning of these vulnerable infants and minimize the impact of their traumatic birth and subsequent fragile health status? Champion (2005) details the brain development of these very-low-birth-weight, pre-term infants and the neurological compromise they face. A Scottish study has shown that many

Figure 2.2 The practice-to-research spiral

Source: Adapted from Carpenter 2012

will have complex health needs, requiring invasive procedures such as supported nutrition, assisted ventilation and rescue medication for complex epilepsy (Brown 2009). Developing countries (e.g. Malaysia) are also reporting an emergence of technologically dependent children as their support for prematurely born infants improves.

Where these children have severe and complex disabilities (and the EPICure study (Wood et al. 2000) suggest this is so far in excess of 50 per cent of surviving infants born extremely pre-term, before 24 weeks gestation), their patterns of learning may be different from those we have previously known in children with learning difficulties. For example, the sensory approaches many teachers have found effective for delivering a relevant curriculum may not engage children whose severe/profound and multiple learning disabilities (S/PMLD) emanate from pre-term birth. Ongoing research in New Zealand has shown that sensory pathways may be not only damaged, but also incomplete and compromised (Champion 2005).

Fetal Alcohol Spectrum Disorders (FASD)

Another group of children causing major concerns are those with Fetal Alcohol Spectrum Disorder (FASD). International estimates suggest that the prevalence could be as many as 1 in 100 children or higher (Autti-Ramo 2002; British Medical Association 2007; May 2009; Sampson et al. 1997) and the disabling effects range across the learning difficulty spectrum from mild to profound (www.nofas-uk.org). In some countries, such as South Africa, prevalence rates of Fetal Alcohol Syndrome (FAS) are very high, with rates of 40 or more children per 1,000 in certain South African wine-producing communities (Molteno 2008; Rendall-Mkosi et al. 2008). An American researcher has shown that the emotional well-being of children with FASD is particularly fragile, and leads to high rates of suicide in later life

(Streissguth 1997). The need for teachers to have a deeper understanding of mental health needs, and how to support emotional well-being and resilience through their everyday teaching, is accentuated by this group of children and others (e.g. those with ASD).

While organizations for FASD produce some excellent materials explaining the condition and warning of the perils of alcohol consumption during pregnancy, the need for a pedagogy specifically designed to embrace these children is vital. Take, for example, the fact that in children with FASD the brain's parietal lobe can be significantly reduced (Goswami 2004). This area controls numeracy and mathematical computation. However skilled a teacher may be in differentiating the Mathematics curriculum, if that part of the brain is compromised just how do we teach Mathematics to the child with FASD? In the UK, a NOFAS-UK project supported by the Training and Development Agency for Schools (now merged with the National College of Teaching and Learning) addressed this issue through a small scale, nine-site, school-based study. The study established a baseline of practice current across all types of schools in England and offered guidance across the four key stages (Blackburn et al. 2012).

This work built upon the previous work of both researchers. In 2009, Blackburn investigated practice related to young children with FASD, and knowledge of the condition among early years practitioners (Blackburn 2009). An Oxford-based study conducted by Carpenter (2011) concluded that school-based practitioners were 'pedagogically bereft' in relation to their understanding of children with FASD and their ability to plan meaningful and relevant learning experiences. Further investigations through the DfE-funded CLDD Project produced guidelines for teachers and teaching assistants (http://complexld.ssatrust.org.uk).

There are many barriers to learning for children with FASD, and engaging them as active and effective learners remains a major challenge in this twenty-first century (Carpenter et al. 2011). At this critical developmental juncture, an interdisciplinary perspective is crucial, combining the respective insights of a whole range of professionals who have experience relevant to seeking solutions across the lifespan (Carpenter et al. 2013).

Chromosomal abnormalities

We need to remind ourselves that parents, as their children's first educator, will be trail blazing approaches which support and engage their child. This is never more pronounced than in the area of chromosomal abnormality. Every day, children are born around the world with genetic abnormalities that are rare. Even if there is a diagnosis, they could be one of only a handful of children in any one country, maybe even worldwide. One in every 200 babies is born with a rare chromosome disorder (www.rarechromo.org). Families search for information, often at great personal expense (Harrison et al. 2007), and become the 'expert' on their children's rare conditions. The need for teachers to be well-trained in family-centred approaches in order to establish a meaningful dialogue and to work closely and collaboratively with parents in evolving pertinent approaches to education is paramount (Jones 2007; Stephenson 2010).

Fragile-X syndrome

Fragile-X syndrome is now the most commonly inherited genetic cause of learning disability in the UK, the USA and many European countries. Again, there are teaching approaches which are not widely communicated or understood by the teaching profession (Saunders 2001). Research in Ireland (Barr and Millar 2003) has shown that parents and professionals will need access to comprehensible information about genetics in general, and specific disorders in particular, if we are to improve the life chances of this group of children with chromosomal disorders. As well as the educational needs of the child with fragile-X, the reverberations of the genetically inherited condition across families has to be carefully thought through, as recent American research has demonstrated (Bailey and Skinner 2007; Bailey et al. 2008). Similarly, the learning spotlight has been shone by groundbreaking Japanese brain research looking at language functioning and impairment in the brains of children with fragile-X syndrome (Hayashi and Tonegawa 2007). These insights provide new platforms for teachers to plan creative and innovative learning pathways for children with these complex conditions.

Autistic spectrum disorders (ASD)

ASD also gives rise to severe, profound and complex learning difficulties in some children. The Medical Research Council (2001) estimates prevalence of ASD in the UK at 1 in 166 children. More recently, Professor Gillian Baird and her colleagues have calculated that children with some form of ASD constitute 1 in 86 of the UK's child population (Baird et al. 2006). Many of these children present with severe and complex learning needs. Often adolescence compounds these difficulties as mental health needs emerge – young people with learning disabilities are six times more likely to have a mental health problem than other children in the UK (Emerson and Hatton 2007).

While we know much about educating children with ASD (e.g. that they are predominantly visual learners), there are lessons emerging from neuroscience (Carpenter and Egerton 2007; Ramachandran and Lindsay 2006) that demand detailed consideration. Similarly there are 'new autisms' being identified which give a different lens with which to view a child's needs profile: Pathological Demand Avoidance (PDA) is one such powerful example which demands critical review. Again, there are new implications for how schools manage the teaching and learning of children with a diagnosis of PDA (Christie et al. 2011). The challenge for teachers is how to translate this information into classroom practices.

Pedagogies for inclusion

The examples of the children cited above demand that we remodel our pedagogy and, furthermore, that we generate teaching strategies which will embrace these children as learners. The debate around personalized learning is surely an ideal opportunity to implement this for all children. If teaching is an evidence-based profession, then special education is its inquiry-based arm.

Effective teaching of children with CLDD can happen in a variety of settings. What we need are 'pedagogies for inclusion' (Lewis and Norwich 2005) that enable all children to be active participants in our school system and receive their entitlement to education. A 'one size fits all' approach to children with profound and complex needs is naïve. We are working with children in that spectrum of learning difficulty/disability associated with unique learning profiles, often linked to the nature of their disorder (e.g. FASD, fragile-X syndrome, ASD), who require specific and specialized teaching approaches. Even where outstanding teaching of children with mild, moderate or severe learning disabilities exists, there is an ever-increasing group of children with CLDD who do not fit the current range of learning environments, curriculum models, or teaching and learning approaches, and who are challenging our most skilled teachers.

Why are our practitioners, skilled in the art of curriculum adaptation, modification and differentiation, unable to address the learning needs of these children? It is because they are a 'new generation' of children with complex learning needs; what Professor Daphne Thomas, University of South Florida (Carpenter 2010a), calls the next frontier of education. The causal base of the difficulties in learning presented by these children is different from that we have traditionally known, and, because we do not have a hotbed of dynamic special education training courses spread across the world, enabling teachers to think, create and evolve the 'new pedagogy', then the in-roads of progress into this issue are limited. In truth, we are failing to offer high-quality education to these children who become alienated as learners from the school system. On a daily basis, skilled teachers know that they have not made a difference to a child through their teaching, but it is not their fault.

With recent research from Canada and Ireland (O'Malley 2007) suggesting that ADHD is a neurological disorder evidenced by a smaller frontal cerebellum, the information that can be gained from neuroscience (Sousa 2007) could significantly influence how we develop future pedagogy. This in turn could raise the attainment of these vulnerable children as our teaching becomes better matched to their learning styles.

There has been much invaluable work around personalized learning (Hargreaves 2006). However, the empirical work of Professor Susan Greenfield clearly indicates the exciting, next-level challenge in this debate when she states (2008: 1): 'The mind is the personalisation of the brain through unique dynamic configurations of neuronal connections, driven by unique experiences.'

Insights from neuroscience

A UK project looking at mental capacity and well-being for children with learning difficulties and disabilities found that:

> Scientific advances in genetics and neuroimaging offer a potential opportunity within the next 20 years to identify children with learning difficulties in infancy. Cognitive neuroscience is already uncovering neural markers or biomarkers for detecting the different learning difficulties measurable in infancy. Such advances will eventually enable environmental interventions from infancy which would alter developmental learning trajectories for these children with consequent benefits throughout the life course.
>
> (Goswami 2008b: 16)

Certainly, there is a strong argument for strengthening the interface between neuroscience and education. In the field of autism alone, through international work in the USA (Mesibov et al. 2006), Holland (Peeters 1997; Peeters and Gillberg 1999) and the UK (Blakemore and Frith 2005; Jordan and Powell 1995), neuroscientific research has generated revolutionary ideas about how to educate this rapidly expanding group of children effectively by mapping the connections between brain states and learning patterns for practitioners. As Frith (2007) discusses (in relation to people with autistic spectrum disorders): 'Evidence from MRI studies showed reduced brain activity in self-reflection and attribution of emotional states to "self".'

Indeed in the context of a recent report for The Royal Society Science Policy Centre (2011), she has stated (Frith 2011): 'Education is concerned with enhancing learning, and neuroscience is concerned with understanding the mechanisms of learning. It seems only logical that the one should inform the other.'

Such insights can greatly aid the process of what has been termed 'pedagogical reconciliation' (Carpenter 2010a), where we seek, through evidence-based, innovative practice, to generate personalized curriculum pathways that touch the child with CLDD at their point of learning need. They could empower our schools to 'provide the strongest possible guidance, counselling and other forms of support for all students as they navigate increasingly complex pathways of learning, especially for students who fall behind or are not experiencing success' (Carpenter 2010b: 43).

To achieve this, we must find ways of implementing structured opportunities for the professional development of school staff to ensure that 'new professional capacities' (Carpenter 2010b) are supported. We have to acquire new professional skills, and more creative and responsive styles of teaching, if we are to meet the challenge of engagement for children with CLDD (Carpenter et al. 2011). If we do not, many children will be lost in, and to, our school system; cognitively disenfranchised, socially dysfunctional and emotionally disengaged.

Conclusion

Children with CLDD are certainly a unique group of learners, and their experiences formulate a unique and, at times, challenging perspective of this world. I hope this chapter has outlined not only the challenge of children with CLDD but also given examples of what complex needs may actually look like in the classroom. In essence, not only are 'new' disabling conditions emerging that present pedagogical challenges previously unknown to teachers, but more children are being diagnosed with co-existing conditions which overlap, compound and interlock, presenting profiles of learning previously not seen (cf. http:// complexld.ssatrust.org.uk). These may be, for example, ASD and ADHD: which is the dominant learning disability? We know much about how to teach either group of children, but do those teaching approaches fit together when the two disabilities influence learning within one child? It is a process which can be termed 'pedagogical reconciliation'. Obvious as it may seem, this takes place when two or more conditions which co-exist in a child need to be reconciled to each other; however, it is not common practice in our schools.

There is much that the international education community can do to resolve these issues for teachers and for children if we marshal our resources, pool our knowledge and come together in a spirit of openness and sharing. We need to create a professional learning community that is committed to inquiry-led practice; we need a new generation of research that is practitioner-led, inquiry-focused and evidence-based. Already there are signs that this approach is emerging strongly, and will form the bedrock for an educational research revolution in the next decade (Jones et al. 2012). Only then will we innovate new, dynamic and personalized learning for children with complex needs, enabling a transformation in their lives, and for our international societies, to meet their responsibilities to their most vulnerable children.

This is a journey of discovery: there will be times when we are lost, and times when we discover new places of learning. We are all navigators of learning, and, for every discovery we make, another child, or group of children, becomes engaged in effective learning. Journey on!

References

Autti-Ramo, I. (2002) 'Foetal alcohol syndrome: a multifaceted condition', *Developmental Medicine and Child Neurology*, 44: 141–144.

Bailey, D. and Skinner, D. (2007) 'Family communications about fragile-X syndrome'. Paper presented to the second conference of the International Society on Early Intervention, Zagreb, Croatia (14–16 June).

Bailey, D.B., Hatton, D.D., Mesibov, G., Ament, N. and Skinner, M. (2000) 'Early development, temperament, and functional impairment in autism and fragile-X syndrome', *Journal of Autism and Developmental Disorders*, 30(1): 49–59.

Bailey, D.B., Skinner, D., Davis, A.M., Whitmarsh, I. and Powell, C. (2008) 'Ethical, legal, and social concerns about expanded newborn screening: fragile-X syndrome as a prototype for emerging issues', *Pediatrics*, 121(3): e693–e704.

Baird, G., Simonoff, E., Pickles, A., Chandler, S., Loucas, T., Meldrum, D. and Charman, T. (2006) 'Prevalence of disorders of the autism spectrum in a population cohort of children in South Thames: the Special Needs and Autism Project (SNAP)', *The Lancet*, 368(9531): 210–215.

Barnett, W.S. and Hustedt, J.T. (2005) 'Head Start's lasting benefits', *Infants & Young Children*, 18(1): 16–24.

Barr, O. and Millar, R. (2003) 'Parents of children with intellectual disabilities and their expectations and experience of genetic counselling'. Paper presented at the Special Olympics International Symposium, Belfast (June).

Blackburn, C. (2009) *Building Bridges with Understanding – Foetal Alcohol Spectrum Disorders (FASD) Project: The acquisition of early years practitioner knowledge in relation to the education and support of children with foetal alcohol spectrum disorders*, Worcester: Worcester County Council/Sunfield.

Blackburn, C. and Carpenter, B. (2012) 'Engaging young children with complex learning difficulties and disabilities in early years settings', *Early Years Educator*, 14(2): 39–44.

Blackburn, C. Spencer, N.J. and Read, J.M (2010) 'Prevalence of childhood disability and the characteristics and circumstances of disabled children in the UK: secondary analysis of the Family Resources Survey', *BMC Paediatrics*, 10: 21.

Blackburn, C., Carpenter, B. and Egerton, J. (2012) *Educating Children and Young People with FASD*, London: Routledge.

Blakemore, S.J. and Frith, U. (2005) 'The learning brain: lessons for education: a précis', *Developmental Science*, 8(6): 459–465.

Bong, M. and Skaalvik, E.M. (2003) 'Academic self-concept and self-efficacy: how different are they really?', *Educational Psychology Review*, 15(1): 1–40.

British Medical Association (2007) *Fetal Alcohol Spectrum Disorders: A guide for healthcare professionals*, London: British Medical Association.

Brown, M. (2009) 'Education and invasive procedures: opportunities and challenges for the future'. Paper to the Invasive Procedures Conference, University of Dundee (June).

Carpenter, B. (2010a) *Curriculum Reconciliation and Children with Complex Learning Difficulties and Disabilities*, London: SSAT.

Carpenter, B. (2010b) 'Disadvantaged, deprived and disabled', *Special Children*, 193: 42–45.

Carpenter, B. (2011) 'Pedagogically bereft!: improving learning outcomes for children with foetal alcohol spectrum disorders', *British Journal of Special Education*, 38(1): 38–43.

Carpenter, B. (2012) 'Leading professional learning in 21st Century schools'. Keynote presentation to the Surrey Headteachers Conference (June).

Carpenter, B. and Egerton, J. (eds) (2007) *New Horizons in Special Education: Evidence-based practice in action*, Clent, Worcestershire: Sunfield Publications.

Carpenter, B., Ashdown, R. and Bovair, K. (2002) *Enabling Access: Effective teaching and learning for children with learning difficulties* (2nd edn), London: David Fulton.

Carpenter, B., Egerton, J., Bloom, T., Cockbill, B., Fotheringham, J., Rawson, H. and Thistlethwaite, J. (2011) 'The Complex Learning Difficulties and Disabilities Research Project: developing pathways to personalised learning', London: SSAT.

Carpenter, B., Blackburn, C. and Egerton, J. (eds) (2013) *Fetal Alcohol Spectrum Disorders: Interdisciplinary perspectives*, London: Routledge.

Champion, P. (2005) 'The at-risk infant – approaches to intervention: the Champion Centre model'. In B. Carpenter and J. Egerton (eds) *New Horizons in Special Education: Evidence-based practice in action*, Clent, Worcestershire: Sunfield Publications, pp. 39–52.

Christie, P., Duncan, M., Fidler, R. and Healy, Z. (2011) *Understanding Pathological Demand Avoidance Syndrome in Children: A guide for parents, teachers and other professionals*, London: Jessica Kingsley.

Conry, J. (1996) *Teaching Students with Fetal Alcohol Syndrome/Effects: A resource guide for teachers*, British Columbia, Canada: Special Programs Branch of the Ministry of Education, Skills and Training. [Online at: www.bced.gov.bc.ca/specialed/fas/ack.htm; accessed: 27.09.09.]

Coughlan, B. (2007) 'Mental health difficulties in people with intellectual disability: integrating theory and evidence-based practice'. In B. Carpenter and J. Egerton (eds) *New Horizons in Special Education: Evidence-based practice in action*, Clent, Worcestershire: Sunfield Publications, pp. 89–109.

Dee, L., Byers, R., Hayhoe, H. and Maudslay, L. (2002) *Enhancing Quality of Life: Facilitating transactions for people with profound and complex needs*, London: SKILL/University of Cambridge.

Dittrich, W.H. and Tutt, R. (2008) *Educating Children with Complex Conditions: Understanding overlapping and co-existing developmental disorders*, London: Sage.

Dossetor, D., White D. and Whatson, L. (eds) (2011) *Mental Health of Children and Adolescents with Intellectual and Developmental Disabilities: A framework for professional practice*, Melbourne: IP Communications

Elliott, E.J. (2013) 'Fetal alcohol spectrum disorders: Australian perspectives' and 'International overview: the challenges in addressing Fetal Alcohol Spectrum Disorders'. In B. Carpenter, C. Blackburn and J. Egerton (eds) *Fetal Alcohol Spectrum Disorders: Interdisciplinary perspectives*, London: Routledge, pp. 294–305.

Elliott, E., Latimer, J., Oscar, J., Fitzpatrick, J. and Carter, M. (2012) *The Lililwan Collaboration: Inquiry into Fetal Alcohol Spectrum Disorders (FASD)*, Fitzroy Valley: The Lililwan Project Collaboration.

Emerson, E. and Hatton, C. (2007) *The Mental Health of Children and Adolescents with Learning Disabilities in Britain*, London: Foundation for People with Learning Disabilities/Lancaster University.

Frith, U. (2007) 'Autism and the difficulty of identifying one's own feelings'. Paper to the 8th International Autism Congress, Oslo, Norway (August).

Frith, U. (2011) 'Royal Society says give neuroscience a greater role in education policy', London: Royal Society. [Online at: https://royalsociety.org/news/2011/neuroscience-role-in-education-policy/; accessed: 01.07.14.]

Fujiura, G.T. (2004) 'Disability epidemiology in the developing world'. Plenary presentation at the Programme of the 12th World Congress of the International Association for the Scientific Study of Intellectual Disabilities, Montpelier, France (June).

Goswami, U. (2004) 'Neuroscience, education and special education', *British Journal of Special Education*, 31(4): 175–183.

Goswami, U. (2008a) *Cognitive Development: The learning brain*, London: Psychology Press.

Goswami, U. (2008b) *Learning Difficulties: Future challenges, mental capital and well being project*, London: Government Office for Science.

Greenfield, S. (2008) 'Expanding minds: the future of the brain, the brain of the future', *NAHT Secondary Leadership Paper 31*. [Online at: www.naht.org.uk/EasySiteWeb/getresource.axd?AssetID=13628&type=full&servicetype=Attachment; accessed: 16.06.09.]

Guralnick, M.J. (ed.) (2005a) *The Developmental Systems Approach to Early Intervention*, Baltimore: Paul H. Brookes.

Guralnick, M.J. (2005b) 'Early intervention for children with intellectual disabilities: current knowledge and future prospects', *Journal of Applied Research in Intellectual Disabilities*, 18: 313–324.

Hargreaves, D. (2006) *Personalising Learning 6: The final gateway: school design and organisation*, London: SSAT.

Harrison, J., Henderson, M. and Leonard, R. (eds) (2007) *Different Dads: Fathers' stories of parenting disabled children*, London: Jessica Kingsley.

Hayashi, P. and Tonegawa, R. (2007) 'Genetics, language impairment and intervention', *Proceedings of the National Academy of Sciences*, 104(27): 11489–11494.

Hirsch, D. (2007) 'Experiences of poverty and educational disadvantage', London: Joseph Rowntree Foundation. [Online at: www.actiononaccess.org/download.php?f=1347; accessed: 24.08.09.]

Johnson, S., Wolke, D., Hennessy, E. and Marlow, N. (2011) 'Educational outcomes in extremely preterm children: neuropsychological correlates and predictors of attainment', *Developmental Neuropsychology*, 36: 74–95.

Jones, P. (2007) 'Involving parents in classroom assessment'. In P. Jones, J.F. Carr and R.L. Ataya (eds) *A Pig Don't Get Fatter the More You Weigh it: Classroom assessments that work*, New York, NY: Teachers College Press, pp. 113–122.

Jones, P., Whitehurst, T. and Egerton, J. (2012) *Creating Meaningful Inquiry in Inclusive Classrooms*, London: Routledge.

Jordan, R. and Powell, S. (1995) *Understanding and Teaching Children with Autism*, London: Wiley.

Lewis, A. and Norwich, B. (eds) (2005) *Special Teaching for Special Children: Pedagogies for inclusion*, Milton Keynes: Open University Press.

McCluskey, J. and McNamara, G. (2005) 'Children in need'. In C. Horton (ed.) *Working with Children 2006–2007: Facts, figures and information*, London: Sage.

May, P. (2009) 'Prevalence and incidence internationally'. In: E. Jonsson, L. Dennett and G. Littlejohn (eds) *Fetal Alcohol Spectrum Disorder (FASD): Across the Lifespan (Proceedings from an IHE Consensus Development Conference 2009)*, Alberta, Canada: Institute of Health Economics, pp. 19–22.

Medical Research Council (2001) *Review of Autism Research: Epidemiology and causes*, London: Medical Research Council.

Mesibov, G.B., Shea, V. and Schopler, E. (2006) *The TEACCH Approach to Autism Spectrum Disorders*, New York, NY: Springer.

Mittler, H. (1995) *Families Speak Out: International perspectives in families' experience of disability*, Cambridge, MA: Brookline Books.

Mittler, P. (2000) *Working Towards Inclusive Education: Social contexts*, London: David Fulton.

Molteno, C. (2008) 'Foetal Alcohol Spectrum Disorder', *Journal of Intellectual Disability Research*, 52(8): 640.

Northern, S. (2004) 'Children's mental health', *Times Educational Supplement* (10 September).

O'Leary, C., Heuzenvoeder, L., Elliott, E.J. and Bower, C. (2007) 'A review of policies on alcohol use during pregnancy in Australia and other English-speaking countries', *The Medical Journal of Australia*, 188(9): 466–471.

O'Malley, K. (2007) *ADHD and Fetal Alcohol Spectrum Disorders*, New York, NY: Nova Science Publications.

Peadon, E., Freemantle, E., Bower, C. and Elliott, E.J. (2008) 'International survey of diagnostic services for children with FASD', *BMC Pediatrics*, 8(12): 1–8.

Peeters, T. (1997) *Autism: From theoretical understanding to educational intervention*, London: Whurr.

Peeters, T. and Gillberg, C. (1999) *Autism: Medical and educational aspects* (2nd edn), London: Whurr.

Pretis, M. and Dimova, A. (2008) 'Vulnerable children of mentally ill parents: towards evidence-based support for improving resilience', *Support for Learning*, 23(3): 152–159.

Porter, J. and Ashdown, R. (2002) *Pupils with Complex Learning Difficulties: Promoting learning using visual materials and methods*, London: David Fulton/NASEN.

Rae, T. (2013) *Developing Emotional Literacy with Teenagers: Building confidence, self-esteem and self awareness (Lucky Duck Books)*, London: Sage.

Ramachandran, V.S. and Lindsay, M.O. (2006) 'Broken Mirrors: a theory of autism', *Scientific American*, November: 63–69.

Ramesh, R. (2010) 'Study shows links between poverty and disability are more pronounced', *Guardian* 20 April, 6. [Online at: www.theguardian.com/uk/2010/apr/19/poverty-disability-warwick-university-debt; accessed: 10.07.14.]

Rendall-Mkosi, K., London, L., Adnams, C., Morojele, N., McLoughlin, J. and Goldstone, C. (2008) *Fetal Alcohol Spectrum Disorder in South Africa: Situational and gap analysis*. [Online at: www.unicef.org/southafrica/SAF_resources_fas.pdf; accessed: 27.08.09.]

Rose, R., Howley, M., Fergusson, A. and Jament, J. (2009) 'Mental health and special educational needs: exploring a complex relationship', *British Journal of Special Education*, 36(1): 3–8.

Royal Society Science Policy Centre (2011) *Brain Waves Module 2: Neuroscience: implications for education and lifelong learning*, London: The Royal Society.

Sampson, P.D., Streissguth, A.P., Bookstein, F.L., Little, R.E., Clarren, S.K., Dehaene, P., Hanson, J.W. and Graham, J.M. Jr (1997) 'Incidence of fetal alcohol syndrome and prevalence of alcohol-related neurodevelopmental disorder', *Teratology*, 56(5): 317–326.

Saunders S. (2001) *Fragile-X Syndrome: A guide for teachers*, London: David Fulton.

Soriano, V. (ed.) (2005) *Early Childhood Intervention – Analysis of Situations in Europe: Key aspects and recommendations* (Summary report), Brussels: European Agency for Development in Special Needs Education. [Online at: www.european-agency.org/publications/ereports/early-childhood-intervention/eci_en.pdf; accessed: 27.07.09.]

Sousa, D.A. (2007) *How the Special Needs Brain Learns*, Thousand Oaks, CA: Corwin Press/Sage.

Stephenson, M.-A. (2010) 'Fathers, families and work: putting "working fathers" in the picture', *The Political Quarterly*, 81(2): 237–242.

Streissguth, A. (1997) *Fetal Alcohol Syndrome: A guide for families and communities*, Baltimore, MD: Paul H. Brookes.

Visser, E. (2009) 'Review of learning difficulty and disability (LDD): an Ofsted perspective'. Keynote presentation to the Croner's 4th Annual Special Needs Conference, London (January).

Webster-Stratton, C. and Reid, M.J. (2004) 'Strengthening social and emotional competence in young children – The Foundation for Early School Readiness and Success: incredible years classroom social skills and problem-solving curriculum', *Infants & Young Children*, 17(2): 96–113.

Wolke, D. (2011) 'Preterm and low birth weight babies'. In P. Howlin, T. Charman and M. Ghaziuddin (eds) *The Sage Handbook of Developmental Disorders*. London: Sage, pp. 497–527.

Wood, N.S., Marlow, N., Costeloe, K., Gibson, A.T. and Wilkinson, A.R. (2000) 'Neurologic and developmental disability after extremely preterm birth', *New England Journal of Medicine*, 343: 378–84.

Woodward, L.J., Mogridge, N., Wells, S.W. and Inder, T.E. (2004) 'Can neurobehavioral examination predict the presence of cerebral injury in the VLBW infant?', *Journal of Developmental and Behavioral Pediatrics*, 25(5): 326–334.

Chapter 3

Engagement and learning

A brief introduction

Why engagement?

Education researchers have long sought to identify and understand why some schools produce better educational outcomes than others, and to discover the learning factors at play (Brooks et al. 2012). Children's engagement in learning has consistently emerged as significant. Many educators now believe that 'the study of engagement has the potential to assist educators and therapists to maximize learning outcomes' (Keen 2009: 136). For Carpenter, engagement is foundational: 'Without [engagement], there is no deep learning, effective teaching, meaningful outcome, real attainment or quality progress' (Carpenter 2010a: 5).

Engagement and children with learning difficulties

Over two decades ago, McWilliam et al. (1985: 60), proclaimed that 'engagement sets the occasion for optimal learning to occur.' For children with disabilities, research has consistently suggested that 'engagement is a gateway to learning and is one of the best predictors for positive student outcomes' (Keen 2008: 1). Consequently, many educators in the field of disability have in recent years come to focus upon engagement as the foundation for effective learning in children with disabilities (Brooks 2010; Carpenter 2010a,b; Guralnick and Albertini 2006; Keen 2009; Mesibov et al. 2004; Ruble and Robson 2007).

For children with disabilities, engaged behaviour is one of the best predictors of successful learning (Iovannone et al. 2003), yet children with disabilities consistently engage for less time and at lower levels than their typically developing peers (Bailey et al. 1993; McCormick et al. 1998; McWilliam and Bailey 1995). This represents a significant problem for the successful education of these children, since 'when unengaged, students lose out on important learning opportunities' (Hume 2006: 1). Furthermore, they are more likely to become distracted, disruptive or demonstrate challenging behaviours.

Consequently, it is now increasingly being recognized that 'to teach children with CLDD [Complex Learning Difficulties and Disabilities] effectively the teacher must penetrate the mask of disengagement generated by many of these children' (Carpenter 2010a: 5). This was also strongly advocated by the schools participating in the CLDD Project, and teachers gave powerful support to this view. As succinctly stated by one teacher involved in the CLDD Project, 'Engagement is essential, absolutely essential. It has to be the central point when looking at our children'. Others commented:

The engagement concept is really valid. If children are not engaged they will not be learning. Watching to see how the students engage is the way forward.

In an ideal world, we would only use engagement, and we haven't used that word or tool until the project. It's opened our eyes to that. It's developed our awareness of the importance of engagement.

Brooks (2010) used interviews and surveys to explore elements of a supportive learning environment for children with autism and complex learning needs with a group of 47 educators at a residential special school. Eighty per cent emphasized that engagement was essential for learning to take place. One stated: '[children] need an environment that is conducive to engagement for learning' (Brooks 2010: 97).

Defining engagement

Over 20 years ago, Newmann (1986: 242) observed that 'engagement is difficult to define operationally, but we know it when we see it, and we know when it is missing.' Newmann was undoubtedly right: engagement *is* difficult to define operationally. A fundamental reason for this is that the way in which children demonstrate engagement varies from child to child and even from lesson to lesson. Consequently, to date 'there is no agreed conceptualization or definition of engagement' (Keen 2009: 137); the term 'engagement' has received many interpretations, and numerous definitions exist.

The National Research Council (2001: 160) defined engagement rather vaguely as 'sustained attention to an activity or person'. However, it is now generally accepted that by limiting engagement to only a measure of how much time a child spends in an activity, one is likely to miss important behaviours critical for learning (De Kruif and McWilliam 1999). Consequently, educators now believe that engagement relates to a far broader concept than simply 'time on task', and that any conceptualization of engagement should recognize the importance of 'the intensity and emotional quality of children's involvement in initiating and carrying out learning activities' (Skinner and Belmont 1993: 572).

As a result, other definitions have expanded the concept of engagement beyond simply *what* children are doing, to considering *how* they are doing it. For example, Ridley et al. (2000: 134) define engagement as 'the amount of time children spend interacting with the environment (with adults, peers, or materials) in a developmentally and contextually appropriate manner'. In this way, the concept of engagement has progressed from considering only the *quantity* of time spent engaged, to considering multiple dimensions of the *quality* of the engagement demonstrated.

Nevertheless, such definitions continue to place primary emphasis on 'time on task' or 'quantity' as a crucial indicator of engagement. Furthermore, they also focus solely upon the role of the child in engaging in learning. In contrast, definitions such as that presented by Kuh et al. (2008: 542) describe how 'student engagement represents both the time and energy children invest in educationally purposeful activities, and the effort institutions devote to using effective educational practices.'

As such, the CLDD Project strived to provide a definition of engagement in learning which emphasized process and quality rather than outcome and quantity. It also recognized the crucial interaction between learner and learning environment described by Kuh that is so fundamental to children's engagement. The following engagement statement and definition emerged through numerous revision processes with a wide array of professionals and educators: 'Sustainable learning can occur only when there is meaningful engagement. The process of engagement is a journey which connects a child and their environment (including people, ideas, materials and concepts) to enable learning and achievement.'

Through describing engagement as a connection between a child and their environment, this definition recognizes the dynamic relationship between learner and learning environment that is fundamental and crucial to children's engagement. In other words, adaptation is required from both the learner and the learning environment for a successful connection to be made.

Children who can learn without the need for personalized adaptations can self-generate and focus the needed effort to achieve learning goals. For children with complex needs, however, educators will need to work with the child to personalize, develop and establish those connections. Personalized learning demands that schools transform their response to the learner from the largely standardized to the profoundly personalized (Hargreaves 2006). He writes: 'If students are to engage in deeper learning, they will need new forms of enriched support' (Hargreaves 2006: 8).

Why is engagement important?

As Chapter 2 highlights, the challenge for schools of meeting the multi-faceted needs of learners with CLDD is immense. Porter and Ashdown (2002) emphasize that if these children are to achieve their full potential, they require educational approaches which stretch beyond differentiation.

Carpenter et al. (2011) address this by suggesting that consideration of children's engagement enables educators to move beyond differentiation to truly personalize learning through utilizing individual children's personal strengths and interests, or in other words, utilizing what engages them as a learner. As Brooks et al. (2012) state: 'The intensity and emotional quality of a child's involvement is key to high quality learning. This intensity can only be achieved through engagement that encourages each child to truly embrace learning.'

In this way, as illustrated in Figure 3.1, engagement can provide the glue which connects the child with CLDD with their often elusive learning outcome (Carpenter et al. 2011).

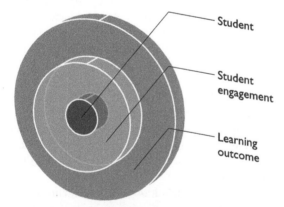

Figure 3.1 The relationship between engagement and learning

Source: Carpenter et al. 2011

The overall goal of the pedagogy is 'engagement for learning'. Our quest is to engage the learner with CLDD in their environment; our challenge is how to achieve engagement (Carpenter 2010a).

What are the teaching strategies that will enable us to engage children with CLDD as active participants in the dynamics of our lessons, programmes or learning environments? How do we recognize when a child is engaged? How do we measure engagement? How do we chart engagement outcomes?

The educator must remain committed to engagement for learning as a core tenet of curriculum experience for the child with CLDD. The permutations of special educational needs presented by some children can send an educator off at a pedagogical tangent or embroil them in a level of detail not helpful to the learning process. With engagement as a focus, the practitioner is equipped to transcend these complexities.

Measuring engagement

With the growing emphasis on engagement as a key indicator for learning, numerous tools for measuring engagement have been created. These have generally been split into two different types of tools: 1) indirect qualitative tools such as questionnaires which facilitate caregivers, practitioners or children themselves to assess global engagement after a learning task has taken place, and 2) direct observation scales which have the benefit of enabling 'observing what children are actually doing' while they are doing it (Kishida and Kemp 2006b: 4). To date these direct observation tools have focused primarily on the quantity of time children spend engaged, with little opportunity to consider the quality of engagement in any detail, or personalize observations.

Consequently, alongside redefining the term 'engagement' to emphasize the quality rather than quantity of engagement, the CLDD Project also recognized the need to develop a novel tool which would allow practitioners to directly measure children's engagement by grounding it in a description of the quality of engagement rather than quantity. Furthermore, in order to acknowledge the very different and individual ways in which children with CLDD demonstrate engagement, such a tool needed to support educators to undertake a process of 'personalising engagement' (Brooks 2010), promoting 'sensitivity to and awareness of the unique engaged/disengaged behaviours of the individual student, thereby facilitating identification of how to enhance engagement for the individual student and thus how to support them to fulfil their learning potential' (Brooks 2010: 293).

To this end, following a period of development and trialling which involved an extensive range of educational settings, including early years services, special schools and mainstream schools in the UK, as well as international special schools across Australia, New Zealand, the USA, Ireland, Scotland and Wales, the CLDD Project developed the Engagement Profile and Scale: an observation and assessment resource which supports practitioners to personalize engagement and learning for the individual child, and track a child's journey towards sustained engagement and deep learning.

Conclusion

How can educators tell if a child is really learning? It is impossible for them to see what a child is thinking or how or what the child is learning. And yet they can see and hear when a child is engaged. This is why strong engagement skills lie at the heart of effective learning.

Children with CLDD need to be taught in ways that match their individual learning styles by educators who recognize their abilities and potential for engagement in learning. Our work must be to transform children with CLDD into active learners by releasing their motivation, unlocking their curiosity and increasing their participation; key to this are relationship processes – warmth, sensitivity and responsiveness (Carpenter 2010a). From there the child becomes engaged, and their personalized learning journey begins. Carpenter (2010b: 6) writes:

> A focus on engagement can underpin a process of personalised inquiry through which the educator can develop effective learning experiences and remove barriers to learning. Using evidence-based knowledge of a child's already successful learning pathways, aptitudes and interests, strategies can be identified, high expectations set, and incremental progress recorded on their journey towards optimal engagement in learning. Their engagement will be the benchmark for assessing whether we have achieved this goal.

Acknowledgement

We would like to thank Tamara Bloom for allowing us to draw on her Ph.D. thesis (Brooks 2010) for this discussion of engagement.

References

Bailey, D.B., McWilliam, R.A., Ware, W.B. and Burchinal, M.A. (1993) 'Social interactions of toddlers and preschoolers in same-age and mixed-age play groups', *Journal of Applied Developmental Psychology*, 14(2): 261–276.

Brooks, T. (2010) *Developing a Learning Environment which Supports Children with Profound Autistic Spectrum Disorder to Engage as Effective Learners* (Ph.D. thesis), Worcester: University of Worcester.

Brooks, T., Law, J., Carpenter, B. and Cockbill, B. (2012) 'Module 3.2: Engaging in learning: key processes'. In Teaching Agency (2012) *Training Materials for Teachers of Pupils with Severe, Profound and Complex Learning Difficulties*, London: Department for Education. [Online at: http://complexneeds.org.uk/modules/Module-3.2-Engaging-in-learning---key-approaches/A/m10p040a.html; accessed: 28.09.14.]

Carpenter, B. (2010a) *Children with Complex Learning Difficulties and Disabilities: Who are they and what are their needs?* (Complex needs series), London: SSAT.

Carpenter, B. (2010b) *Curriculum Reconciliation and Children with Complex Learning Difficulties and Disabilities* (Complex needs series), London: SSAT.

Carpenter, B., Egerton, J., Brooks, T., Cockbill, B., Fotheringham, J. and Rawson, H. (2011) *The Complex Learning Difficulties and Disabilities Research Project: Developing pathways to personalised learning*, London: SSAT.

de Kruif, R.E.L. and McWilliam, R.A. (1999) 'Multivariate relationships among developmental age, global engagement, and observed child engagement', *Early Childhood Research Quarterly*, 14(4): 515–536.

Guralnick, M.J. and Albertini, G. (2006) 'Early intervention in an international perspective', *Journal of Policy and Practice in Intellectual Disabilities*, 3(1): 1–2.

Hargreaves, D. (2006) *A New Shape for Schooling?*, London: SSAT.

Hume, K. (2006) 'Get engaged!: designing instructional activities to help students stay on task', *Reporter*, 11(2): 6–9.

Iovannone, R., Dunlap, G., Huber, H. and Kincaid, D. (2003) 'Effective educational practices for students with autism spectrum disorders', *Focus on Autism and Other Developmental Disabilities*, 18: 150–165.

Keen, D. (2008) 'Engaging children with autism in learning activities', *Griffith Institute for Educational Research Newsletter*, 1(2): 1–3.

Keen, D. (2009) 'Engagement of children with autism in learning', *Australasian Journal of Special Education*, 33(2): 130–140.

Kishida, Y. and Kemp, C. (2006b) 'Measuring child engagement in inclusive early childhood settings: implications for practice', *Australian Journal of Early Childhood*, 31(2): 14–19.

Kuh, G., Cruce, T.M., Shoup, R. and Kinzie, J. (2008) 'Unmasking the effects of student engagement on first-year college grades and persistence', *Journal of Higher Education*, 79(5): 540–563.

McCormick, L., Noonan, M.J. and Heck, R. (1998) 'Variables affecting engagement in inclusive preschool classrooms', *Journal of Early Intervention*, 21(2): 160–176.

McWilliam, R.A. and Bailey, D.B. (1995) 'Effects of classroom social structure and disability on engagement', *Topics for Early Childhood Special Education*, 15(2): 123–147.

McWilliam, R.A., Trivette, C.M. and Dunst, C.I. (1985) 'Behaviour engagement as a measure of the efficacy of early intervention', *Analysis and Intervention in Developmental Disabilities*, 5: 59–71.

Mesibov, G.B., Shea, V. and Schopler, E. (2004) *The TEACCH Approach to Autism Spectrum Disorders*, New York, NY: Plenum.

National Research Council (2001) *Understanding Dropouts: Statistics, strategies, and high-stakes testing*, Washington, DC: National Academies Press.

Newmann, F. (1986) 'Priorities for the future: toward a common agenda', *Social Education*, 50(4): 240–250.

Porter, J. and Ashdown, R. (2002) *Pupils with Complex Needs: Promoting learning through visual methods and materials*, Tamworth: NASEN.

Ridley, S.M., McWilliam, R.A. and Oates, C.S. (2000) 'Observed engagement as an indicator of child care program quality', *Early Education and Development*, 11(2): 133–146.

Ruble, L.A. and Robson, D.M. (2007) 'Individual and environment determinants of engagement in autism', *Journal of Autism and Developmental Disorders*, 37: 1457–1468.

Skinner, E.A. and Belmont, M.J. (1993) 'Motivation in the classroom: reciprocal effects of teacher behavior and student engagement across the school year', *Journal of Education Psychology*, 85: 571–581.

Chapter 4

Evidencing engagement for learning

The Engagement Profile and Scale

It goes without saying that the learning needs of children and young people with CLDD are complex! These children are often either disengaged or show low levels of engagement in one or more areas of learning. Often their educators have become discouraged after repeated, unsuccessful attempts to engage them; simple, 'off the peg' solutions have not worked; the children have not responded consistently to teaching strategies that have successfully engaged other learners with learning difficulties and disabilities.

This chapter will introduce the two core engagement for learning resources – the Engagement Profile and Scale – that were developed during the CLDD Project to support educators in engaging children with CLDD in learning. Children with CLDD who are persistently disengaged or minimally engaged in one or more curriculum areas need educators to develop personalized, strengths-based approaches to support their engagement for learning. To do this, educators will need to carry out multiple adaptations – in some cases breaking new ground – in consultation with families and other professionals involved with the child. Using the Engagement Profile and Scale, schools can record these learning and teaching developments for children with CLDD, and provide evidence of their endeavours to engage the child in learning.

The Education Profile and Scale together form a systematic and deductive framework for incrementally developing, trialling and modifying personalized learning pathways for children with CLDD. They support multidisciplinary solution-finding, and the opportunity to take a graduated approach to optimizing children's engagement in learning (Rome wasn't built in a day!). They are also a means of monitoring and demonstrating the learning adaptations and progress made through maximizing the child's learning opportunities. This evidence can be shared with colleagues, families, the young person themselves, local authorities or schools inspectorates (see Figure 4.1).

One school described a situation when, prior to taking part in the CLDD Project, school inspectors had asked to see evidence of the strategies they had used to try to support the learning of a child who was largely disengaged from learning. Despite having trialled numerous different approaches with him, they had kept no record of outcomes for unsuccessful interventions, so were unable to provide evidence of what they had done or why. The Engagement Profile and Scale subsequently offered them a way of providing evidence of both successful and unsuccessful intervention outcomes for children, how they responded and the reasons for the decisions and actions taken. As the DfE (2010: 9) states: 'It is important to have an understanding of both how well a learner has been progressing and how effectively barriers to progress have been identified and minimized or removed.'

SEN UK trial school – case study

Harry is a young man, aged 8 years, who attends a UK special school. His identified conditions are moderate/severe learning difficulties, attention deficit hyperactivity disorder, obsessive compulsive disorder, oppositional defiant disorder, mental health issues and speech and language difficulties. He has involvement with the occupational therapist, speech and language therapist and play therapist.

At the start of the SEN trial school phase, Harry was entirely disengaged from cookery lessons. He had not been able to participate in group cookery sessions for a couple of years because he was too disruptive during the lesson.

Using the inquiry process it was identified that Harry responded very well to puppets. Puppets were introduced during Harry's cookery lessons as a means for Harry to communicate with the group. Harry engaged with this and used the puppets successfully.

Harry then started using a peer's communication book to participate. In response to this Harry was given his own book. He gradually progressed from using the puppet to using the communication book. Harry is now fully engaging in cookery sessions and has been able to successfully re-integrate with his class group for these sessions.

Target: To engage in food technology and reading lessons.

The following strategies were put in place:
Strategy 1: (27/9, 1/10, 4/10) Cooking session relocated to the classroom. Puppet introduced.
Strategy 2: (11/10, 18/10) Puppet not brought out until Harry independently requested it.
Strategy 3: (5/11) Communication book introduced IN ADDITION to puppet available.
Strategy 4: (12/11) Communication book INSTEAD of puppet.
Strategy 5: (15/11, 19/11, 22/11, 29/11) Cookery relocated to the Kitchen.

Following interventions and subsequent monitoring using the Engagement Profile and Scale, Harry's engagement record's showed a significant increase in engagement in food technology, evidenced in the table and chart below.

Session	BASELINE		INTERVENTION	
	DATE	SCORE	DATE	SCORE
1	10.09.10	0	27.09.10	27
2	13.09.10	9	01.10.10	26
3	17.09.10	9	04.10.10	25
4			08.10.10	24
5			11.10.10	25
6			18.10.10	27
7			05.11.10	23
8			12.11.10	28
9			15.11.10	28
10			19.11.10	26
11			22.11.10	28
12			29.11.10	27

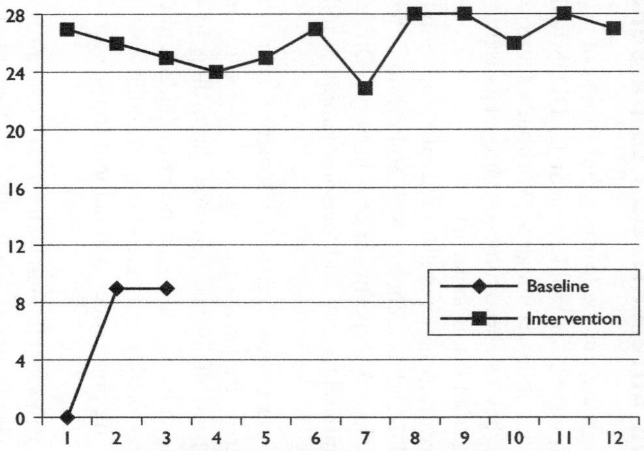

Harry's engagement journey evidenced using the Engagement Profile and Scale

—◆— Baseline
—■— Intervention

Figure 4.1 Exemplar evidence for increased engagement generated using the Engagement Profile and Scale

Beyond differentiation to personalization

All children are unique learners, but most can adapt their learning to the way educators teach. However, for children with CLDD, whether they attend mainstream or special schools, this ability is impaired. Without educators who can help them build bridges into learning, they risk becoming educationally disenfranchised and disengaged both at school and later, as adults, from society.

Most educators are familiar with differentiation. However, to meet the needs of learners with CLDD, adjustment needs to go beyond differentiation to personalization (Carpenter 2010a). The US Department of Education, Office of Educational Technology (2010: 12) defines 'differentiation' and 'personalization' as follows:

> **Differentiation** refers to instruction that is tailored to the learning preferences of different learners. Learning goals are the same for all children, but the method or approach of instruction varies according to the preferences of each child or what research has found works best for children like them.
>
> **Personalization** refers to instruction that is paced to learning needs, tailored to learning preferences, and tailored to the specific interests of different learners.

To achieve this for children with CLDD, educators will need to wrap the curriculum around the child (Carpenter 2010a,b, 2012; Carpenter et al. 2011) by:

- re-engineering and reconciling existing pedagogies;
- adopting new and innovative teaching strategies; and
- personalizing children's learning pathways.

Examples

For a child with ADHD and ASD who needs regular kinaesthetic and sensory stimulation to remain focused on learning, this might mean providing them with 10 minutes structured exercise before a class, access to a sensory 'fiddle kit' during the lesson to enable them to focus and scheduled short 'choice or errand' activity breaks to accommodate their short attention span in a directed way. They may also require visually structured learning activities geared to their concrete learning needs.

For a child with mild physical as well as learning disabilities, the occupational therapist may advise a foot-rest and specific seating support before that child is comfortable enough to focus on learning; the child's learning resources may need to be customized to reflect a personal interest in order to stimulate their curiosity.

Although schools may provide these interventions, they often find it difficult to assess how effective each intervention is individually, and if additional adaptation can make them more effective. The Engagement Profile and Scale provides a means of doing this.

It is easy to assume that because a child's learning barrier is long-standing, it is permanent. However, when the combined minds of educators, families and colleagues from other professions are brought to bear on an entrenched learning issue in a focused and systematic way, the discoveries made can be life-changing for the child. The focus on trialling possible solutions in the quest to increase a child's engagement rather than on instant success frees educators to try out and evidence creative solutions.

Case study: Abby

One class, supported by the Engagement Profile and Scale, started working with Abby, a young woman with quadriplegic cerebral palsy and impaired vision and hearing. She presented as having little interest in engaging with people or activities and was easily distracted. She would startle and hit out when anyone approached. Her aggression was a serious long-term barrier to her learning and had become more challenging with age.

Following initial observations using the Engagement Profile and Scale, the class teacher, teaching assistants and occupational therapist (OT) brainstormed and prioritized possible barriers and solutions to Abby's engagement for learning. As a result, the OT assessed Abby's seating to improve her head positioning. Abby's new headrest improved her line of vision so she was able to anticipate people's approach and new activities. The teaching staff also developed consistent strategies to alert Abby to their approach. As a result of the interventions, she became calmer, started to interact with staff and show an interest in her peers and other activities, and began to show greater confidence when using switches to communicate and make choices.

Using a collaborative, solutions-based approach to overcoming learning barriers, supported by the Engagement Profile and Scale, educators were empowered to make a few simple changes resulting in a massive leap forward in Abby's learning engagement and future life opportunities.

The Engagement for Learning Framework: the tools and how to use them

Although this chapter will mainly describe the Engagement Profile and Scale, which are the core Engagement for Learning Framework tools, it is important to set them in the context of the whole Engagement for Learning Framework.

There are five tools within the Framework:

Core tools

- **Engagement Profile**: used to describe a child's 'highest possible engagement for learning' behaviours during their 'most absorbing-interest' activity or activities; this may be in any environment (e.g. school, home, therapies, community activities, etc.).[1]
- **Engagement Scale**: allows assessment and documentation of a child's progress on a journey from minimal engagement in a priority learning activity to high engagement as a result of adjustments made.

Supplementary tools

- **Engagement Ladder**: helps educators to identify a priority learning focus for children with CLDD (see Appendix A).
- **CLDD Briefing Packs**: provide information on the learning profiles and evidence-based teaching approaches associated with a range of ten conditions commonly co-existing in CLDD (see Appendix B).
- **Inquiry Framework for Learning**: provides 'inquiry-starter questions' in 12 key areas (e.g. communication, emotional well-being) to promote discussion and identify possible investigations for educators as they explore pathways to increase children's engagement (see Appendix C).

All the Engagement for Learning Framework tools complement one another, and Figure 4.2 shows diagrammatically how they come together.

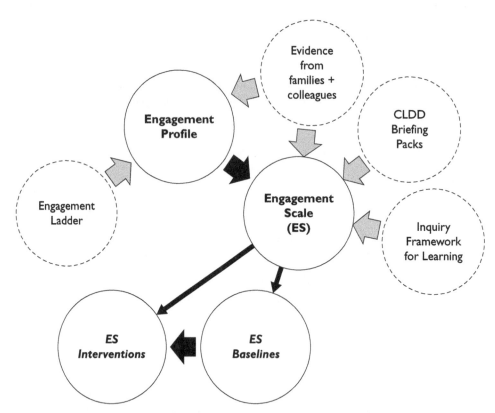

Figure 4.2 A diagram showing how the use of the Engagement for Learning Framework tools can be sequenced. The principal tools (solid outline) – the Engagement Profile and Scale – are used to collect evidence. The supplementary tools (broken outline) – 'Engagement Ladder', 'CLDD Briefing Packs', 'Evidence from families + colleagues' and 'Inquiry Framework for Learning' – are information sources that support use of the core tools.

The Engagement Profile and Scale

As stated above, the Engagement Profile and Scale are the core tools of the Engagement for Learning Framework. They encourage educators to build on children's pro-learning behaviours to overcome learning barriers, and they provide a means of scoring, reporting and presenting the evidence for increasing or decreasing engagement for learning.

The Engagement Profile and Scale together form a classroom observation and assessment resource that enables educators to shape child-centred, personalized learning pathways through:

- identifying children's engagement for learning behaviours during their highest-interest activity;
- reflecting on and implementing strategies to increase children's sustained engagement and 'deep learning' in low-interest activities (Cogill 2002; Hargreaves 2006; Hennessy et al. 2007);
- evidencing the impact of the resulting incremental adjustments to the children's learning environment; and
- scoring the children's current engagement for learning in the light of their own 'highest engagement' activities.

By focusing on a child's engagement for learning, instead of their disengaged behaviours, educators and learners can celebrate their incremental progress towards a priority learning target.

Understanding 'engagement': the seven Engagement Indicators

The term 'engagement' can be used either in a 'passive' sense or in a 'dynamic' sense.

The passive sense treats 'engagement' as a simple, unproblematic label – as something a child is or something they are not. When used in this way, there is little understanding of what behaviours contribute to engagement or that educators can creatively support a child's engagement for learning.

The dynamic sense recognizes 'engagement' as a complex concept, with components that relate to child *actions* which educators can support and change. In consultation with a Clinical Psychologist, the following seven Engagement Indicators or actions which underpin the engagement for learning tools were identified as core to the dynamic concept and management of engagement for learning (see Figure 4.3).

When educators recognize engagement as a complex concept made up of different learner actions, this enables them to identify a child's areas of engagement weakness and to keep a consistent focus on increasing engagement in that area through trialling possible solutions. The Engagement Profile and Scale provides structure and a means of recording. The step-by-step successes enable educators to construct a personalized approach to learning for the child that may also be generalized to other learning situations.

For example, starting with questions based on the Indicators, educators can ask 'How can I change the learning activity to stimulate Robert's *curiosity*?' and 'What can I change about the learning environment to encourage Nina to *persist*?'. In this way, educators can

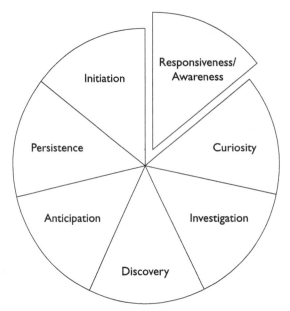

Figure 4.3 The dynamic understanding of engagement: seven Engagement Indicators relating to learner actions

propose, explore and trial, in a very focused way, possible solutions to a child's learning barriers.

One teacher from the CLDD Project commented:

> Focusing on engagement has really opened my mind to the impact of my teaching to the pupil's learning. Time needs to be taken to observe and focus on the Indicators that show a pupil is engaged. Once we have addressed this we can then personalise the pathways of learning for our pupils. We need to ensure that our pupils are engaged before learning can take place and we can help to reinforce this through Engagement Profiles.
>
> (CLDD Project class teacher)

The following two sections will describe how the Engagement Indicators and engagement qualities are used in relation to the Engagement Profile and Scale.

The Engagement Profile

Having identified a child with CLDD who is disengaged from an area of learning and would benefit from working with the engagement approach (see the Engagement Ladder for guidance – Appendix A), the first step is to discover the ways they *do* engage in learning. For many teachers, this is instinctive; others need to make a considered decision (Wright 2014).

When completed, the Engagement Profile provides a quick-access summary of a child's 'fully sustained' engagement behaviours for each of the Engagement Indicators or actions. Using the template (see Figure 4.4), educators can gain evidence of a child's potential for high-level engagement, and use it as a reference throughout their work with the child and the Engagement for Learning Framework. If the Engagement Profile is completed properly,

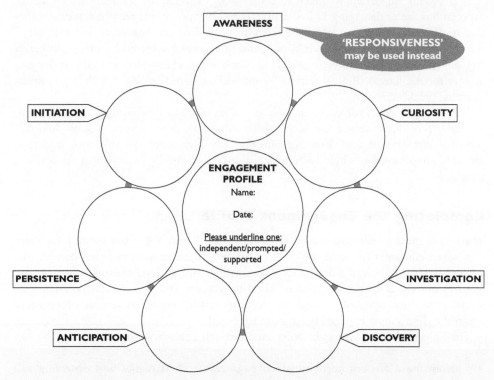

Figure 4.4 The Engagement Profile template ('Responsiveness' and 'Awareness' may be inter-changed depending on its appropriateness for the child)

it will support all educators to develop high expectations of a child's potential engagement, and show areas of high interest for the child which can be introduced into other, less favoured, learning activities to raise their engagement for learning.

Developing high expectations

It is important to involve as many people as possible in creating the child's Engagement Profile. If a child finds their classroom or school environment challenging, it is unlikely that educators will ever see them demonstrate their most highly engaged behaviours. Based on their observations in school, educators may therefore have low expectations of the child's potential for engagement for learning and achievement.

However, all children are learners. Somewhere and in some way, a child will demonstrate engagement in learning. The child's family[2] and the child themselves, will often have insights into what activities the child engages highly with. Education colleagues and colleagues from other disciplines (e.g. psychologists, therapists) who work with the child in different subjects or outside the classroom environment can offer different perspectives on a child's engagement.[3] A child who is disengaged from learning at school may show highly engaged behaviours during an important leisure interest which may be noticed only by a brother or sister. A colleague may have discovered a way of keeping the child focused at the beginning of a lesson until the class has settled.

It is equally important to make sure that high expectations are realistic. Over-high expectations are as damaging as low expectations. If expectations are not achievable they lead to discouragement and low self-esteem for both child and educators. For example, if the maximum length of time a child can concentrate when involved in their most highly engaging activity is 10 minutes, then it is unrealistic to expect them to focus on a challenging activity for the length of a 30-minute lesson without interspersing it with high-interest 'learning break' activities.

The Engagement Profile, because it describes a child's behaviours at their most engaged, provides evidence for both raising educators' low expectations of children's potential engagement and lowering unrealistically high ones. In this way, educators are able to personalize their high expectations of a child's engagement in learning activities.

Completing the Engagement Profile

The Engagement Profile is formed of seven circles (see Figure 4.4) – one for each Indicator – in which educators can note the child's observed high engagement behaviours. At the centre, the child's name, the date of form completion[4] and the level of support they needed to carry out the activity are recorded. The Engagement Profile is completed once from scratch, and then updated throughout the intervention period as further observations about the child's most engaged behaviours are noted.

The Engagement Profile can be completed through a combination of:

- identifying a favourite activity which engages the child highly, and observing and recording the behaviours they show during that activity;
- observing the child's engagement behaviours across a range of favourite activities, and adding the engagement observations to the profile on an ongoing basis;
- talking to others who are closely involved with the child – other education colleagues, family/carers, the child themselves, therapists, etc. – and noting their recollections of the child's behaviours when they are highly engaged; and
- asking the family and colleagues to complete their own Engagement Profiles for or with the child, and then collating the information into one profile.

TOP TIP: One way to gather the information for the Engagement Profile

- Enlarge the Engagement Profile template to A3, place it on the classroom wall and give an A3 copy to anyone else contributing outside the classroom.
- Ask *all* who are involved with the child's learning (including family, therapists, etc.) to note the child's engagement actions on Post-It notes over the course of a week, saying when and how the child demonstrated different Indicators (e.g. investigation).
- Ask them to stick the Post-It notes on the A3 Engagement Profile next to the relevant Indicator.
- At the end of the week, discuss the Post-It comments and the best way of recording them on the profile.

Riverside School, Bromley, a special school for pupils from 4–19 years who have severe, profound and complex learning difficulties and disabilities (SLD, PMLD and CLDD) or severe autism, was one of 12 schools involved in the development phase of the CLDD Project. They use the Post-It note system and an Engagement Profile wall display (see Figure 4.5) in each PMLD classroom. Charlotte Parkhouse, Speech and Language Therapist, who led the CLDD Project at Riverside, writes:

> Having the Engagement Profile on permanent view acts as a visual mnemonic for all to see, prompting the class team to make targeted observations as well as encouraging them to offer extended activity opportunities to show pupil development in these areas. For example, if a pupil is engaged in an activity such as reaching into a box to get a desired resource, rather than the activity finishing there, a supporting adult might be prompted by the visible descriptors to, perhaps, shut the box lid to create an air of anticipation, or promote curiosity. Thus a simple reaching activity can be transformed and extended. The display is also a powerful Assessment for Learning system for the teacher as, when they come to reflect on the pupil's development, they are able to show attainment in specific areas that relate to engagement for individual learning.

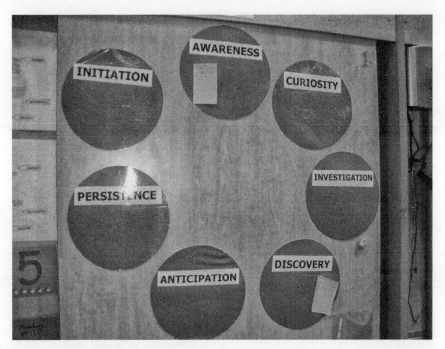

Figure 4.5 An Engagement Profile wall display with Post-It evidence capture at Riverside School, Bromley

Understanding the Engagement Indicators

Often when educators come to complete the Engagement Profile, they begin to ask 'What exactly do the Indicator words mean?', 'When is a behaviour "awareness" and when is it "curiosity"?'.

To help answer these questions, the CLDD Project team developed an 'Indicator definitions' guidance sheet (see Figure 4.6).

It is not enough, however, to take the guidance 'definitions' and apply them to a child. The dynamic use of 'engagement' is about children's engagement *actions*. One child's 'awareness' behaviour might be to orientate their body towards an activity; another's may be to flick their eyes towards it once; yet another might not appear to notice an activity until they are left alone. One child might be aware of the activity from across the room; while their peer might not be aware until their hand is placed upon it. Not all staff will have the opportunity to see or recognize all a child's engagement behaviours, especially for children with CLDD; hence the importance of pooling and writing down collective knowledge about the child's potential engagement behaviours so everyone working with them can recognize and encourage their engagement for learning.

For some children, it is difficult to distinguish behaviours between different Indicators. If this is the case, then the same behaviour description is written in the different sections. Some schools found that as educators became more attuned to the Indicators, and the child's engagement behaviours, they began to distinguish between the Indicators which they had been unable to do initially.

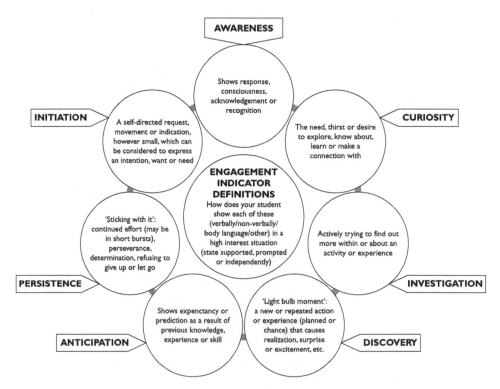

Figure 4.6 The Engagement Profile – Indicator definitions

Summary

Using the Engagement Profile to describe how the child demonstrates and displays high engagement fulfills a number of uses:

- All teaching staff can review the profile, assisting them to recognize the child's high engagement behaviours.
- The profile provides evidence to all educators that it is possible to engage the child at a high level, and therefore it supports them to develop high expectations for the children's engagement in learning.
- The profile supports educators to discover what elements of the high engagement activity/activities engage the child so that the principles may be transferred in some form to the child's low engagement activities with the aim of increasing their engagement in those also.
- The behaviours described represent the highest possible score on the Engagement Scale.

The Engagement Profile and Scale: key differences

The Engagement Scale (see Figure 4.7) is an assessment and scoring tool that, used together with the Engagement Profile, allows educators to plan, describe and score the engagement journey of a child towards a desired learning outcome. Like the Engagement Profile – its companion tool – it is based on the seven Engagement Indicators.

There are key differences between the Engagement Profile and the Engagement Scale:

- The **Engagement Profile** is used to describe a child's behaviours during a favourite activity or activities when they *are at their most engaged*. It is filled in once during the intervention period, but can be added to as new fully engaged behaviours emerge.
- The **Engagement Scale** is used to record the child's journey from a point of *low engagement in a prioritized focus activity* in which the child is minimally engaged to a point of high engagement in that activity. Engagement Scales are filled in once or twice each week to keep a record of the changes made to the activity, and the impact they have on the child's engagement. If the focus activity is carried out in the interim, the adaptations need to remain in place, even when the activity is not scored.

How the Engagement Profile and the Engagement Scale relate

The relationship between the Engagement Profile and the Engagement Scale can be likened to a journey. As with any journey, educators working with the child are starting in one place (low engagement) and want to be somewhere else (high engagement). To do this, they need a destination and a way of getting there.

The engagement for learning behaviours described in the child's Engagement Profile can be thought of as the child's engagement for learning destination. It describes their highly engaged behaviours, which, ideally, educators would like to see demonstrated in every learning activity.

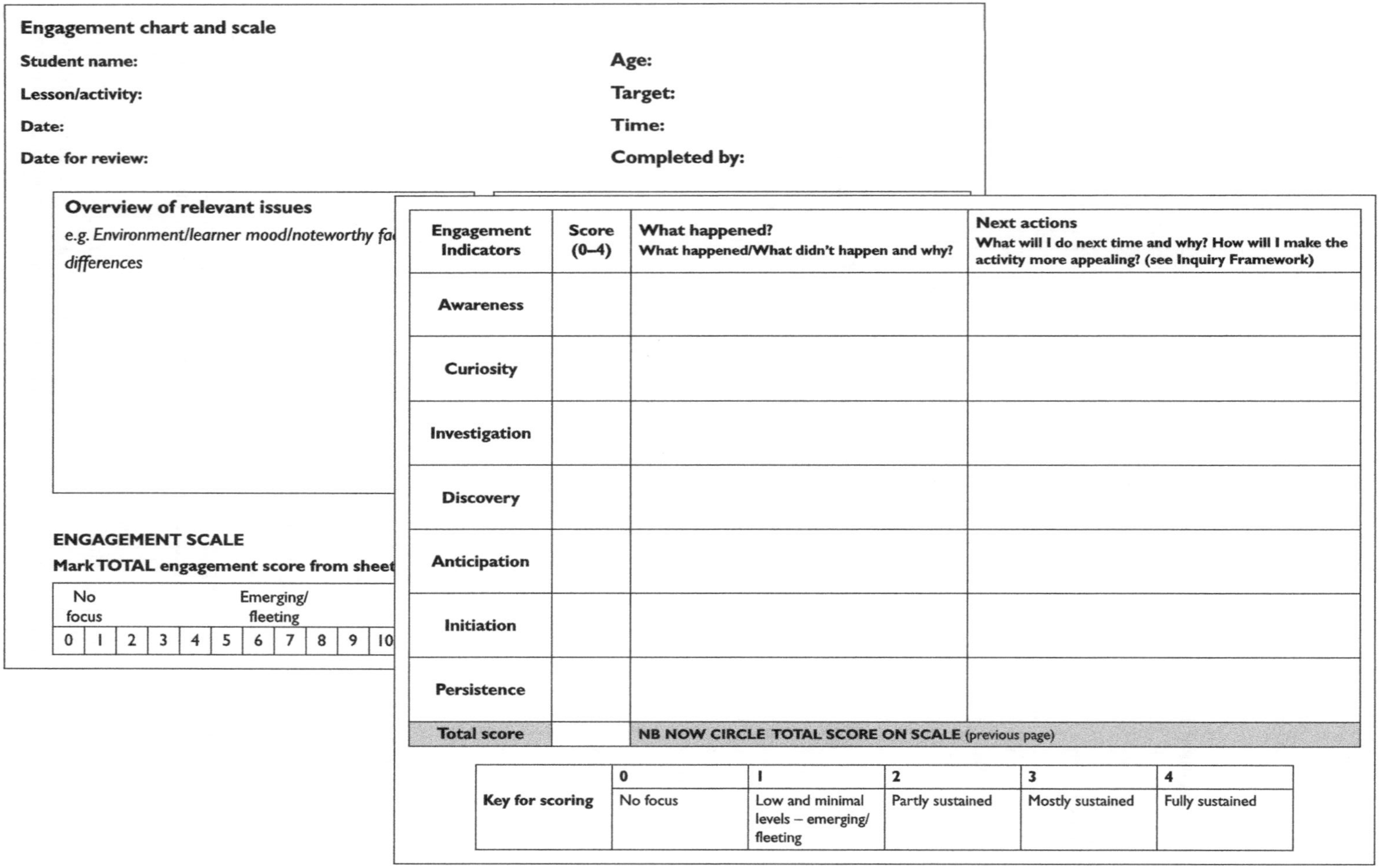

Engagement chart and scale

Student name:

Lesson/activity:

Date:

Date for review:

Age:

Target:

Time:

Completed by:

Overview of relevant issues

e.g. Environment/learner mood/noteworthy fa... differences

Engagement Indicators	Score (0–4)	What happened? What happened/What didn't happen and why?	Next actions What will I do next time and why? How will I make the activity more appealing? (see Inquiry Framework)
Awareness			
Curiosity			
Investigation			
Discovery			
Anticipation			
Initiation			
Persistence			
Total score		NB NOW CIRCLE TOTAL SCORE ON SCALE *(previous page)*	

Key for scoring	0	1	2	3	4
	No focus	Low and minimal levels – emerging/ fleeting	Partly sustained	Mostly sustained	Fully sustained

ENGAGEMENT SCALE

Mark TOTAL engagement score from sheet

No focus				Emerging/ fleeting						
0	1	2	3	4	5	6	7	8	9	10

Figure 4.7 The Engagement Scale (pages 1 and 2)

When the educator and the child with CLDD begin working on a topic the child finds difficult, they will be a long way from this ideal. The path to high engagement will be an unknown. The educator's aim is to discover and record the strategies that are successful in engaging the child in learning, step by step, on their journey towards high or higher engagement. Using the Engagement Scale, educators can systematically evidence this exploration of optimum strategies to engage the child.

Keeping this record of strategies and impacts (positive and negative) prevents the 'revolving door' situation for the child, where every subsequent teacher revisits the same unsuccessful strategies as their predecessor. The successful strategies can then be applied not only to the child's present learning situation, but also tried out in many others, and may transform the child's experience of learning across their school career. Strategies that make no difference or have a negative effect can be abandoned, with the evidence to support that decision recorded.

Preparing to use the Engagement Scale: five steps

In this section, it is assumed that the child has at least some emerging or fleeting engagement in the activity. (An example of using the Engagement Scale with a child who is completely disengaged from learning in school is given in Chapter 5.)

When using the Engagement Scale, the preparation period is as important as the intervention period. The preparation period can be described in five steps; the intervention period does not start until Step 6!

Step 1: Prioritize

Educators need to identify the learning activity, key skill or situation that the child has most difficulty with. If educators have difficulty in prioritizing an activity (e.g. a lesson, a key skill, etc.) of low engagement for the child, they can use the Engagement Ladder (see Appendix A) to support this.

Once the activity has been selected, a specific target or desired outcome within that activity needs to be identified. It is important not to make the target too broad or too ambitious. Remember time and resource constraints and be realistic about expectations. One way of ensuring 'do-ability' is to align the engagement work with one of the child's existing targets. In this way, it can take place within educators' existing work schedules, instead of adding to them. It is better to focus on an achievable outcome instead of aiming to make a big impact and failing through lack of time or resources.

Keeping the target small and focused will make it achievable for both educator and child. This may mean:

- using the Engagement Profile and Scale with only one child to start with (so that educators can get used to working with the tools);
- carrying out observations once or twice per week instead of every day;
- focusing on a short period (e.g. 5–10 minutes) or a specific activity within the lesson, instead of trying to monitor the child throughout the whole lesson (e.g. the introductory activity).

See the SMART check in Step 2.

The priority activity and target must remain consistent throughout the intervention period, and all the evidence collected needs to relate to them.

Step 2: SMART check

S: The target, and the evidence collected, need to be **specific** so that the evidence relates directly to the target. If it does not, it will be useless. The target must stay the same throughout the intervention period; a new target means starting again.

M: The outcomes have to be **measurable**. Everyone involved with collecting evidence needs to be clear about and agree how to score the child's engagement behaviours (see the 'Scoring children's engagement' section later in this chapter).

A: It is important to ensure that the learning target is **achievable** (e.g. manageable; developmentally appropriate; all Engagement Scale observations are target-focused; etc.).

R: To do this, educators will need to be **realistic** about what they can achieve with the resources they have. They may need to: reduce the number of children involved; focus on a smaller learning activity; share the work with a colleague; request non-contact allocation; etc.

T: **Timing**: Educators need to plan how long the intervention period is going to be (e.g. one half term, two terms, etc.), when they are going to take observations (e.g. once or twice a week, during which lesson) and for how long (e.g. 5 minutes at the beginning of a lesson) (Leach 2014).

Step 3: Baselines!

Observe the child engaging in the chosen learning activity *without any intervention* using the Engagement Scale. These initial observations are known as 'baselines' – the starting point for the educator and child.

Baseline observations are essential. Without knowing the child's level of engagement before any adaptations are made, the full extent of their progress will not be apparent (see Figure 4.8). It is important to carry out at least two or three baseline observations so that any unusual results (i.e. if the child is unusually well or poorly engaged) will be balanced out by the other baseline observations.

In the graph in Figure 4.8, the 'Pre-intervention' line represents the baseline observation engagement scores – Ivan's starting point before any interventions were put in place. The 'Post-intervention' line represents Ivan's engagement scores following different interventions. Without the baseline scores as a point of comparison, Ivan's progress would be unremarkable; with them, his improvement is meteoric!

Step 4: Detective work

Access teaching and learning advice related to the child's difficulty or condition through reading the child's files, talking to knowledgeable colleagues/specialists and/or reading professional magazines or journals with a good reputation.

Review the child's Engagement Profile and identify anything that could be included in the low engagement learning activity to encourage the child to engage more.

Ask families and colleagues (teaching and non-teaching) about successful strategies they have for engaging the child. (See Appendix D for questionnaires used during the CLDD Project.)

Look back into the child's educational file for helpful specialist reports or information that might have been missed or forgotten. (It is surprising how common this is!)

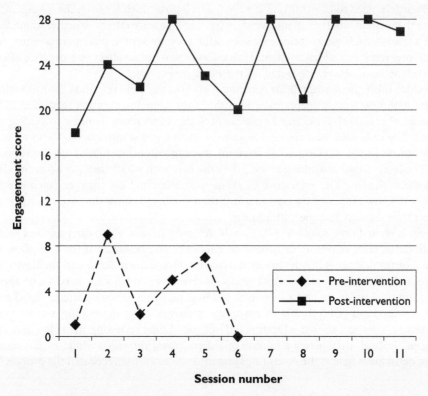

Figure 4.8 Engagement Scale graph for Ivan for pre- and post-intervention lessons

Step 5: Prioritize adaptations

The University of Exeter (2011) suggests that for a child to achieve a personalized target, teaching staff should establish the starting point, try to see through the eyes of the child and concentrate on the barriers that prevent the child from learning.

Prioritize the most promising intervention ideas relating to the Engagement Indicators. This will be a guide only. Educators often find that during the intervention period they discover new and more relevant ideas which take priority.

Step 6: Starting interventions – one change at a time

Once the baseline (i.e. no intervention) observations have been completed, it is time to begin putting in place interventions – one at a time – to support the child's engagement for learning. An 'intervention' in this context is any change or adaption to the child's learning environment made with the intention of increasing their engagement for learning. Each time a new intervention is introduced, its impact on the child's engagement for learning is observed using the Engagement Scale.

Other than the one prioritized change, try to keep all other aspects of the child's learning environment as consistent as possible; for example, time of day, the lesson or activity, communication, teaching approach, etc.

Interventions need to be made one at a time, so it is possible to see from the Engagement Scale for that session whether an intervention has had a positive effect – whether immediate or over a few weeks. If interventions are successful, they are kept in place permanently, and the next intervention is added to them. If an intervention has no effect or a negative effect, it is abandoned, and the reason noted on the Engagement Scale.

Introduce subsequent adaptations depending on how the child responds. Some children can cope with new weekly adaptations; for others, the same intervention may need to be maintained over several weeks and Engagement Scale observations before introducing the next one. The child may even respond negatively when it is first introduced. Children with CLDD can be found working at all levels of the curriculum, including age-appropriate levels. The level a child is working at will affect the ease with which they can accommodate or assimilate change. The educators working with the child on their engagement for learning will know them well enough to gauge their needs and adjust the pace of adaptation to reflect their capacity to cope with change.

If there is limited time to observe during the learning activity, video can provide a useful back up. Often child responses or issues that educators do not notice at the time show up on video, or the educators may be briefly distracted by someone walking into the classroom during a task at the point that a child responds. However, video clips need to be short, focused and used sparingly, and a time limit put in place when reviewing them. Woodlands School, Leatherhead (Curreli 2014), made this manageable by developing a strict 'play, pause, record' protocol so that educators did not spend time reviewing the video over and over again. Instead, they *played* a minute of video, *paused* the video while the class team *recorded* behaviours against the seven Engagement Indicators, then repeated the process for

Case study: the power of video

One young woman seemed to be completely disinterested in any learning activity which was put in front of her, and became aggressive if staff tried to support her engagement. Her class team had tried several adaptations, including temporarily moving her to a screened area of the classroom to reduce the noise and disturbance from other children. It seemed to have no effect. The teaching assistant decided to set up a video camera of the activity in the screened area to try to capture any of the young woman's behaviours that she might be able to build engagement on, and had arranged with the rest of the class team to view and discuss the 5-minute video over lunch. She introduced the adapted activity to the young woman – no response. She was briefly called out of the screened area to help another child, but returned to find the young woman sitting passively in front of the task as before. However, when the class team came to review the video, they had a shock. At the point on the video when the teaching assistant went to help the other child, the young woman leaned forward and began to inspect the task closely. The moment she heard returning footsteps, she slumped back in her chair. This extraordinary discovery gave the class team a way forward to engage the young woman in learning. They began to demonstrate activities, then leave the girl on her own to do the activity with the video running, and re-demonstrate in line with the video outcomes. They had discovered a pathway to learning for this young woman.

the next minute of video. Then everybody pooled their observations and came to a joint decision on scoring.

Exeter House School, Salisbury, together with AnalysisPro and Cardiff Metropolitan University, are developing an effective video capture, tagging (similar to 'bookmarking') and analysis computer software program that will allow educators to analyse and track a child's engagement over time. Using the seven Engagement Indicator categories, the research team are able to track and count points in video clips when a child's objectively observable behaviours link with one of the Engagement Indicators. (More information is available from the school's website: www.exeterhouseschool.co.uk/ground-breaking-research/.)

Scoring children's engagement

The Engagement Profile and Engagement Scale are designed to be used together. Although the Engagement Profile can stand alone as an information document, it only becomes a tool for change when it is teamed with the Engagement Scale:

> When used with the Engagement Scale the Engagement Profile provides the benchmark against which the child's engagement in all other activities can be measured.

The Engagement Scale charts the child's engagement for learning journey, both as a series of scores and descriptively. As noted above, both the Engagement Profile and the Engagement Scale are based on the seven Engagement Indicators or actions. For each, there are five **qualities of engagement** to score as follows:

None (Score = 0)	Emerging or fleeting (Score = 1)	Partly sustained (Score = 2)	Mostly sustained (Score = 3)	Fully sustained (Score = 4)

The behaviours described in the Engagement Profile are the child's behaviours when they are at their maximum engagement. Therefore, for the child described, the Engagement Profile behaviour descriptions represent 'Fully sustained', and, if the child was being observed during their highest engagement activity using the Engagement Scale (which they would not be!), such behaviours would rate a maximum score of '4' for each Indicator on the Engagement Scale.

If the child being observed in an activity shows none of the behaviours associated with any of the Engagement Indicators, this would result in a score of '0' for each Indicator on the Engagement Scale (see Figure 4.9).

It is up to all the adults working with the child, and who know them well, to decide what behaviours represent the remaining three levels of engagement – 'emerging/fleeting', 'partly sustained' and 'mostly sustained' – for each Engagement Indicator. One effective way of doing this is to video several short clips of the child showing different levels of engagement and discuss as a team how to rate the child's behaviours *compared to their 'fully sustained' behaviours* described in the Engagement Profile descriptions. This preparation

Engagement Indicators	Score (0–4)	What happened? What happened/What didn't happen and why?	Next actions What will I do next time and why? How will I make the activity more appealing? (see Inquiry Framework)?
Awareness			
Curiosity			
Investigation			
Discovery			
Anticipation			
Initiation			
Persistence			
Total score		NB NOW CIRCLE TOTAL SCORE ON SCALE (previous page)	

	0	I	2	3	4
Key for scoring	No focus	Low and minimal levels – emerging/ fleeting	Partly sustained	Mostly sustained	Fully sustained

Figure 4.9 Engagement Scale observation template (page 2)

will take time and discussion, but must not be skipped. For the Engagement Scale scoring, it is important that all the adults using the Engagement Scale to observe the child come to an agreement on how to score their learning behaviours.

Observing engagement using the Engagement Scale

Engagement scores are recorded in Column 2 of the Engagement Scale observation template (see Figure 4.8) – one for each of the Engagement Indicators. Once scores have been decided on for each of the Engagement Indicators, these can be totalled. This provides an 'overall engagement' score out of a maximum of 28, which is then recorded overleaf on page 1 of the Engagement Scale.

As with the Engagement Profile, sometimes educators find it difficult to tell the difference between the child's behaviours relating to two or more Engagement Indicators (curiosity and investigation, for example). In this case they should enter the same score for each of the Engagement Indicators. In time, the educators may come to distinguish between behaviours associated with different Indicators.

Column 3: What happened, what didn't happen and why?

Column 3 of the Engagement Scale observation template allows space to describe the child's behaviours in relation to the target – both engaged and non-engaged behaviours.

The description should contain enough detail to justify the score given in Column 2, without becoming too time consuming by recording detail that is not relevant to the child's learning target (however interesting!).

Column 4: Next Actions

The score in Column 2, and the descriptive observation in Column 3, will influence the decisions made by educators about possible 'next actions' to be written in Column 4. Educators may decide to prioritize next actions in relation to one of the seven Indicators; for example, asking themselves, 'Next time, how will I change this activity, environment or context to improve the child's curiosity [or other of the Engagement Indicators]?'

If the educational team cannot think of a way forward for at least one of the Indicators, they may find inspiration by consulting with colleagues and the child's family, using the Briefing Packs (see Appendix B) or the Inquiry Framework for Learning (see Appendix C).

Engagement Scale: essential context

The Engagement Scale observations need to be firmly embedded within a learning context. When pressed for time, it is easy to imagine that 'tomorrow' there will be time to complete the contextual details for the observation. However, the old adage is true – tomorrow never comes! Educators should complete the Engagement Scale as soon as possible after the activity otherwise their previous effort will be wasted. Figure 4.10 shows the essential contextual information needed for the observation.

Engagement chart and scale

Student name: **Age:**

Lesson/activity: **Target:**

Date: **Time:**

Date for review: **Completed by:**

Overview of relevant issues

e.g. Environment/learner mood/noteworthy factors or differences

What 'next action' are you using from the last scale you completed?

e.g. Introduce a computer-based initial activity to reduce demands on student when s/he first arrives at lesson; explain individually to student before lesson what s/he will be doing.

ENGAGEMENT SCALE

Mark TOTAL engagement score from sheet overleaf:

No focus						Emerging/ fleeting							Partly sustained							Mostly sustained								Fully sustained
0	1	2	3	4	5	6	7	8	9	10	11	12	13	14	15	16	17	18	19	20	21	22	23	24	25	26	27	28

Figure 4.10 Engagement Scale observation template (page 1): providing context

In addition to the child's name, the critical details are the *'Date'* of the observation and the *'Target'* they are working towards. Without these details, however good the observations, they will be meaningless to anyone else wanting to learn about the child's engagement journey. If someone picked the observation out of the child's file they would have no idea of the progress made in relation to earlier or later observations; nor could they make a judgement on how appropriate the interventions were to the target selected.

During the CLDD Project, one error often made was losing sight of the target. Educators would become so fascinated by another area of the child's development, other than the target, that they would start making intervention changes that had no relation to the original target. This meant that when they came to evaluate the intervention in relation to the target, they had nothing to say because they had changed their focus to something completely different. If educators decide to change the focus of intervention, they need to identify a new target and start a new sequence of observations related to the new target.

Ideally *'Lesson/activity'* and *'Time'* will be consistent throughout the intervention period. A child may be more engaged earlier in the day due to medication, or may enjoy one lesson/activity better than another, and so without consistency, what might look like an increase in engagement relating to an intervention may just be a reflection of the preferred lesson or time of day. A similar issue is covered by *'Completed by'*. The Engagement Scale recording will be most consistent if one person is responsible for all the observations during the intervention period. However, this is often impractical. If there is more than one educator involved, all need to be trained in the use of the Engagement Profile and Scale, all need to have agreed on the level to score behaviours, and all need to keep to the same approach (e.g. the way the activity is presented, the language used, etc.).

'Relevant issues'

As mentioned above, apart from the planned intervention, educators should try to keep strategies and conditions as consistent as possible for the intervention so any changes in the child's engagement behaviour are likely to be as a result of the planned intervention; for example, keeping the intervention specific, within one particular lesson, during the same period of the day. However, some things are beyond control. For example: the child may have had an argument with their parent before school; they may have had a bad night or a change in medication. The form therefore has a box to record 'relevant issues' which may account for a child's unexpectedly low or high engagement.

'What next action . . .'

The 'What next action . . .' is completed before carrying out the observation. It records the prioritized change made to the activity since the last observation. If there has been no change made this should also be recorded together with the reason (e.g. more time needed by the child to accommodate to the change).

'Engagement score'

The 'Engagement score' is completed after the observation has taken place by taking the total engagement score from page 2 (see Figure 4.9) and recording it on page 1 (see Figure 4.10). This makes the paperwork quicker and easier to refer back to.

'Date for review'

This is a reminder to diary the next observation. Unless the next observation is set, the momentum of the project is lost.

Bringing together the evidence

The Engagement Profile and Scale is designed to be used with a child over a defined period. Once an intervention period has been completed for a child, there will be five to ten, or more, completed Engagement Scales relating to the child's target. The information is now ready to be brought together as evidence for the progress made by the child relating to the different interventions. Chapter 5 contains case study examples illustrating how schools have done this.

The engagement approach: top tips

The process of personalizing engagement and learning for a child with CLDD is not one which always progresses smoothly. Often children may reach a plateau or educators may struggle, through no fault of their own, to identify the motivators and adaptations which a child requires in order to increase their engagement in learning. It is important to remember that for some children with CLDD, progression can be lateral rather than vertical. The DfE's *Progression 2010–11* (2010: 7) document acknowledges that 'preventing or slowing a decline in performance may be an appropriate outcome' of intervention.

The CLDD Project revealed a few key tips which the schools developing and trialling the Engagement for Learning Framework found to be key to their success:

1. Collaborate

The Engagement Profile and Scale is most beneficial when a team (including educators – teachers and teaching assistants – other professionals and the child's family) collaborate to discuss how a child shows their engagement in terms of each of the seven Engagement Indicators. Once the team working with the child develops a shared and consistent perspective of how the child shows engagement, they can share observation and recording. Collaboration also encourages the enrichment of the child's learning experience through sharing ideas and strategies from different perspectives. Different people will have different, yet equally valuable, insights and interpretations. For more information on collaboration see Chapter 7.

2. Video

If you are struggling to observe a child, filming them will allow you to reflect in more detail later. Many of the schools involved in the CLDD Project noticed that through videoing a child, they were able to see behaviours relating to the Indicators which initially they had not spotted. Videoing can also facilitate collaboration, allowing many individuals to watch the child's lesson.

The use of video is now considered to be a most powerful observational tool when used in conjunction with data-based tools. It assists and highlights steps towards the target. It may reveal a child's need for more processing time or emphasize sensory issues that may go unnoticed in a busy classroom. It can enable staff to self-evaluate the impact of their own practice in relation to a child's learning.

Conclusion

The learning needs of children with CLDD go beyond the expectations for classroom differentiation, challenging the teaching skills of even our most experienced and effective educators. A key element to consider is that 'Engagement is the connection between the student and their learning outcome. Students cannot create that connection for themselves; it is educators, families and colleagues who must construct it with and for them' (Carpenter et al. 2011: 59).

Educators need to be critical observers, writing down what they see, and reflecting on this with colleagues, perhaps using video to clarify and confirm: what happened; what didn't happen; why should it have happened; was the intervention successful; if not, should it be re-presented or discarded and why?

Notes

1 When children's 'most absorbing interest' is detrimentally obsessional or socially inappropriate, educators should select an alternative highest interest activity.
2 Here, the term 'family' includes the self-defined family in its widest sense – not only the nuclear family, but also grandparents, neighbours, friends, etc. (Carpenter and Filmer 2015).
3 The questionnaires in Appendix D are one way in which this information can be collected.
4 Recording the date is essential on all paperwork; without a date, it is impossible to track changes in child behaviours or achievement over time.

References

Carpenter, B. (2010a) *Curriculum Reconciliation and Children with Complex Learning Difficulties and Disabilities* (Complex needs series), London: SSAT.

Carpenter, B. (2010b) *Children with Complex Learning Difficulties and Disabilities: Who are they and what are their needs?* (Complex needs series), London: SSAT.

Carpenter, B. (2012) 'Children with complex learning disabilities: a 21st century challenge'. [Online at: http://hwb.warwickshire.gov.uk/files/2012/04/Professor-Carpenter-Children-with-complex-learning-disabilities.pdf; accessed: 20.06.14.]

Carpenter, B. and Filmer, H. (2015, forthcoming) 'Working with families: partnership in practice'. In P. Lacey, H. Lawson, P. Jones and R. Ashdown (eds) *The Routledge Companion to Severe, Profound and Multiple Learning Difficulties*, London: Routledge.

Carpenter, B., Egerton, J., Brooks, T., Cockbill, B., Fotheringham, J. and Rawson, H. (2011) *The Complex Learning Difficulties and Disabilities Research Project: Developing pathways to personalised learning*, London: SSAT.

Cogill, J. (2002) 'How is the interactive whiteboard being used in the primary school and how does this affect teachers and teaching?'. [Online at: www.virtuallearning.org.uk/whiteboards/IFS_Interactive_whiteboards_in the_primary_school.pdf; accessed: 17.05.09.]

Curreli, L. (2014) 'Engagement = learning: a toolbox for the inclusive classroom'. In Innovation Teaching School (ed.) *Developing a Finding Out Culture: Teachers evidencing interventions and impact*, Farnham: Innovation Teaching School, pp. 67–72.

DfE (Department for Education) (2010) *Progression 2010–11: Advice on improving data to raise attainment and maximise the progress of learners with special educational needs*, London: DfE.

Hargreaves, D. (2006) *A New Shape for Schooling?*, London: SSAT.

Hennessy, S., Deaney, R., Ruthven, K. and Winterbottom, M. (2007) 'Pedagogical strategies for using the interactive whiteboard to foster learner participation in school science', *Learning, Media and Technology*, 32(3): 283–301.

Leach, S. (2014) 'Jumpers, lip-balm and music: the management of engagement'. In Innovation Teaching School (ed.) *Developing a Finding Out Culture: Teachers evidencing interventions and impact*, Farnham: Innovation Teaching School, pp. 73–79.

University of Exeter (2011) 'Setting and achieving personalised learning outcomes/targets'. [Online at: www.education.exeter.ac.uk; accessed: 28.07.11.]

US Department of Education, Office of Educational Technology (2010) *Transforming American Education: Learning powered by technology*. Washington, DC: US Department of Education. [Online at: http://planipolis.iiep.unesco.org/upload/USA/USA_NETP_2010.pdf; accessed: 10.07.14.]

Wright, B. (2014) 'Complex children: enhancing engagement'. In Innovation Teaching School (ed.) *Developing a Finding Out Culture, Teachers evidencing interventions and impact*. Farnham: Innovation Teaching School, pp. 12–19.

Chapter 5

Personalizing engagement

Case studies

Chapter 4 introduced the Engagement for Learning Framework and described how to use the Engagement Profile and Scale. This chapter explores in more depth how educators can use the tools and develop personalized teaching and learning strategies for children and young people with CLDD. It presents a range of case studies from schools, and shows how they used the Engagement Profile and Scale to facilitate personalized learning pathways and generate reliable, high-quality evidence of learning progress.

As we saw from Chapter 4, a child's Engagement Profile can provide the missing information needed for educators to engage a child in a learning activity in which they currently have minimal engagement. Educators can:

- find out about innovative and incidental strategies used by families and other colleagues to engage the child;
- integrate features from favourite activities that engage the child into a learning activity in which they currently have low engagement;
- take inspiration from strategies known to work with children who have the same disability or an allied condition; and
- make adjustments based upon the child's perspective on what they enjoy doing and what changes that could help them learn better.

Each of the following case studies takes one of the above routes as their focus. The children in these case studies were brought into the CLDD Project by their schools because they had very minimal engagement with learning, and educators were struggling to move their learning forward. When the educators became sensitized to what they themselves, the child's family and their colleagues did know about the child, they were empowered to make the changes that re-engaged the child as a learner.

Case study: Sarah

Find out about innovative and incidental strategies used by families to engage the child

Sarah is a nine-year-old girl with a diagnosis of ADHD and Asperger syndrome who attends a mainstream primary school. She has support from a range of professionals, including the local educational psychology service, the assessment and care management team, the communication/autism team, a consultant paediatrician, a clinical psychologist (Child and Adolescent Mental Health Services, CAMHS) and an occupational therapist.

Following discussion, and after observing one of her low engagement activities – a Numeracy lesson – the target chosen for Sarah's intervention was 'to engage in the first part of a Numeracy lesson'. It was apparent that Sarah could concentrate in short bursts only, and that the expectation that, along with her class, she would sit and attend to the one-hour Numeracy session was unattainable for her.

The teacher had already put in place some positive interventions for Sarah. Sarah had responded well to increased positive reinforcement and the introduction of visual timetables, but the use of visual prompt cards had not worked as Sarah had either hidden them or given them away. She also liked being given tasks/jobs to do.

Sarah's Engagement Profile

Sarah's teacher created an Engagement Profile for Sarah using her favourite lesson – English – as a high-interest activity, and noted her behaviours against each of the seven Engagement Indicators. The Engagement Profile is shown in Figure 5.1.

Although Sarah's Engagement Profile shows that she is capable of behaving appropriately in a lesson she likes (English), it is not as useful as it could be. When completing the Engagement Profile under time pressure, it is tempting to take the easy option and settle for describing the child's best lesson as Sarah's teacher did here. This is unlikely to show the

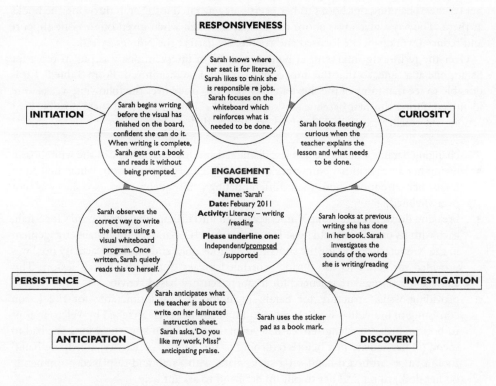

Figure 5.1 Sarah's Engagement Profile

high-quality engaged behaviours that a favourite activity for the child will show. If the child is not displaying *highly engaged* behaviours in school, educators will get a real insight into the child's capacity for engaged behaviours only if they talk to the child's family and/or other teaching and multidisciplinary colleagues and complete the Engagement Profile together.

When Sarah's teacher came to use the Engagement Profile as a resource describing Sarah's high engagement activities, she realized that all it showed was the learning behaviours expected of any child, and did not tell her anything about how Sarah herself engaged most strongly, so she thought again. She rang Sarah's mother for a chat. Sarah's mother was able to tell her that Sarah's favourite of all activities was making collages from different materials. Whereas her attention span was usually 5–10 minutes for other activities, she could spend up to 20 minutes working on her collages. Sarah's collage work would have been a much more useful activity to use as a basis for her Engagement Profile. The teacher was subsequently able to integrate this activity to raise Sarah's engagement in her lessons.

Sarah's Engagement Scales

Sarah's baseline Numeracy lesson (i.e. before any interventions had been introduced) led to a score of '10' on the Engagement Scale (maximum score: 28) (see Figure 5.2). Although initially she appeared ready to learn (sitting quietly; correct equipment on her desk; looking focused), Sarah quickly disengaged and was largely disengaged throughout the lesson – listening to peers' jokes, playing with equipment on her desk, etc. A job given to Sarah by her teacher – handing out books to her peers – degenerated into Sarah throwing the books at them. The work given was above her ability, although when given one-to-one support and reduced workload, she focused and tried really hard at the Numeracy task.

Over the term-long intervention period, a series of interventions was put in place for Sarah, one at a time, so that the impact of each could be monitored. From Table 5.1 it is possible to see that most of the 'next actions' put into place over the following weeks were identified during this first baseline session (see final column). From all these possible next actions, the teacher created a prioritized list. It included:

- changing Sarah's seat so she was less distracted and had a clear view of the whiteboard;
- giving her an easy initial Numeracy activity at the start of the lesson, which helped to focus her attention, and then differentiating subsequent work so she was not overwhelmed;
- breaking down the one-hour Numeracy lesson into manageable time chunks for Sarah, each with its own tasks/activities. Due to her ADHD, Sarah could sustain engagement in the Numeracy lesson for the short time periods only, and a collage 'activity box' was provided for Sarah to use during scheduled breaks during the hour's lesson. This allowed her to regulate her need for frequent sensory-based activity.
- providing visual structure for Sarah, including: a visual timetable for the lesson consisting of individual symbols representing activities each attached by Velcro in top-to-bottom order to a length of card; a visual timer so Sarah knew how long she had to spend on her activity box before returning to the Numeracy activity; a 'helping hand' tool (a large cardboard hand-on-a-stick, made with Sarah and displayed prominently on her desk) to remind her to put up her hand to ask for help.
- working with a peer, which gave opportunity for focused social interaction; and

Engagement Indicators	Score (0–4)	What happened? What happened/what didn't happen and why?	Next actions What will I do next time and why? How will I make the activity more appealing? (see Inquiry Framework)
Responsiveness	3	Very aware what the lesson was about. Sat down with correct equipment in front of her. Looked focused, ready to start.	Make the most of her readiness to engage – have a simple work sheet until the whole class is ready to work.
Curiosity	1	Slightly interested. Symbol cards given for visual prompts. Sarah laughed, looked at them, then turned them over.	Symbols to be in front of her on the table or fixed to wall beside her.
Investigation	0	No questions re lesson. Played with equipment – disengaged. Responded to Teacher question with *'Don't know the answer'*.	Only allowed the equipment needed for that lesson.
Discovery	1	Teacher used the word, 'estimation'. Sarah made a 'don't understand' sound. Discovered she could rub the pen marks off the laminated sheet with her jumper sleeve.	Make helping-hand-on-a-stick as a reminder for Sarah to put up her hand if she doesn't understand.
Anticipation	1	Sarah asked, *'What are we supposed to be doing?'*, then waited for response.	Sarah likes to know what happens next. Use written 'to do' list with tick boxes to tick when complete instead of laminated board.
Initiation	1	Sarah began the job of handing out the books which ended in her throwing them to her peers. Not much opportunity to initiate work as it appears too complicated. Sarah asked for help with maths; needed 1:1 support.	Sarah clearly loves jobs – should she earn the job and only be allowed if she understands the rules of the job? Sarah needs a differentiated maths sheet.
Persistence	3	Began to disengage; sighed and said, *'I'm bored'*. Given worksheet; asked to do fewer questions. After 1:1 support, focused on task and tried really hard.	Example demonstrated and left on her work table to remind her what to do.
Total score	10	NB NOW CIRCLE TOTAL SCORE ON SCALE (previous page)	

Key for scoring	0	1	2	3	4
	No focus	Low and minimal levels – emerging/fleeting	Partly sustained	Mostly sustained	Fully sustained

Figure 5.2 Sarah's baseline (no interventions) Engagement Scale for 17 February 2011 [this is page 2 of a completed Engagement Scale; page 1 is not shown, but would provide essential contextual information for observation analysis]

Table 5.1 Sarah's engagement scores (intervention period: 26 January–17 March 2011)

Session No.	Baselines		Interventions	
	Date	Total score	Date	Total score
1	26 January	10		
2			17 February	22
3			3 March	24
4			4 March	20
5			10 March	28
6			11 March	27
7			17 March	28

- providing motivators, such as responsibility for jobs, to be earned by completion of Numeracy tasks, and reward stickers for using her 'helping hand'.

Table 5.1 and Figure 5.3 show Sarah's engagement scores as each intervention was introduced. There was only one baseline session scored, and ideally there would have been two more to check that the first was not out of character. The graph provides a strong visual presentation of the initial leap in Sarah's engagement.

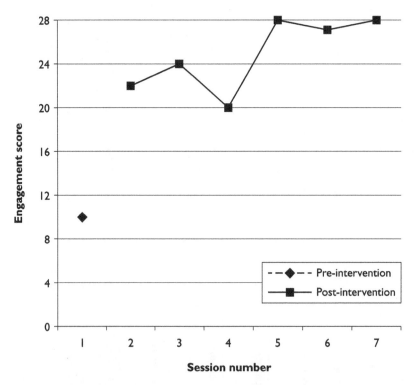

Figure 5.3 Sarah's engagement scores (intervention period: 26 January–17 March 2011)

Intervention postscript

The interventions were successful, and Sarah was able to complete focused work during her Numeracy lesson, interspersed with specific times for self-regulatory sensory activities (activity box). Her class teacher was considering extending the intervention by reducing the length of Sarah's self-regulatory periods, and increasing the time she was engaged in Numeracy. From a lesson in which she had had a low level of engagement, Sarah was now able to engage for most of the Numeracy lesson with the support of interventions. Following the period of implementation of the Engagement for Learning Framework, Sarah's teacher gave feedback about Sarah's continuing engagement in learning:

> There is a way to engage even the 'most difficult child' through the use of what can be very simple strategies. . . . With both of the children [Sarah and a peer] taking part in the research, the approach has had a very positive result. In previous years and during the first part of this school year both the children were not accessing the curriculum successfully, rarely completed tasks and were causing concern by showing extreme behaviours or behaviours that were difficult to cope with within a classroom. Through the participation in the research, gaining insight into complex learning difficulties, and being given tools to develop personalized learning pathways, both children have successfully moved forward in their learning.
>
> Sarah has become more settled in class. She will listen and focus on her work. She does not shout out during a lesson. It has also helped her to develop social skills. Sarah has found that she can work with other children and is not so isolated. She rarely shows aggression towards others and her self-esteem has developed.
>
> Making resources for [Sarah] was not a big issue, and actually involving [her] in making the resources was a positive thing. The response of the other children was interesting in that they accepted that 'something different' was happening. Strategies used have become an integral part of the lesson. Other children who do not have complex needs but behaviour issues have used some of the ideas to improve their engagement.
>
> A member of the communication and autism team who supports the school [one or two visits a term] has been made aware of the research taking place and shown some of the ideas we have used with Sarah. They have had copies of some of the resources used with the children and are suggesting their use in other schools!

Case study: Harry

Find out about innovative and incidental strategies used by other colleagues to engage the child.

Harry is a young man, aged eight years, with diagnoses of moderate/severe learning difficulties, attention deficit hyperactivity disorder, obsessive compulsive disorder, oppositional defiant disorder, mental health issues and speech and language difficulties. He is involved with the occupational therapist, speech and language therapist and play therapist.

Harry found it difficult to engage with learning across the curriculum, but he was entirely disengaged from food technology lessons, and had not been able to participate in group sessions in this lesson for two years because he was too disruptive during the lesson. Harry's teacher wanted to begin to explore re-engaging Harry with this lesson as a focus. Using the Engagement Profile and Scale, as described in the Chapter 4, she began to explore ways to achieve this.

Harry's teacher talked with her colleagues about strategies they had found successful in engaging Harry. One colleague had found that Harry engaged highly in sensory story sessions and had become enthralled when puppets were involved. His engagement in this activity was of such a high level that his teacher decided to use sensory stories as the basis for his Engagement Profile.

Following her baseline observations using the Engagement Scale, Harry's teacher began to introduce interventions one at a time. Puppets were introduced during Harry's cookery lessons, with Harry using them as a means to communicate with the group, albeit indirectly. This strategy proved very successful. Harry then independently started taking an interest in how one of his peers was using a communication book to participate, and one lesson, he picked the book up and started to explore it. His teacher capitalized on Harry's interest in communicating more directly. She gave him his own communication book, and he gradually progressed from communicating indirectly using the puppet to using the communication book to interact with staff and peers. With this support, Harry achieved his target – 'To engage in food technology lessons' – and was able to re-integrate successfully with his class group for these sessions, and is using the communication book to support his learning activities across the school day. Through the initial close focus on improving Harry's engagement in one small area of the curriculum, his educators were able to develop a personalized pathway to learning which could be generalized across all his other learning activities.

Looking at Table 5.2 which shows the timetable of baseline and intervention observations, you can see that:

- session outcomes were recorded once or twice weekly depending on Harry's and staff attendance, with a break for half-term;
- interventions were introduced one at a time with one exception for the first session. This is important for the reasons explained in Chapter 4.
- some interventions were in place for more than one session before introducing another intervention, giving Harry the time he needed to become confident in using them successfully.

Following interventions and subsequent monitoring using the Engagement Profile and Scale, Harry's engagement records showed a significant increase in engagement in food technology, evidenced in Table 5.3 and Figure 5.4.

Table 5.2 Implementation record of strategies supporting Harry's engagement (intervention period: 10 September–29 November 2010)

Intervention strategy	Session dates														
	September				October					November					
	10	13	17	27	1	4	8	11	18	5	12	15	19	22	29
No intervention (baseline sessions for comparison)	X	X	X												
Session relocated from cookery room to classroom				X	X	X	X	X	X	X	X				
Puppet introduced				X	X	X									
Puppet not brought out until Harry requested it independently								X	X						
Communication book										X	X	X	X	X	X
Cookery session relocated to the kitchen												X	X	X	X

HALF TERM

Table 5.3 Harry's increase in engagement scores over time (intervention period: 10 September–29 November 2010)

Session No.	Baseline		Intervention	
	Date	*Total score*	*Date*	*Total score*
1	10 September	0		
2	13 September	9		
3	17 September	9		
4			27 September	27
5			1 October	26
6			4 October	25
7			8 October	24
8			11 October	25
9			18 October	27
10			5 November	23
11			12 November	28
12			15 November	28
13			19 November	26
14			22 November	28
15			29 November	27

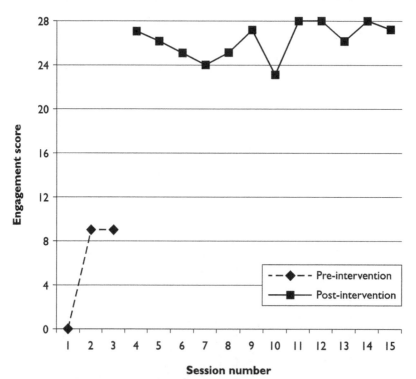

Figure 5.4 Chart displaying Harry's increase in engagement scores over time (intervention period: 10 September–29 November 2010)[1]

Case study: Alfie

Integrate features from favourite activities that engage a child in a learning activity in which they currently have low engagement.

Alfie is a four-year-old boy with profound and multiple learning difficulties (PMLD), including global developmental delay, epilepsy and physical disabilities. His teacher and the class team were at a loss as to how to engage him. Alfie would self-induce sleep during most of the day's activities: he would be asleep within minutes of the beginning of a lesson and wake up once the lesson had finished. This was especially so in food technology lessons, when he would disengage within seconds! Although he seemed passive, the class team found through close observation that Alfie did have likes and dislikes and seemed content to be in his own space; he did not invite others in.

One of Alfie's Statement of SEN Objectives was to improve his attention and listening skills, and the class decided to work on this in the context of enabling him to be actively engaged during food technology. Consequently the aims of the CLDD Project intervention were: (1) to maintain Alfie's attention during a food technology lesson; (2) to encourage his understanding of what others were communicating and develop appropriate responses; and (3) to build up his social interaction skills with the eventual long-term aim of appropriate interaction with peers.

Alfie's teacher identified key barriers to his learning, such as not being interested in people or his immediate environment, having little understanding of his world and having very delayed attention and listening skills.

One of Alfie's only activities in which he showed active engagement was pouring water. In this, Alfie would show high levels of interest and interaction as he watched and listened to water being poured into a tin from a height. The class team used the water-pouring activity to write an Engagement Profile for Alfie (see Figure 5.5). They noted his interest in the container, the enjoyment of water, of watching the way the water poured and where it came from, and of the sound. They also noted how his behaviour showed that he was engaged – his body stilled, he paid close attention and tracked the water from its source to its destination, he vocalized and made babbling sounds showing anticipation when the water was moved away.

Alfie's behaviour during the water pouring activity demonstrated to the class staff team how intently he could be engaged. They now knew how he could respond if he was interested in an activity – and they had an idea of what interested him. Completing the Engagement Profile and looking for evidence of all the Engagement Indicators during the observation enabled Alfie's class team to understand how *he did* demonstrate engagement for learning, rather than how they *expected* him to.

Interventions

As described above, during food technology Alfie would self-induce sleep at the beginning of the lesson within 1–2 minutes. The summaries below (Table 5.4) describe the outcomes of observations carried out using the Engagement Scale by the class in two food technology lessons before any intervention was introduced at all. This gave a starting point for comparing Alfie's progress in future sessions after interventions were introduced. The questions represent the observer's musings about future strategies to engage Alfie.

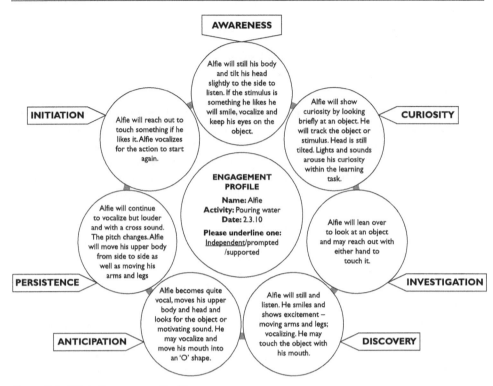

Figure 5.5 Alfie's Engagement Profile

Table 5.4 Summary of Alfie's baseline Engagement Scales 1 and 2

Session No.	Date	Total score	Summary of Engagement Scale observation
1	10 March	2	• Alfie appeared comfortable in his chair. • How much verbal communication does Alfie understand? Lots of verbal communication from staff – some to Alfie, some to his peers, some to each other. Does he need more processing time? If so how much? • How aware is Alfie of activity around him? He shows awareness: of staff wiping his table and of his chair being moved. (Does this need to be moved? If so where and why?) He showed no awareness of food in front of him. Possibly use more motivating foods? • Alfie was asleep within 1 minute.
2	26 April	3	• Similar to above. Alfie did not open his mouth to taste until the toast was put to his lips. No initiation seen. Alfie showed no obvious signs that he wanted to continue the experience.

The beginnings of these two food technology lessons were videoed until Alfie fell asleep. Later, the class team reviewed the video and discussed the demands placed on Alfie during food technology activities. They suddenly realized what a busy and noisy environment their classroom was for Alfie. He was seated close to his peers, which made him uneasy; he was also expected to listen to and process verbal communication, make choices, smell and eat the food presented and interact with staff. The class team began to understand why he was so overloaded by all the sensory stimulation and staff demands that he needed to sleep!

In deciding upon what interventions they might introduce, the class team considered:

• adjusting Alfie's seating position to make him more comfortable and give him better balance and stability to make exploring the food easier;
• reducing the invasiveness of the learning environment for Alfie (e.g. moving Alfie to the periphery of the class group where he could see his peers but was not surrounded by them);
• transferring features from his high-interest Engagement Profile activity (water-pouring) to his focus low-interest activity of food technology (e.g. transferring the idea of a pouring substance, and the high-level pouring action to the food technology context);
• how to increase his interaction with adults and peers – although he appeared to interact with adults during the water-pouring activity, the teacher felt that his connection was with the activity, not the adult. Alfie did not interact with his peers at all. The teacher talked to Alfie's mother who told her that when his family wanted Alfie to pay attention or listen to them, they sang the words to nursery tunes instead of talking to him.

Completing Alfie's Engagement Scales

Alfie's class team then prioritized the interventions they had thought of, and began to introduce them into the food technology sessions for Alfie. They carried out scheduled observations using the Engagement Scale. Also, through these observations, they began to gain ideas about additional interventions that they might introduce. These became part of the prioritized list of possible interventions for Alfie. They completed one Engagement Scale weekly during the food technology lesson.

Figure 5.6 shows the first intervention observation. The length of observations noted on the Engagement Scale is ideal. The observations are short and to the point, yet include enough information to be useful. Not including unnecessary detail (however interesting!) makes the records quicker to write at the end of a busy session.

The proposed 'next actions' are similarly short. It is not necessary always to include a next action for every Engagement Indicator.

To save space, information from the post-intervention Engagement Scales completed by the class team is summarized in Table 5.5. Together with the baseline summary (Table 5.4) and the timetable of all baselines and interventions (Table 5.6), they tell Alfie's 'engagement story'. Figure 5.7 illustrates that story visually.

From Table 5.5 it is possible to see that the successful interventions were maintained after their introduction. The third intervention – a teaching assistant sitting behind Alfie, instead of in front of him, to support his learning – was unsuccessful, so it was quickly abandoned. The fourth intervention – providing only one ingredient for Alfie to explore – was modified in following weeks (e.g. providing hand-over-hand support for Alfie's exploration, introducing a more engaging food substance first) to extend Alfie's experience

Engagement Indicators	Score (0–4)	What happened? What happened/what didn't happen and why?	Next actions What will I do next time and why? How will I make the activity more appealing? (see Inquiry Framework)
Awareness	1	New positioning helped, although he fixed his gaze on the ceiling light.	Ensure ceiling light is off.
Curiosity	2	Smiled when he saw the dish. Watched the adult mash the banana. Curious when showed but would not touch.	Offer motivating food item first.
Investigation	1	Allowed adult to help him to wash hands using hand over hand. Also to help him explore mashed banana after tasting.	Give time to explore food and present in dish.
Discovery	1	Stilled, leaned forward and looked intently when introduced to water bowl for hand washing. Tracked with eyes when taken to next person.	
Anticipation	0	No anticipation seen.	Put bowl on table in front of him; give time for response.
Initiation	0	No initiation seen.	
Persistence	1	Showed no obvious signs that he wanted to continue the experience. Stilled when shown food. Vocalized when he didn't want to do something.	
Total score	6	**NB NOW CIRCLE TOTAL SCORE ON SCALE (previous page)**	

Key for scoring	0	1	2	3	4
	No focus	Low + minimal levels – emerging/fleeting	Partly sustained	Mostly sustained	Fully sustained

Figure 5.6 Alfie's Engagement Scale for the first intervention session (10 May 2010). This is page 2 of the Engagement Scale; page 1 is not shown, but provides essential contextual information.

Table 5.5 Timetable of interventions supporting Alfie's engagement (intervention period: 10 March–5 July 2010)

Session No.	Intervention strategy	Session dates								
		March	April	May		June				July
		10	26	10	24	7	14	21	28	5
1	No intervention ('baseline')	X								
2	Adjusted seating position		X	X	X	X	X	X	X	X
3	Bowl of water instead of wipes introduced for Alfie (and his peers) to wash hands before lesson			X	X	X	X	X	X	X
4	Teaching assistant sat behind instead of beside him to aid his concentration				X					
5	Alfie given a single ingredient for independent sensory experience instead of being required to touch/taste multiple sandwich ingredients				X	X	X	X	X	X
6	Alfie supported hand-over-hand to experience and explore the single food ingredient					X	X	X	X	X
7	Instead of speaking instructions to Alfie, staff sang the instructions to simple tunes to gain his attention, give repetitions of the instruction and increase processing time for him						X	X	X	X
8	Introduced a bowl (icing sugar, then adding water). Clinked spoon on bowl when stirring to gain Alfie's interest.							X	X	X
9	Using the spoon, poured the icing from a height into the bowl so Alfie could see it pouring – replicating the high engagement pouring water							X	X	X
10	Took action to reduce light distraction for Alfie								X	X
11	Interventions maintained; no new interventions									X

HALF TERM (between the 24 May and 7 June sessions)

Table 5.6 Summary of Alfie's Engagement Scales 3–9 (intervention period: 10 March–5 July 2010). These post-intervention observations follow on from the baseline (pre-intervention) sessions in Table 5.4.

Session No.	Date	Total score	Summary of Engagement Scale observations
3	10 May	6	• Being mindful of Alfie's fascination for water, as demonstrated in his Engagement Profile activity, a bowl of water was introduced at the beginning of the lesson for him to wash his hands, instead of staff wiping them clean with a cloth. This purposeful activity (hygiene) immediately engaged his interest right at the start of the lesson. • Alfie stilled when he saw the bowl of water, leaned forward in his chair and looked into the bowl. Staff positioned him to make it easier for him to reach the bowl, and he allowed staff to place his hands in the bowl. He tracked the bowl with his eyes when it was taken to the next child.
4	24 May	12	• To try to increase Alfie's engagement in the activity, the teaching assistant began the session sitting behind Alfie instead of in front of him to see if this mode of instruction was more successful for him, but Alfie was unsettled and kept trying to look behind him to see where she had gone. He responded better when she moved back in front of him. • Instead of experiencing making a sandwich, Alfie was given a single food item (i.e. a peeled banana) in his hand, allowing him to have sensory/tactile experience of foods.
5	7 June	17	• Alfie was supported hand-over-hand to touch and explore a preferred single food (i.e. icing sugar) before going on to the banana. Alfie was supported to taste the sugar.
6	14 June	20	• Staff began to sing instructions to Alfie instead of saying them. Alfie was more responsive, looking towards staff.
7	21 June	20	• Staff introduced the single ingredient (i.e. icing sugar) in a bowl. The teaching assistant encouraged Alfie's curiosity in the bowl by making sounds with the spoon and bowl when mixing in the water. She encouraged Alfie to indicate 'more' by stopping stirring, then re-starting when he leant forward. By using the spoon to pour some of the runny icing into the bowl from a height, staff introduced a key characteristic of Alfie's high-engagement 'pouring water' activity to gain his full interest in the properties of the icing.
8	28 June	19	• Staff made changes to the environment to decrease the play of light which was distracting Alfie from the learning activity. The window blinds were drawn. (Alfie was also getting used to a new type of chair.)
9	5 July	16	• No additional intervention took place on this date. Alfie seemed tired and closed his eyes a lot. He became more alert when water was brought to wash his hands.

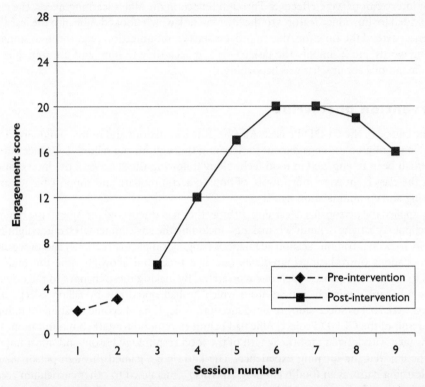

Figure 5.7 Engagement Scale graph for Alfie pre- and post-interventions (intervention period: 10 March–5 July 2010)

and increase his engagement. All other interventions were successful and were retained unchanged following their initial introduction.

It can be seen that more than one intervention was introduced in the early sessions (e.g. interventions 1, 2 and 3). This is not ideal. If more than one new intervention is introduced at a time, it could be that only one of them is successful, and the others have no impact, but there would be no way of telling which intervention made the difference. There is also the possibility that multiple changes to the activity at one time could confuse the child and lower their level of engagement in the activity.

Interventions overview

In food technology lessons, between March and July 2010, Alfie's engagement score increased from two to 20 as a result of introducing the ten interventions described above. Sessions 3–5 show steady increases in Alfie's engagement levels from his baseline scores (Sessions 1 and 2), going from fleeting to sustained engagement.

Sessions 8 and 9 show a downward trend in engagement. This can be explained from the commentary on the Engagement Scales for those weeks. In Session 8, he was getting used to a new wheelchair, which might have impacted on his levels of engagement for learning. In Session 9, Alfie had been ill which could explain his sleepiness and the drop in his engagement score to 16.

Most interventions were effective. Through reflection on Alfie's learning needs, the class team decided to: introduce features to the learning task which hooked Alfie into the learning experience; extend the time for Alfie to process staff communication (e.g. through singing, repeating words, etc.); simplify the task to make it accessible to him; and use strategies to make him curious about what was happening.

Intervention postscript

Over the course of the CLDD Project, Alfie became less anxious and more confident within lessons, impacting on his engagement for learning throughout the school day. Once Alfie's interest had been re-engaged in food technology following the success of the intervention period, the class team were more aware of how to accommodate and support his sensory, processing and communication needs.

They applied the personalized learning pathway they had discovered for Alfie to the original food technology activity of sandwich-making – including the environmental changes (lighting, proximity to peers), communication adaptations (singing simple instructions) and processing accommodations (introducing ingredients one at a time, and allowing Alfie the time he needed to explore and process each one separately). By making these changes to the original 'making a banana sandwich' activity from which he had opted out by falling asleep, staff members were able to successfully re-introduce it to Alfie. It had become meaningful to him.

As a result of the CLDD Project, Alfie had begun to respond to staff communication. He now engaged with learning for the length of the food technology lesson, and, most importantly, he enjoyed the learning experience. The knowledge gained through personalizing Alfie's learning pathway in food technology was also generalized to other curriculum areas. The curriculum developed for Alfie as a result provided sensory learning experiences which included materials that had different textures and made unique sounds, stimulating his curiosity and his desire to explore, and leading to discoveries which delighted him. Alfie's expectations of his learning experiences were also raised, encouraging him to initiate, persist and anticipate. Having a record of high-engagement behaviours for Alfie allowed all educators to recognize the level of engagement that he could show in activities/lessons.

Teacher feedback

In summarizing her experience of using the Engagement Profile and Scale, the teacher who had worked with Alfie throughout the project concluded:

> I am much more observant now of the different factors that can stop children engaging . . .
>
> I think that this approach is an ideal way of helping the teacher/teaching assistant to have a starting point and a focus which hopefully will enable them to plan a relevant learning pathway for their pupils. To be engaged shows an interest and that interest can be built upon in a personalized way . . .
>
> The Profile gives good indication of progress. It is a record of what has happened and informs the teacher/teaching assistant. It also shows what strategies have been tried and what has been successful or not . . .
>
> The framework helps you to focus on questions that you need to answer or investigate further in order to help resolve issues. The framework also acts as a record which can inform planning and assessment . . .

Use the format and make it your own. It does work! You can't always have the amount of staff you need for videoing etc, but you adapt it to what you can do. It is surprising how enterprising you can become!

Case study: Annabelle

Integrate features from favourite activities that engage a child into a learning activity in which they currently have low engagement.

This case study has been contributed by Parkside School, Pukekohe, New Zealand.

Annabelle is eight years old and has a formal diagnosis of Jacobsen Syndrome and bilateral extropia (a vision impairment). She attends a New Zealand special school satellite class at a mainstream primary school. The satellite class promotes inclusive education while affording the students the necessary individualized programming, specialist support and high staffing ratios required to support their learning and behavioural needs.

Annabelle was in the emerging stages of learning how to read and write. She showed an interest in books by looking at pictures, listening to stories and engaging in educational iPad applications. She was at the pre-writing stage and used a template to practise making horizontal, vertical and circular lines.

In the class environment, however, it was often challenging to engage her in learning activities. She would not attend to tasks, choosing rather to move away and wander around the room. She did respond positively to short and focused one-to-one structured sessions; however, this intensive adult support was not always possible.

In the playground, however, Annabelle was highly motivated by the swing and slide, often spending up to 40 minutes on these activities. The vestibular movement that these activities provided for Annabelle enabled her to self-calm. For the same reason, she would seek movement in the classroom, such as spinning on a chair or bouncing on the exercise ball. These behaviours were, at times, disruptive to the class and disengaged her from her learning. Our challenge was to find a way to allow Annabelle to engage in her required self-regulatory behaviours appropriately within the class in order to remain engaged in learning activities.

Profiling the student

All those who worked with Annabelle were asked to complete a preliminary profile form (see Appendix D). This included the family, specialists involved in her programme (occupational therapist and a speech and language therapist) and the class teacher. This provides an excellent starting point for investigating the child's strengths and interests.

It was clear that Annabelle required a large amount of sensory input. She would remain seated for extended periods of time while playing with play dough on her desk top while rocking back and forth in her chair and rhythmically vocalizing. This activity included vestibular, tactile and auditory sensory input and was an activity that she was able to access within the class that was less disruptive than her other vestibular seeking behaviour. The team completed an Engagement Profile for Annabelle based on this high-engagement activity, categorizing her different engaged behaviours against each of the seven engagement indicators (see Figure 5.8).

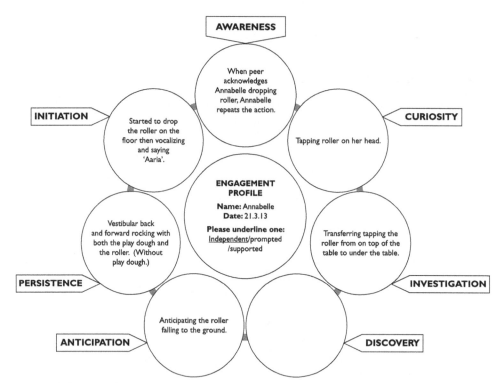

Figure 5.8 Annabelle's Engagement Profile based on her high-engagement play dough activity

The team decided to explore increasing Annabelle's engagement in her learning through this and similar sensory activities. They decided to use a familiar task of writing skills, both familiar and unfamiliar, to create a standardized activity to explore in different learning settings.

Following the baseline observation (no interventions) as a first intervention, the team decided to introduce a peanut ball for Annabelle to sit on during lessons to see if it would help her to fulfil her sensory needs while remaining engaged in learning.

Engagement Scale observations

Table 5.7 briefly summarizes the Engagement Scale observations throughout the intervention period, together with the 'next steps' which were actioned. Figure 5.9 provides a chart of her scores.

Findings

Through the inquiry process of the Engagement Profile and Scale programme it became clear that when Annabelle's sensory need for vestibular regulation was met, she was able to focus on a task and remain engaged. It became evident that Annabelle required only minimal vestibular movement in order to actively engage in her learning and that this could be provided for her by ensuring that she was seated on a peanut ball when working on a table top task or activity, during morning circle or other programmes such as during the music lesson.

Table 5.7 Summaries of Annabelle's Engagement Scale sessions

Session No.	Date	Score	'Next step'	Summary of the observation
1	22.04.13	8	*Baseline data hence no 'next step' was actioned.*	Annabelle was presented a familiar pre-writing skill task at a desk and left to complete the task independently.
2	30.05.13	15	Provide the familiar play dough activity with the addition of a peanut ball to be seated on.	In the next observation, Annabelle was working at a table, seated on a peanut ball and independently explored the play dough. She was observed at this time to be bouncing on her ball and more focused on the task. There was high engagement and a notable difference in eye contact and language content expressed by Annabelle.
3	06.06.13	17	Present a familiar writing worksheet activity to Annabelle while she has access to play dough and is seated on the peanut ball. Teacher to provide intermittent support and not continuous 1:1 support. Teacher to 'check in' with Annabelle.	Annabelle was trialled on the peanut ball at a table, working firstly with the teacher and then independently on a pre-writing skill worksheet activity. Play dough was still provided at this stage to provide proprioceptive feedback for Annabelle. She was able to focus on her writing activity and complete the task independently.
4	27.06.13	21	Present an unfamiliar writing worksheet activity to Annabelle while seated on the peanut ball. Begin the task with 1:1 teacher support then the teacher moves away so as to observe Annabelle's independent engagement in the task.	For this session the peanut ball was retained but the play dough was removed. This was to ascertain whether it was the vestibular or the proprioceptive feedback that allowed Annabelle to self-regulate and maintain focus during learning activities. She was observed to be very focused in her worksheet activity. We queried whether the unstable surface of the peanut ball was enough to provide the feedback that Annabelle required in order to stay focused on a task.
5	24.07.13	20	Present a familiar writing worksheet activity to Annabelle while working in a group setting with her peers.	Annabelle was observed to be working with her peers at her own desk, whilst seated on a peanut ball. She was able to retain her focus and work for a period of time on the learning task of paper and pen appropriately.

(Continued)

Table 5.7 (Continued)

Session No.	Date	Score	'Next step'	Summary of the observation
6	31.07.13	16	Annabelle was presented with a matching activity worksheet with pictures under paper flaps. She was seated on a standard chair on her own (not in a group setting). The teacher provided minimal support apart from the initial modelling of the task.	Annabelle was able to sit at her desk on her chair and complete an activity. She started to investigate what was under the flaps after she was modelled. Annabelle was focused on her task for some of the time and didn't appear to rock/swing on her chair. What was notable about this session was that it occurred at the end of the day during which the class had been involved in horse riding, swimming and a Tac Pac session.
7	06.08.13	18	Annabelle was presented with a fine motor activity of posting while seated on the peanut ball.	Annabelle was seated on a peanut ball and working at her table. Initially this was by herself and then her peers joined her at their tables. Annabelle was able to retain her focus on the fine motor activity of posting for an extended period of time.

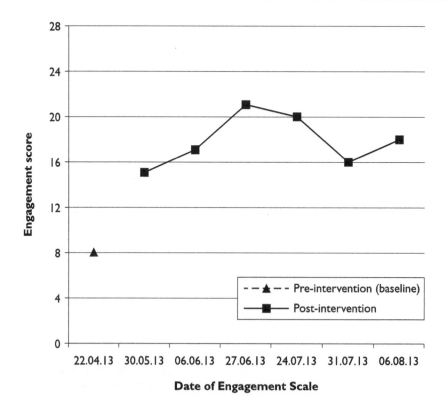

Figure 5.9 Annabelle's Engagement Scale scores (intervention period: 22 April–6 August 2013)

Following the intervention, Annabelle's teacher commented:

> Prior to starting the Engagement Profile programme it was difficult to engage Annabelle in individual or group activities for any length of time. She needed support to complete or start any activities. Through the Engagement Profile [and Scale] programme we found that Annabelle needed to be seated on a peanut ball and once she was, Annabelle was more settled and able to engage in her learning. She would use the peanut ball before starting her lesson and then during her activity when required. Annabelle was able to complete familiar tasks independently.

Since Annabelle's inclusion in the Engagement Profile programme she has moved to a new class. As part of her transition the new teacher was informed of Annabelle's learning need. The Dean of Engagement also met with the whole teaching team and presented her Engagement Profile and Scale evidence and findings to them to show what her 'personalized learning pathway' involved. Below are comments from her current teacher and her parents:

> Annabelle does enjoy using the peanut ball during class time. She will sit on it well and, when needed, bounces for a while to regulate herself and then go back to focusing on her task without bouncing. The peanut ball has also been used during music sessions. During this time Annabelle is able to stay completely focused for the duration of the session. If Annabelle sits in a chair she will often lean forward, make noises and not be able to focus completely.
>
> (Current class teacher)

> The findings from the Engagement Profile programme were interesting and informative. We are pleased that the study has found a way to engage Annabelle in her learning. We adopt this practice at home from time to time when we need Annabelle to concentrate on something.
>
> (Annabelle's parents)

Case study: Eva

Taking inspiration from strategies known to work with children who have the same disability or an allied condition.

Eva is a six-year-old girl with tuberous sclerosis (TS), epilepsy and global learning and communication delay, in addition to major social and communication difficulties and associated behavioural difficulties. She also has cardiac rhabdomyoma (a heart tumour associated with TS) which requires monitoring. She lives with her family, and is dependent on carers for all aspects of care in all environments, and requires access to trained staff for acute management of multiple daily seizures.

Eva attends a leading edge day special school which offers many specialisms. She currently has multidisciplinary support from a community nurse, family support worker, occupational therapist (to address sensory issues), a speech and language therapist, music therapist and numerous consultants, one being a neurologist. Eva's teacher supports an interdisciplinary approach, and makes it a priority to communicate with these colleagues and Eva's parents.

Eva is currently working towards P1(i) in all subjects, although her teacher and parents feel that she is functioning slightly above this level, which reflects Eva's behaviour difficulties during the assessment process. (Her attention skills and alertness vary depending on seizure activity and her interest in the task.)

Using the Engagement Profile and Scale

As described in Chapter 4, the Engagement Profile and Scale works on the principle of enabling a child's engagement through personalization of an activity or learning task which enables them to attain their learning targets. It offers a way of recording the pathways and monitoring outcomes of personalizing learning through an engagement score.

Before structuring the intervention mediated by the Engagement Profile and Scale, the teacher needed to identify Eva's individual strengths, motivators and difficulties, and to establish her priority learning need as a focus for the intervention, so that they could personalize the activity to increase Eva's engagement with it.

Completing the Engagement Profile

A high-Engagement Profile was drawn up for Eva by observing her involved in water play – a favourite activity – and describing her actions against each of the seven Engagement Indicators. This allowed all teaching staff to recognize the level of engagement that Eva was capable of and the kind of behaviours they were aiming for in other activities. It helped them to develop high expectations for Eva.

Establishing a priority learning need

Eva's teacher and her class team identified communication needs, self-harming and lack of motivation as the three key factors preventing Eva from fulfilling her learning potential. From informal observations, they felt that the first two were linked.

Eva's current three main strategies for communicating with adults were: reaching towards something she wanted to eat; backing herself on to an adult's lap to request a cuddle; and screaming and self-harming/biting to express frustration and to communicate what she did *and* did not want. Consequently teaching staff were often confused about the cause of her distress.

Due to Eva's regressive condition, many strategies that had been successful in the past were no longer working, and both staff and her parents were finding it difficult to come to terms with this. Observation showed that while she used to be able to understand symbols, they now appeared to have no meaning for her.

Both Eva's teacher and her parents selected her priority learning need as establishing meaningful communication/choice-making. This priority learning need accorded with a number of Eva's learning objectives:

- *Statement of SEN learning objective*: To develop communication skills
- *Long-term target*: To initiate communication in a variety of situations to help relieve frustrations
- *School targets focus*: Student autonomy and self-advocacy

Eva had been using rebus symbols (Detheridge and Detheridge 2002) to communicate based on the Picture Exchange Communication System (PECS) (Bondy and Frost 1994).

The class team discussed and researched the communication options for her in relation to her reduced levels of understanding and functional communication. As a result, they decided to replace the symbols in her communication system with True Object Based Icons (TOBIs). The tactile quality of these thick, cut-out photographic images allowed Eva to not only see the photograph, but also to feel its shape and therefore to better focus on and understand the image (Bell 2013).

Identifying a motivating context

Although Eva's interests were very limited, she was highly motivated by food. She could finger feed and drink from a spouted cup. Therefore snack times were chosen as an initial context for communication.

Prior to the intervention, at snack times Eva was seated at the table with peers to either side of her. She needed close and constant staff support to prevent her self-harming, and reaching and grabbing at what she wanted. She made no attempt to use her PECS board when it was offered. When there was no more food on her plate, she would become distressed, then get up from the snack table and wander around the classroom. Both Engagement Scale total engagement scores during the two snack sessions prior to any intervention (i.e. the baseline scores) were 2 of a possible 28.

Identifying and addressing the barriers to engagement

From the two baseline observations, subsequent review of video and discussion by the teacher and teaching assistants, barriers and possible solutions to Eva's engagement were identified. The interventions were prioritized during one to two sessions each week, one adaptation was made to the activity and the Engagement Scale was used to score her engagement level. At the end of these sessions, further decisions were made about how the activity could be further personalized in the next session to increase her engagement still more. Periodically, staff would take short video clips during the session which were reviewed. These clips gave a full and accurate record of events and allowed the staff team time to notice things which they may otherwise have missed.

The following list summarizes Eva's barriers and the solutions that were introduced over the course of the intervention period.

- *Lack of understanding.* As Eva was not able to understand symbols, her choices were not currently meaningful. She needed a personalized choice board which used TOBIs instead of symbols to indicate choice. Once choices were no longer available, they needed to be removed from the choice board. Eva also needed specific teaching in relation to PECS to help her understand how to communicate using the system. The number of choices on the board needed to be reduced so she was not overwhelmed.
- *Using challenging behaviour to get her needs met.* Teaching staff minimized their response to Eva's behaviour while using hand-over-hand, gentle physical prompt and/ or gesture to direct her to use the TOBIs to exchange for snack items.
- *Raised anxiety levels.* Eva is auditory and tactile defensive. Sitting at the table with peers to either side meant her space was invaded, and the noise levels were high. She was unable to focus on learning the new communication system. Therefore Eva was temporarily moved away from the rest of the group, giving her a calm environment in

which she was able to attend to the exchange of a TOBI for her chosen food item. When she had learned the system, she would be seated at the periphery of the group.
*   *Auditory processing issues and processing time.* Eva finds it difficult to process spoken language, therefore verbal communication was minimized. Staff also gave her longer to process simplified speech/TOBIs and to make choices.
*   *Self-harming.* Prior to the CLDD Project, Eva had to wait for longer than she was capable of for her turn at snack time, resulting in episodes of self-harming. Therefore intervals between waiting for her turn needed to be reduced.

The post-intervention scoring increased as changes were. Outcomes are shown in Table 5.8 and Figure 5.10.

Table 5.8 Engagement Scale summaries for Eva (intervention period: 30 March–7 July 2010)

Session No.	Date	Total score	Observation summary
Baseline			
1	30 March (AM)	1	Eva showed distress and lack of understanding of the communication system or staff verbal instructions. She indicated what she wanted by reaching towards it, and made repeated attempts to grab food from other children.
Intervention			
2	30 March (PM)	13	TOBI choice board introduced and modelled hand-over-hand.
3	19 April	14	Eva remained focused on the TOBIs for the duration of the
4	21 April	15	activity, and showed curiosity and investigation. Although she became cross and anxious when the food on the plate was nearly finished, she remained sitting when normally she would lose interest in the snack activity and walk around.
5	17 May	15	Eva showed anticipation by seating herself at her snack table
6	19 May	6	as she saw the TOBI choice board being set up. Eva started to
7	20 May	10	use eye pointing to the TOBIs to indicate a choice, so eye
8	24 May	5	contact was reduced during snack time to encourage her to refocus on picture exchange. Eva stopped reaching out to grab
9	25 May	10	food, although was still anxious when her plate was empty.
10	28 May	11	
11	9 June	15	Although a gentle physical prompt was still given at times for
12	10 June	13	Eva to pick up the TOBI from the communication board, she
13	14 June	18	became more independent in using it and less anxious when the food came to an end. On 14 June, for the first time, Eva
14	17 June	16	vocalized at a TOBI, then laughed. She became more confident
15	21 June	15	when using the TOBIs. Staff now gave her more processing
16	28 June	22	time, and a clear start and finish for the snack.
17	30 June	22	
18	1 July	2	Although on 1 July Eva was distressed all day, and could not
19	2 July	23	focus on PECS, by 7 July she showed sustained engagement
20	5 July	24	throughout the snack activity.
21	7 July	28	

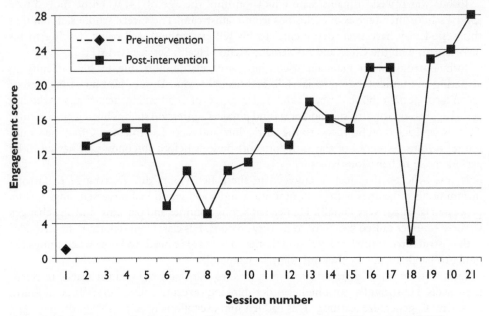

Figure 5.10 Engagement Scale chart for Eva (intervention period: 30 March–7 July 2010)

Intervention postscript

Using the Engagement Profile and Scale, Eva's teacher and class team were able to increasingly personalize the activity to Eva so that she became able to engage and achieve communication and choice-making within the snack activity. The scoring across the seven Engagement Indicators highlighted different areas that needed attention, which led to an overall increase in engagement scoring over a number of weeks. Eva's teacher was very pleased with how the Engagement Profile and Scale had helped her structure and monitor the intervention for Eva. Eva's parents were also keen to use the choice system and TOBIs at home, so the CLDD researcher made a home visit to explain and demonstrate the choice and communication system to them. The next step for Eva was for the class team to begin to extend her choice-making using TOBIs from food into other areas of learning.

Case study: Joshua

Make adjustments based upon the child's perspective on what they enjoy doing to create learning opportunities.

Joshua is a 16-year-old boy with a diagnosis of DiGeorge Syndrome, a rare chromosome disorder caused by a missing section of chromosome 22. The condition can cause a wide range of health problems, cognitive delays and socio-emotional problems, and Joshua presents with communication difficulties, high emotional responses and moderate learning difficulties. He is also described by his teachers as 'very outgoing, very caring and very good at looking after people that are less able then him.'

Joshua was placed in mainstream education until the age of 14, when he moved to a special school after a series of exclusions from mainstream. The special school staff felt that this period may have been detrimental to his self-esteem and well-being, leading to his involvement with the Child and Adolescent Mental Health Service (CAMHS).

Joshua struggled to maintain friendships and relationships due to his difficulty in acquiring and understanding social skills and his behaviour. During his time at his present secondary special school, Joshua exhibited a range of challenging behaviours including verbal aggression towards staff and peers and physical aggression such as hitting and kicking. This also impacted on his access to the curriculum and school attendance. Often, he would refuse to come to school or stay only for short periods before absconding or having to be excluded due to behaviour issues.

It was believed that Joshua engaged in these behaviours due to a range of factors, including his difficulties with communication and socio-emotional understanding. Joshua processed language very literally. He needed strong routines and patterns, and any changes to these routines caused him to become very anxious. His class team reported: 'he struggles with unstructured times like break and dinner time. . . . He needs to know when things are going to happen and why they are going to happen.'

Joshua also needed increased processing time to learn new tasks and rehearsal to retain these skills. He struggled with higher order thinking (executive function) skills, and found it difficult to generalize learning. This had left him exceptionally vulnerable in the past. His father said: 'I have to teach him how to cope in every situation that he comes across. Every new situation is difficult.'

Engagement for learning intervention – a different use of the Engagement Scale

The school recognized the need for a personalized provision for Joshua. He was so minimally engaged with the school curriculum at the time of the CLDD Project that he was not at a stage where it was possible to assess his engagement within lessons. The school decided to use the Engagement Scale in a different way to assess, score and compare Joshua's engagement across the different learning experiences of a personalized curriculum so they could compare his engagement in different activities.

As Joshua was actively disengaging from the school environment and curriculum, this meant that he was not achieving deep learning and was extremely demotivated. The school also realized that Joshua's lack of engagement with school would compromise his emotional well-being and put him in socially vulnerable situations.

A series of interventions were put into place to improve Joshua's self-esteem and his perception of himself as a successful learner. A meeting was held between Joshua, his father and the school. Here Joshua was asked what could be done to make him 'happier' in school. With his father's support, Joshua was able to share his career aspirations to be a builder or car mechanic. The school decided that a reduced timetable that concentrated on providing Joshua with activities that played to his strengths and interests would give him opportunities to achieve qualifications, increase his self-esteem and begin to re-engage him in learning.

The school used areas of the Inquiry Framework for Learning (see Appendix C) as a basis for reflection on Joshua's learning issues. The school realized that Joshua needed more support for his communication, and it was noted that a higher level of visual structure would help Joshua to learn his routines and be able to cope better with change. Next, the amount of exercise and physical activity that Joshua was involved in was reviewed. They felt that if Joshua took part in more physical activities outside the classroom, it may increase his engagement in learning across his curriculum.

The school also acknowledged that a more flexible curriculum approach would be beneficial when it came to supporting Joshua's behaviour. Joshua was asked to attend only science and media studies within school as they would provide him with opportunities to work within curriculum areas he could achieve and would be most likely to obtain qualifications in. Joshua was also placed on 'alternative curriculum days', which involved him attending a construction site and a working agricultural centre to gain employment and manual skills.

Due to the nature of the intervention, and Joshua's dislike of being formally observed, engagement evidence was discussed and recorded retrospectively. The Engagement Scales were used to record overall engagement scores for the different 'alternative curriculum' settings rather than focusing on specific tasks within these settings. The outcomes are summarized in Table 5.9 and Figure 5.11. The three sessions each represent a 1-hour observation of Joshua.

Table 5.9 Engagement Scale summaries for Joshua (intervention period: Autumn Term 2010)

Session No.	Total score	Observation summary
I	7	**Initial science lesson observation: pre-alternative curriculum** Joshua entered late. I explained what Joshua needed to be doing and he understood the purpose and recalled learning from the previous lessons. He engaged straight away with the slime and jelly bath activity, but then wanted to do his own thing with the items. He had no desire to use the products for the purpose and did not use the objects appropriately. He left the classroom without permission.
2	14	**Initial science lesson observation: post-alternative curriculum** Joshua was fully engaged … He was actually asking questions that needed higher level thinking and asked questions throughout the lesson. He challenged the science evidence and asked 'why', 'what' and 'how'. His effort was superb – a massive improvement. Next action: to find a better way for him to communicate and understand.
3	20	**Agricultural centre observation** Joshua shows persistence in attendance at the agricultural centre, arriving and leaving promptly. Joshua was interested, observant, listening and happy. His eye contact was stronger. He felt more confident and understood the task, so this made him more aware. He asked a lot of questions about the animals. He was aware of the placement timetable, so he knew when to have break and make the tea, and also how and when to clean out the animals. He followed the timetable, made a cup of tea, then sat and chatted. He needed to be continually directed with low level prompts. He persists with strategies to manage his behaviour and maintain relationships with adults and also with the learning activities that he engages in.

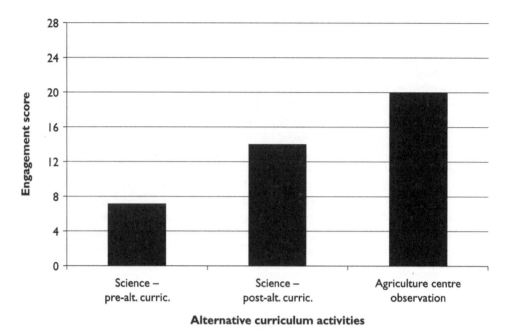

Figure 5.11 Engagement Scale graph for Joshua (intervention period: Autumn Term 2010)

Explanation

The graph in Figure 5.11 indicates an increase within Joshua's engagement for learning. As the pre-alternative curriculum score suggests, Joshua was mostly disengaged throughout the science lesson and showed only fleeting signs of engagement. During this lesson Joshua left without permission and removed himself from the lesson.

After the alternative curriculum was put into place Joshua's engagement score increased from seven to 14. Staff felt this was due to the fact that Joshua was more relaxed and the lesson was motivating. The lesson was also personalized to Joshua through providing more practical activities and written instructions to ensure he knew what he was expected to complete within the session.

Joshua's engagement for learning score increased to 20 during the agricultural centre observation. Joshua was engaged for the majority of the time in activities that involved showing younger children around the centre, making morning snack and tending to lambs. Joshua appeared to be proud of what he was able to accomplish, and to thoroughly enjoy himself while at this provision.

Intervention postscript

Although there was a limited amount of data that could be collected in this instance, it was noted in school that Joshua was more engaged and less anxious throughout the day. This enabled staff to introduce more demands without the strong emotional responses that have occurred previously. It also meant that Joshua was able to build relationships and trust in peers in similar educational placements and staff supporting him.

The change in his behaviour and learning is evident and staff felt this was due to the CLDD Project. The project allowed staff to sit down and really think about Joshua as a learner and as a person and to adapt the curriculum delivery to enable him to become engaged and achieve deep learning.

The level of visual support introduced to his science lesson led to a large increase in engagement. Joshua no longer became disengaged and lost within the lesson, and his new visual structure enabled him to self-check his work, ensuring he completed each element of the tasks. This visual structure was generalized successfully to Joshua's other lessons.

It is also important to acknowledge the skill base that was present at the alternative placements. The flexibility that is allowed in these provisions allowed Joshua to be able to adapt and feel supported. The need for more external providers to work collaboratively with schools is evident when presented with a range of disabilities and behaviours that are now being seen in twenty-first-century CLDDs. It is also important to integrate the behavioural approaches and activities that can be offered by these provisions into schools to be able to offer consistent and adaptable support.

The use of the Engagement Scale allowed staff to provide evidence that justified the use of an alternative curriculum with Joshua by being able to demonstrate clearly that the adaptations to his curriculum increased his levels of engagement. This evidence was used in reviews along with curriculum assessments to reflect the progress that he has made.

Based on this evidence, the school planned to use alternative curriculums with other children in similar situations to re-engage them with a curriculum. They also aimed to introduce the Engagement Profile and Scale into their pupil profile documents to prompt all staff to think about the engagement for learning of the children within their educational settings.

Conclusion

In these case studies, educators have observed *how* the child with CLDD engaged in learning. They reflected on what engagement interventions enabled the child to reach and achieve their learning outcome, and which of those could be adapted for all the child's learning environments. In doing so, they transformed the child's learning potential.

In each of the cases, it was the educators and families who held the key to engaging the complex learner through recalling and sharing things that collectively they already knew about the child. They began to notice, value and explore what they and their colleagues did know about when the child engaged and what they enjoyed, and to realize its learning significance. Once they had reflected on this, they were able to integrate it into the child's learning activities in new and creative ways. The CLDD Engagement Profile and Scale provided the observation, recording and assessment framework in which this knowledge could be put to work. Some practitioners have adapted the tools further to suit their needs (Jones 2013; Chapter 10, this publication).

So often, what a child can do becomes obscured by what they cannot – a kind of 'educational overshadowing'. As educators, we need to push back that shadow by focusing on the child's interests and strengths so we can reclaim the child for the engaged learner that they can be.

Note

1 For instructions on creating graphs using CLDD data, turn to Appendix F.

References

Bell, I.P. (2013) 'Providing a total communication approach'. [Online at: http://ianpbell.wordpress.com/communication-in-vi-children/; accessed: 29.06.14.]

Bondy, A. and Frost, L. (1994) 'The picture exchange communication system', *Focus on Autistic Behavior*, 9: 1–19.

Detheridge, T. and Detheridge, M. (2002) *Literacy through Symbols: Improving access for children and adults*. London: David Fulton.

Jones, S. (2013) 'Call on your inner detective: engagement with students on the autism spectrum' (PowerPoint presentation). [Online at: http://barrycarpentereducation.com/tag/engagement/; accessed: 28.09.14.]

Chapter 6

Learning with families

Partnership with families

Families are key to our ability to achieve effective educational approaches for children with CLDD. Educating a child with CLDD is a collaborative venture, and the parent is the child's first educator, laying the foundation for the child's social, physical, emotional and intellectual development (Beveridge 2005; World Health Organization 2011). By the time their child enters school many parents will have researched, inquired, visited and discussed their child's condition and future development with a multitude of people and organizations. Many will have pioneered interventions and supported their child through them. They will understand their child in a way that no professional can ever do (Carpenter 1997, 2010; Carpenter and Filmer 2015).

While for a typically developing child the route from birth to adulthood is so integrated into our societal systems that families are scarcely aware of it, for a child with CLDD it is anything but. Their unique needs mean that families have to carve out this pathway, not only breaking new ground, but often having to fight for it as well at every level from school to government. Such experiences can leave a lifelong emotional legacy.

This chapter will help educators appreciate the life journeys that families engage in with their child with CLDD, the day-to-day pressures they live with and why they may be far shorter of resources – energy, time, resilience, finance and sometimes patience – than families of typically developing children. It will explore the experiences and insights of families with a child with CLDD through case studies and examples of how families and schools can work collaboratively to engage these children in learning. Having this understanding will enable educators more effectively to listen to and work with families of children with CLDD.

The family journey

Diagnosis at birth

The birth of a child should be a celebrated occasion, one that brings feelings of joy, pride and excitement. However, when a child is born with a disability, many different reactions are described, and it is important to remember that not all families react in the same way (Carpenter and Egerton 2007; Young 2007). For many it can be an experience which brings feelings of shock, anger, grief, denial, jealousy and worry (Attfield and Morgan 2007; Chesney and Champion 2008; Young 2007). One mother remembers: 'When I was given the severe diagnosis, one of the nurses ... suggested I was suffering a bit from depression, which I wasn't. I was just suffering from shock – grieving with shock – which was very natural' (Kingston 2007: 55).

For parents of children born extremely prematurely, the most significant stressor can be the loss of the early mothering and fathering opportunities with their child (Chesney and Champion 2008). Some parents, however, are delighted at the birth of their baby with disabilities from the start. One mother, whose baby was born with Down's syndrome, stated: 'If someone had offered their commiserations I would have been very upset' (Davies 2005: 5).

Later diagnosis

However, it is not just from birth that families receive news of diagnosis. Families may learn of diagnoses as their children get to 12–18 months, when there is a realization that developmental milestones are not being met, or families have an inkling of something not feeling 'right'. Other conditions such as autistic spectrum disorders (ASD) and Fetal Alcohol Spectrum Disorders (FASD) may not be diagnosed until their child is at school age, some as late as their early teens.

Later diagnosis can be difficult for some families, but for others it can be a relief to finally have a reason for their child's atypical development and behaviours. A named condition can bring families practical information as well as emotional support, reducing their feelings of isolation and confusion. A mother speaks of the point of diagnosis for her son when he had started school: 'It took a long time to get over the initial shock. But then it was a relief. We could start to understand him and talk to him so that he could understand us' (Kingston 2007: 62).

Children may have difficulties that become apparent soon after birth but receive no diagnosis, leaving families with uncertainty and worry for the short and long term (Statham et al. 2010). Other families may have a child who has a regressive disorder, where they have to cope with watching their child's condition deteriorate.

For some children, their condition may be acquired as a result of a road traffic accident or brain injury due to an illness such as meningitis or a stroke, for example. This can be particularly hard for the child and the family as they cope with the loss of what once was.

After diagnosis

After diagnosis, families' resilience contributes to their overall outlook and ability to cope, manage stress and function day-to-day (Seligman and Darling 2007). One parent involved in Contact a Family research (2009: 12) described one of their strategies: 'We have had to develop a very thick skin where outsiders are concerned. We are incredibly proud of our disabled child regardless of how difficult life may be.'

Over time, as families develop, the actual diagnosis seems to be less of a defining issue for them. As the child grows up, the focus moves to more practical issues around education, health and access to services, which parents often approach with 'devoted vocation rather than . . . burdensome obligation' (Oulton and Heyman 2009: 313).

As part of the CLDD Project, family members of the initial 59 children involved in the research were interviewed to gain their perspective on their child's learning, education and wider family issues. The main theme to arise from the interviews was that of the joy their child with a disability brought to the household: 'It's the little things . . . I just love taking him out because he buzzes, even just driving in the car. I like just seeing him happy.'

Other studies also discuss the inspiration and pride a child can provide not only to parents, but to siblings and grandparents (Contact a Family 2009; Meyer and Vadasy 1997). For example, families recounted the first time their child spoke, defying all medical beliefs; or when they overcame anxieties and took part in a school production.

Family priorities

For families involved in the CLDD Project interviews, communication was the dominant priority for their children's development, and some wanted more of a focus on appropriate communication strategies for their child. One mother said her most important memory was when her daughter started using a *DynaVox* speech device to communicate: 'For years I'd dreamt that she could speak to me and now she can answer you and she has a voice. It brings tears to my eyes. Communication is a massive part of our lives, but you don't know if you don't have it.'

Families appreciated communication systems, both low and hi-tech, for their child, but said they needed to have their use properly explained to ensure consistency between school and home.

Family struggles

Other issues parents raised in the interviews were more negative, and often secondary to the child's disability. Families spoke of the continual fights for appropriate placements at every juncture and significant point in their child's lives – for education and housing, statements, resources, funding, practical and emotional support including respite/short breaks and therapies. One parent described what this meant:

> The stress, anxiety, frustration and exhaustion that I have experienced is categorically initiated from the extended world – namely, the service providers and educators. Central policies and initiatives are very reassuring, but the cruel reality is that they are to little effect as service providers and educators continue to operate within their comfort zones. I will readily refer to my family situation as the new generation of disability, and the brutality of it is that you learn to survive on your own.
>
> (Godden, in Carpenter 2010: 2)

Families also struggled when schools failed to recognize the learning and social/ emotional implications of a child's condition. The impact of premature birth on children's learning is only now beginning to be acknowledged by schools. Instead of burdening the family with sole responsibility for the difficulties their child experiences at school, educators need to work with them. This mother wrote:

> My son was born at 24 weeks. He is five years old, and commenced a mainstream primary school this September. He has a statement of special educational needs. He has been diagnosed with global learning delay and has difficulty with his behaviour and attention . . . I would like to be able to say that my son has 'additional needs of extreme prematurity', but that condition does not exist in the medical or teaching world.

I often dread picking my son up from school to be informed of his antics. I will dutifully go through the motions of discussing his behaviour with him and the teacher, but really I feel very sad for him because it is not all his fault. The teachers do not understand that sometimes he just cannot help his behaviour. He is definitely wired differently to his peers!

(Ricks, in Carpenter 2010: 1)

At secondary school age, the implications can be even more serious. The following case study shows how premature birth affected a 12-year-old boy's social understanding, and how a diagnosis led to solution-finding and support:

Case study: Adam

Adam was a young man in Year 7 of a mainstream secondary academy. While academically, he was on a par with his peers, he had little sense of social appropriateness, and his unacceptable comments and behaviours threatened to alienate him from both peers and staff. The academy's SEN Director rang Adam's mother to discuss Adam's behaviour with her, and asked whether she knew of any past learning or health difficulty that could be linked to his current difficulties with social understanding.

Adam's mother recalled that he had been born extremely premature at 24 weeks, and had subsequently suffered a serious brain bleed. Adam's GP referred him for a brain scan, which revealed that there had been damage in the brain area associated with socio-emotional development.

It was a massive relief to Adam and his mother to have evidence of a physiological cause for his social difficulties, which had plagued him since junior school. The school quickly responded by putting pastoral mentoring in place to support Adam with socio-emotional guidance and strategies. Without the knowledge gained from talking to Adam's mother, and the SEN Department's support in approaching their GP, Adam would have been penalized for behaviour of which he had no understanding. Without subsequent support from the academy's pastoral team, he would not have understood why his behaviours were unacceptable or what he needed to do to change them. He is now successfully integrated within his class.

Understandably continual negative, drawn out and often fruitless experiences influence how families function and interact with professionals, including educators, day-to-day. Having gone through these stressful experiences, families may show cynicism and disillusionment with the system and services on offer.

As practitioners, we need to appreciate families' perspectives – both the joyous and too often difficult circumstances and experiences that have shaped them throughout their child's life. It is frequently those with a 'thick skin' and determination that manage to achieve what they want for their child, despite obstacles and adversities. This is not easy, and sometimes this thick skin can make parents appear over protective, wary or 'stand offish'; many families who are less resilient, knowledgeable and able to battle become overwhelmed. Mencap (2006) reported that eight out of ten families with a child with a disability are at breaking point.

Defining the family and their needs

When we talk about the family, who do we actually mean? Schools and organizations speak of 'partnerships with parents', but by definition this excludes people who play a key role in the child's life. In the twenty-first century, it is not just parents, but grandparents, step-families, foster-families, siblings, aunts, uncles and friends who act as core family members (Carpenter and Egerton 2007; Carpenter et al. 2012; Rawson 2010), either taking on a parental role for differing reasons, or providing invaluable informal practical and emotional support to the child and family. For example, families report neighbours offering lifts to appointments and childminding for a couple of hours when difficulties arise, work colleagues arranging flexible work hours to accommodate difficulties and friends offering shoulders to cry on. This is particularly the case for families who do not receive formal support from outside agencies (Contact a Family 2009). Other children may have no close family contact, relying on carers and social workers to fulfil this role.

When working with families, it is important to be aware of the differing needs and experiences of family members; for example:

Mothers

Mothers, often being the primary care-giver, are said to feel the greatest burden of responsibility and problem-solving for their child with disabilities, even if they have support from other family members (Kurt et al. 2004). This mother describes the pressures often put upon mothers:

> During my son's short 12 years I have dealt with 12 psychologists, six psychiatrists, seven speech therapists, three social workers and numerous teachers, tutors, home support workers and special needs assistants. Despite all this army of professionals he still ends up being suspended from his special needs school and sent back home to me – the mother, who is expected to do the job nobody else can manage.
>
> (Kingston 2007: 14)

Only 16 per cent of mothers with disabled children work, compared to 61 per cent of other mothers (Contact a Family 2011). One mother interviewed for the CLDD Project spoke of the resentment she felt at having to give up her career; this was not towards her son, but towards a society and system unable to cope with a child with such complex needs. Mothers who do give up their work have reduced social contact, and may lose their identity as an earner, a worker, a colleague and a friend. For mothers of life-limited children, stress levels are higher than mothers of healthy children (Brown 2007).

By automatically making the mother the first and main point of contact, many services may unintentionally contribute to mothers' burden of responsibility. Reaching out to both parents and other family members who are willing can help to share the practical and emotional responsibilities.

Fathers

Fathers have reported that professional structures and expectations make involvement difficult, resulting in fathers maintaining or taking on traditional, emotionally uninvolved, bread-winner roles (Carpenter and Towers 2008). Fathers may be perceived as not involved if they are not seen in school or when practioners do home visits – this could be because meetings are arranged at times when fathers are at work. When fathers do attend meetings, the focus might be put more on the mother.

Fathers also have emotional needs; it may be that fathers take longer to come to terms with their child's diagnosis and have unrealistic expectations about their child's ability. They may also take on the emotional burden of the whole family, yet have limited support networks themselves.

Research has found that fathers tend to not be asked what support they might need, unlike mothers (Carpenter and Towers 2008). Practically, fathers may struggle to find a job that is flexible enough to fit with the responsibilities of family life, in terms of getting time off for appointments and meetings. Encouraging fathers to be involved may prove advantageous as a father's interest in their child's schooling is strongly linked to positive educational outcomes for the child (DfES (Department for Education and Skills) 2003).

Siblings

The sibling relationship is often the longest and most enduring relationship of the family, perhaps spanning 30 years longer than that of the parent–child relationship (Conway and O'Neill 2004). This relationship may adjust over time, with some siblings taking on additional responsibilities relating to their brother's or sister's health, finances and care. Siblings with a brother or sister with a disability may experience a range of emotions, including pride, resentment, guilt, isolation and concern (Meyer and Vadasy 1997).

There are a range of supports that siblings may want, including understanding of their needs, reassurance that what they feel is okay and information (Rawson 2010). Some schools offer sibling specific support. Sibshops (www.siblingsupport.org/sibshops), for example, include games and activities that encourage discussion, reflection, honesty and fun between siblings of people with disabilities.

However, not all siblings may want an involvement in the life of their brother or sister with a disability. Opportunities for involvement should be made available and clear, but without pressure.

Grandparents

Although not every family will have close bonds with grandparents, many grandparents regularly offer vital emotional and practical support to families, whether a child has a disability or not. However, when a child is born with a disability, grandparents are said to experience a 'dual grief' not only for their grandchild, but also for their own child whom they may see as burdened for life (Mirfin-Veitch and Bray 1997). Some grandparents may struggle to come to terms with the diagnosis. For grandparents, and perhaps older relatives, the process of coping with the diagnosis may be compounded by outdated views of disability, quality of life and interventions. This in turn can put pressure on the parents.

By creating an environment that is receptive of grandparents and other extended family members, schools can encourage and sustain support for parents (Mirfin-Veitch and Bray 1997).

Extended family

Schools also need to specifically welcome other family groups (e.g. step-families, foster-families). Step-family members, for example, may take time to adapt to having a new member of their family with a disability. Research shows that step-families tend to not make use of family support services, often not perceiving themselves as core family members (Smith et al. 2001) and therefore unsure of their welcome.

Addressing extended family needs

- **Be inclusive** – think 'partnership with families', not 'partnership with parents'. (Is the school 'families' room' still called a 'parents' room'?) Include specific invitations to siblings, grandparents and friends for events, open days and reviews; use Skype or video to enable family members physically unable to attend a meeting to contribute; address informal home correspondence to 'The Smith family' rather than 'Mr and Mrs Smith'.
- **Consider ways to encourage fathers** – Many feel alienated as a male among so many mothers and females. Offer informal contact to fit their schedules; 'structured conversations' (DCSF (Department for Children, Schools and Families) 2009; Humphrey and Squires 2011), and 'lads and dads' mornings with a practical focus.
- **Demonstrate that you are listening** – Establish listening opportunities for families, and provide routes for different family members to help educators work with their child (e.g. through regular emails/conversations; a sibling place on the school advisory board or parent/teacher group?)
- **Communicate with families and keep them in the loop** – In what ways can families be regularly informed with general goings-on around school and those relating to their child? Ofsted (2010) note that 'excellent' communication supports consistent home–school ways of working with children with CLDD. Some CLDD Project families interviewed asked for home–school diaries to focus more on positives and the content of the school day, rather than just behaviours. Social communication is also important. Core family members and others (including step-family members and absent parents when appropriate) appreciate email updates or photographs from school.
- **Provide opportunities for families to meet** – Family-to-family support is invaluable. Consider creating regular opportunities – whole-family events such as a family picnic, or specific events such as a 'mum's day' or regular coffee morning, a sibling support weekend or a 'lads and dads' computer club. These can provide informal emotional support from people in a similar situation, or just a time to relax and enjoy a laugh!
- **Provide information** – Whether specific to your school or service, or pulled from other sources, family members may appreciate information about the child's needs, wider support or information regarding the future. This will increase knowledge and alleviate some of their feelings and anxieties. Workshops or training could also be a way of doing this.
- **Encourage participation** – Different family members may also be keen to contribute knowledge, skills and support (e.g. disability training for staff, DIY/crafts, ICT, policy development, governing board or volunteer support for events or trips).

The importance of partnerships with families

Families have always held key information about their children, and professionals in different fields have had much to share with them regarding their child's learning and development. Whilst this is still the case, children are being born and diagnosed with conditions so unique and complex that existing medical, social and education practices can shed very little light on the child's needs or make projections for the future. Instead, families of children with CLDD have become the experts, charting new care practices, therapeutic interventions and education pathways (Carpenter 2010). As practitioners we have much to learn from families to improve our practice. Lamb (2009: 3) writes:

> Face-to-face communication with parents, treating them as equal partners with expertise in their children's needs is crucial to establishing and sustaining [parent] confidence. Where things go wrong, the root causes can often be traced to poor communication between school, local authority and parent.

Partnership with families is about building a bridge between a child's home and school to allow for formal and informal correspondence and co-operation. When effective, partnerships establish a collaborative, equal relationship, providing:

- consistency between home and school;
- insights into the child as an individual;
- further information on the child's interests and preferences;
- opportunities to create and facilitate shared targets;
- more responsive relationships (when one requests action from the other); and
- support for families.

We also know that direct involvement of families can have a beneficial long-lasting impact on the development, achievement and well-being of the child during their school

Case study: Ali

Ali's attendance at his special school was particularly poor. When he did attend, he would arrive at school stressed, tired and struggled to engage. School found the behaviours he displayed difficult to manage, despite trying several different strategies to try to reduce them and improve his engagement. After a staff meeting concerning the issue, a conversation was arranged with his family to find out more about this young man's home life. Through this dialogue, school learned that he would stay up late playing computer games which meant he was getting little sleep. In collaboration with his parents, a visual timetable was implemented to structure the young man's free time at home. This ensured he finished playing computer games at a reasonable hour and gave him a selection of alternative options such as reading, bathing and watching TV to help him relax before bed. The difference in his engagement at school was dramatic, going from 0–28 (maximum score) on the Engagement Scale over a period of just 2 months.

life (Beveridge 2005; Carpenter et al. 2007; DfES 2003; Lamb 2009; Rix 2007; Sylva et al. 2004).

Effective communication between school and home is essential for a child's education, and is particularly important when a child has a disability or special educational need. Below is an example of how collaboration between home and school provided a significant improvement in engagement with education for one young man with CLDD.

Children with CLDD are often disengaged from learning, and educators can find themselves overwhelmed by the complexity of their barriers to learning. As part of the CLDD Project, schools discovered through working in partnership with families that the deep knowledge of their child and the advice that they could give was key to being able to engage or re-engage children as learners and transform their learning experiences. For example, children's interests in collage, music, water pouring, car racing on TV, puppets, and the reasons they found these activities so motivating, were used creatively to enhance children's engagement *within* the activity.

Case study: finding inspiration

One school was at a loss to find an activity to motivate a young woman with hemiplegia and profound and multiple learning disabilities to 'reach and grasp' as her next motor developmental objective. She appeared almost completely passive, showing no apparent interest in reaching for any person, object or food. The school shared their difficulty with the girl's family, who agreed few activities interested her. 'However,' her mother said, 'she thinks it is hilarious when we throw the ball for the dog.' With the parents' and the family dog's support, the girl's learning target became to reach and grasp a light plastic ball. In the context of exercising the dog, within a short time, the girl was not only reaching and grasping the ball, but also releasing it for the dog to pounce on and return. This was an achievement that the school had despaired of reaching, and it was only through bringing together the family's knowledge of their daughter and the school's learning focus that this educational milestone became achievable.

While working on the CLDD Project, we discovered that families were often overwhelmed if asked about their child's educational strengths or for their advice on engaging their child without a specific context. However, if educators showed them a planned approach or activity, families would often comment and suggest innovative ideas about how it could be personalized and made more effective for their child.

Parents' often deep connection with their son or daughter can give their child the confidence and support to articulate their learning needs and aspirations when involved in educational decisions increasing the school's ability to meet the child's needs, as in Joshua's story from Chapter 5.

Establishing partnerships

Partnerships are important for families, staff and the development of the child, but how do we establish them? While being systematic, at a practice level partnerships need to reflect each family's unique needs, alongside those of their child.

There are some key principles of practice for empowering families to become involved in their child's education:

- welcoming all families and family members
- mutual respect (non-patronizing)
- an open, honest approach
- regular and thorough communication with opportunities for all parties to contribute
- understanding family situations, particularly during times of change
- sharing of thoughts, feelings and decisions
- maintaining high expectations
- remaining positive and constructive – CLDD Project families felt there was often too much negative feedback from school;
- being flexible
- not assuming what a family can or cannot contribute.

(Carpenter 2002; Davis 2007; Garrigan 2011)

Davis (2007) also shares key staff partnership skills:

- concentration/active listening
- prompting and exploration
- empathic responding
- summarizing
- enabling change
- negotiating
- problem solving.

We may not realize how much parents need positive contact with schools when so much of the communication about their son or daughter with CLDD is likely to be negative.

Case study: Fiona

As part of the CLDD Project, one mainstream primary teacher invited the mother of Fiona, an 11-year-old child with ADHD and complex health needs, to come into school so she could explain the new ways they were working with her daughter in the classroom to engage her in learning, and show the progress that her daughter was making as a result. The mother found this a very emotional experience. She told the teacher that it was the first time she had been invited into school to discuss something positive about her daughter. She was a single mother who did not feel able to discuss Fiona's difficulties with her own family. Having had the opportunity to meet with the teacher, she felt she now had someone alongside her who was committed to Fiona's success, and with whom she could talk about her hopes and fears for Fiona in the future.

Engaging 'hard to reach' families

Working with families can be difficult when put into practice. While some issues will be common across all families with children with CLDD, families are as unique as their children – no two will have identical needs; 'families can be diverse in terms of their experience, resources and expectations as well as their cultural, religious and linguistic influences' (DfES/DH 2003: 9). This needs to be reflected in systems for working with families.

There are children within every school whose families are considered 'hard to reach', including families with their own needs.

Families with their own needs

Families may have their own needs – needs which can be multiple; for example due to poverty, physical or mental health problems, physical or learning disability or substance dependency. These families may be reluctant to engage with their child's school due to their worries about:

- **Judgement or stigmatization** (Blewett et al. 2011) – especially if parents have a mental health problem or drug/alcohol problem.
- **Confidentiality** – schools need strong policies and protocols to safeguard families.
- **Access** – difficulties may be practical (e.g. transport, timings, finances, language or childcare) or psychological (e.g. anxiety).
- **Understanding** – family members (particularly if they also have a learning disability), may not want to reveal their difficulties to the school (Blewett et al. 2011).

When working with these families, these principles and potential barriers are also important to consider:

- **Accessibility of well-informed, approachable staff** (Blewett et al. 2011; Maguire et al. 2009).
- **Building trusting relationships** through sensitive and understanding communication and having a single, trusted contact person.
- **A more relaxed, informal approach** to offset parents' own negative school experiences. Playground conversations and first name terms can help perceptions of informality.
- **Having a flexible system** which is adaptable to parents' needs – e.g. some parents may benefit from meetings and target setting being carried out on home visits rather than in school.
- **Being accommodating for all** – Can schools accommodate the child or their siblings while their parents are in a school meeting?
- **Ensure information is understood** – some parents may need information in Plain English, larger text or symbols, with a follow-up phone call or home visit to explain important events and information.
- **Empower families** to become active partners in their child's education. Using 'structured conversations' can be effective.

It is important that staff remain mindful of potential issues within the home that may affect the child's own emotional well-being and education.

Supporting families from BME communities

Some families from black and minority ethnic (BME) communities can also be 'hard to reach', and may be wrongly perceived as passive in relation to their child's education (Diniz 1997). These families may be struggling to overcome multiple access issues, including language barriers (Hatton et al. 2004), and a related lack of knowledge about services (Hatton et al. 2004; Mir et al. 2001) and disability/special education systems (Diniz 1997), including disability concepts, terminology and professional roles. Despite non-community perceptions that these families of children with disabilities automatically receive strong family and community support, in many situations this is not the case (Mir et al. 2001). As a result, these families may be particularly vulnerable to negative experiences with their child with CLDD yet may be among those least likely to seek and access practical and emotional support.

Schools can establish partnership with minority-ethnic families by:

* **acknowledging the experience** of the family as a whole and their unique needs;
* **providing written support** materials in different languages;
* **utilizing staff language skills;**
* **employing staff** who can speak a relevant second language or a dedicated key worker;
* **providing home visits** for families who cannot access school;
* **ensuring families are aware** of the opportunities available for support in school and more widely (e.g. Contact a Family), particularly if aimed at minority ethnic families; and
* **offering opportunities to link with families** from similar cultural backgrounds – this may provide them with more information about services available and offer companionship of others in comparable situations.

However, Diniz (1997: 113) warns:

> I cannot stress too strongly the view gained from the research that stereotyped assumptions about ethnic groups (e.g. that Muslim men will not allow their wives to have their say) can damage access to ethnic minority families, many of whom will have had negative experiences with officialdom.

Structured conversations

Schools who used the Achievement for All programme's 'structured conversations' (DCSF 2009; Humphrey and Squires 2011) as a way of engaging parents of children with special educational needs and disabilities in primary, secondary and special school settings have seen a significant improvement in parental engagement and the relationship between staff and parents.

Structured conversations between parents and schools establish a shared dialogue about the child and their needs, and provide a more holistic view of the child. They led to a culture shift, where parents felt included and empowered, and engaged with and contributed more positively to their child's education. The structured conversations gave parents a better understanding of the difficulties their child was facing and gave them ways of working with their child at home. Through this, relationships between parents and children also improved and there was an increase in children's school progress and self-esteem.

A flexible approach in meeting organization was seen as key to maximizing attendance of family members. While there was a small group of hard-to-reach families that did not engage with the programme, the schools persisted, looking at changes to timings and locations of the meeting, as well as providing transportation.

Case study: Family Support at The Milestone School

The Family Support Team at The Milestone School consists of two Family Support Workers, who between them have extensive knowledge and experience of working with children with disabilities and their families. This enables them to have an understanding of the difficulties and challenges that families encounter, and to support and empower them, providing them with the information they require to access appropriate supportive networks and services.

The Family Support Team has encouraged the involvement of parents and extended family members by inviting them into school for social groups. The Parent Café has given parents the opportunity to discuss the issues they experience within a supportive and empathetic atmosphere. About the Café, parents have said: 'It enables parents of children with special needs to come and relax and share their experiences' and 'Coming to the Parent Cafe has made me realize I am not the only one with problems'.

Parent Workshops and training from professionals and guest speakers have been a tremendous success. Sessions have included 'Promoting Positive Behaviour', 'Benefits Advice', 'Looking after Yourself', 'Makaton Signing' and 'Home Safety', with families being encouraged to suggest additional topics. Parents have reported feeling more confident and relaxed after gaining knowledge about services available to them.

Support given to ethnic minority families has been extensive, with the involvement and assistance for parents to set up their own Black and Minority Ethnic group, accessing interpreter services to support families with English as an additional language, and building relationships and supporting 'hard to reach' families such as those from the Travelling and Multi-Cultural communities.

Other family members have also been supported by opportunities for them to access groups, such as the 'Siblings Group', 'Makaton Signing' and 'Grandparents and Autism' groups.

The Grandparents and Autism Group has been facilitated by the Family Support Workers over the past two years. It is delivered by a grandparent of children with autism who has a wealth of knowledge and experience also gained through further inquiry and education. Grandparents said this has helped them to 'Gain much needed information', and commented on its 'friendly and relaxed atmosphere', and grandparent perspective.

Other work the Family Support Team do is: liaise with services to help children and families access out-of-school activities and provision for short breaks, in terms of gaining the support and funding required; facilitating positive parenting courses, such as Webster-Stratton (2007) and Webster-Stratton and Redi (2009), which has been adapted to meet the needs of our families; supporting parents with benefit appeals and at tribunals; and completing forms, signposting, completing referrals to appropriate agencies and applying to charities to gain specialist equipment for their children.

In recent questionnaires on the impact that the Family Support Team has had on children with SEN, their parents/carers, siblings and extended family have been extremely positive. Teachers have expressed the impact this has had on children's development and attainment in school as being evidenced in:

- improved attendance and behaviour;
- closer links with home; and
- increasing emotional well-being, educational achievement and confidence.

Conclusion

Partnerships can be challenging, and families of children with CLDD may be among the most vulnerable to work with. However, with encouragement, support and an appreciation for the personal and emotional investment families put in to the upbringing of their child, schools can develop positive and proactive collaborative partnerships which benefit all.

References

Attfield, E. and Morgan, H. (2007) *Living with Autistic Spectrum Disorders*, London: Paul Chapman.

Beveridge, S. (2005) *Children, Families and Schools: Developing partnerships for inclusive education*, London: RoutledgeFalmer.

Blewett, J., Noble, J., Tunstill, J. and White, K. (2011) *Improving Children's Outcomes by Supporting Parental Physical and Mental Health*, London: Centre for Excellence and Outcomes in Children and Young People's Services (C4EO).

Brown, E. (2007) *Supporting the Child and the Family in Paediatric Palliative Care*, London: Jessica Kingsley.

Carpenter, B. (ed.) (1997) *Families in Context: Emerging trends in family support and early intervention*, London: David Fulton.

Carpenter, B. (2002) 'Enabling partnership: families and schools'. In B. Carpenter, R. Ashdown, and K. Bovair (eds) *Enabling Access: Effective teaching and learning for pupils with learning difficulties*, London: David Fulton, pp. 269–285.

Carpenter, B. (2010) *The Family Context, Community and Society* (Complex needs series), London: SSAT.

Carpenter, B. with Egerton, J. (2007) *Working in Partnership through Early Support: Family structures*, Nottingham: DfES Publications.

Carpenter, B. and Towers, C. (2008) 'Recognising fathers: the needs of fathers of children with disabilities', *Support for Learning*, 23: 118–125.

Carpenter, B. and Filmer, H. (2015, forthcoming) 'Working with families: partnership in practice'. In P. Lacey, H. Lawson, P. Jones and R. Ashdown (eds) *The Routledge Companion to Severe, Profound and Multiple Learning Difficulties*, London: Routledge.

Carpenter, B., Conway, S., Whitehurst, T. and Attfield, A. (2007) 'Journeys of enquiry: working with families in a research context'. In B. Carpenter and J. Egerton (eds) *New Horizons in Special Education: Evidence-based practice in action*, Clent, Worcestershire: Sunfield Publications, pp. 145–154.

Carpenter, B., Filmer, H. and Egerton, J. (2012) 'Talking to families; listening to families'. In Department for Education (2012) *Training Materials for Teachers of Pupils with Severe, Profound and Complex Difficulties*. [Online at: www.complexneeds.org.uk; accessed: 14.07.14.]

Chesney, A. and Champion, P. (2008) 'Understanding the dynamics between preterm infants and their families', *Support for Learning*, 23: 144–151.

Contact a Family (2009) *What Makes My Family Stronger: A report into what makes families with disabled children stronger – socially, emotionally and practically*, London: Contact a Family.

Contact a Family (2011) *Statistics: Information about families with disabled children*. [Online at: www.cafamily.org.uk/professionals/research/statistics.html; accessed 17.08.11.]

Conway, S. and O'Neill, K. (2004) 'Home and away', *Learning Disability Practice*, 7: 34–38.

Davies, J. (2005) 'First impressions: emotional and practical support for families of a young child with a learning disability'. In B. Carpenter and J. Egerton (eds) *Early Childhood Intervention: International perspectives, national initiatives and regional practice*, Coventry: West Midlands SEN Regional Partnership, pp. 97–106.

Davis, H. (2007) 'The helping relationship: understanding partnerships'. In P. Limbrick (ed.) *Family-Centred Support for Children with Disabilities and Special Needs*, Clifford: Interconnections, pp. 7–23.

DCSF (Department for Children, Schools and Families) (2009) *Achievement for All – The Structured Conversation: Handbook to support training*, Annesley: DCSF Publications.

DfES (Department for Education and Skills) (2003) *The Impact of Parental Involvement on Children's Education*, Nottingham: DfES Publications.

DfES/DH (Department for Education and Skills/Department of Health) (2003) *Together from the Start: Practical guidance for professionals working with young disabled children (birth to third birthday) and their families*, Nottingham: DfES Publications.

Diniz, F.A. (1997) 'Working with families in a multi-ethnic European context: implications for services'. In B. Carpenter (ed.) *Families in Context: Emerging trends in family support and early intervention*, London: David Fulton, pp. 107–120.

Garrigan, P. (2011) 'Engagement must not stop at the gate', *The Sydney Morning Herald*. [Online at: www.smh.com.au/national/education/engagement-must-not-stop-at-the-gate-20110612-1fz3x.html; accessed: 30.08.11.]

Hatton, C., Akram, Y., Shah, R., Robertson, J., and Emerson, E. (2004) *Supporting South Asian Families with a Child with Severe Disabilities*, London: Jessica Kingsley.

Humphrey, N. and Squires, G. (2011) *Achievement for All National Evaluation*, Nottingham: DfE Publications.

Kingston, A. (2007) *Mothering Special Needs: A different maternal journey*, London: Jessica Kingsley.

Kurt, O., Cavkaytar, A. and Kircaali-Iftar, G. (2004) 'The correlations between perceptions of mothers of children with mental retardation about their families and various family variables'. Paper presented at the 'European Dimension of Special Education: Emergence of a Different Profile' conference, Thessaloniki, Greece (date unknown).

Lamb, B. (2009) *Lamb Inquiry: Special educational needs and parental confidence*, Nottingham: DCSF Publications.

Maguire, R., Brunner, R., Stalker, K. and Mitchell, J. (2009) *Supporting Disabled Parents' Involvement in their Children's Education: Good practice guidance for schools*, Reading: CfBT Education Trust.

Mencap (2006) *Breaking Point*. [Online at: www.mencap.org.uk/case.asp?id=542; accessed 11.04.11.]

Meyer, D. and Vadasy, P. (1997) 'Meeting the unique concerns of brothers and sisters of children with specials needs'. In B. Carpenter (ed.) *Families in Context: Emerging trends in family support and early intervention*, London: David Fulton, pp. 62–75.

Mir, G., Nocon, A., Ahmad, W. and Jones, L. (2001) *Learning Difficulties and Ethnicity*, London: DH.

Mirfin-Veitch, B. and Bray, A. (1997) 'Grandparents: part of the family'. In B. Carpenter (ed.) *Families in Context: Emerging trends in family support and early intervention*, London: David Fulton, pp. 76–88.

Ofsted (2010) *The Special Educational Needs and Disability Review: A statement is not enough*, London: Ofsted.

Oulton, K. and Heyman, B. (2009) 'Devoted protection: how parents of children with severe learning disabilities manage risks', *Health, Risk and Society*, 11: 313–319.

Rawson, H. (2010) '"I'm going to be here long after you've gone": sibling perspectives of the future', *British Journal of Learning Disabilities*, 38: 225–231.

Rix, J. (2007) 'Knowing yourself and the family'. In Early Support (ed.) *Working in Partnership through Early Support: Distance learning text*, Nottingham: DfE Publications, pp. 1–30.

Seligman, M. and Darling, R.B. (2007) *Ordinary Families, Special Children*, New York, NY: Guildford Press.

Smith, M., Robertson, J., Dixon, J., Quigley, M. and Whitehead, E. (2001) *A Study of Stepchildren and Step-parenting: Final report to the Department of Health*, London: Thomas Coram Research Unit.

Statham, H., Ponder, M., Richards, M., Hallowell, N. and Raymond, F.L. (2010) 'A family experience of the value of diagnosis for intellectual disability: experiences from a genetic research study', *British Journal of Learning Disabilities*, 39: 46–56.

Sylva, K., Melhuish, E., Sammons, P., Siraj-Blatchford, I. and Taggart, B. (2004) *The Effective Provision of Pre-school Education (EPPE) Project: Final report*, Nottingham: DfES.

Webster-Stratton, C. (2007) 'Tailoring The Incredible Years Parenting Program according to children's developmental needs and family risk factors'. In J.M., Briesmeister and C.E. Schaefer (eds) *Handbook of Parent Training*, Hoboken, NJ: Wiley, pp. 305–344.

Webster-Stratton, C. and Reid, M.J. (2009) 'The Incredible Years Program for children from infancy to pre-adolescence: prevention and treatment of behavior problems'. In R. Murrihy, A. Kidman and T. Ollendick (eds) *Clinician's Handbook for the Assessment and Treatment of Conduct Problems in Youth*, New York, NY: Springer Press, pp. 117–138.

World Health Organization (2011) *World Report on Disability*. Geneva: World Health Organization.

Young, S. (2007) 'When parents are in denial'. In P. Limbrick (ed.) *Family-Centred Support for Children with Disabilities and Special Needs*, Worcester: Interconnections, pp. 33–44.

Chapter 7

Together everyone can achieve more

Collaborating with other professionals

Collaborative approaches are key to unlocking the innate abilities of children with CLDD, and close partnership between the adults working with them is essential. This can mean teachers working in new ways with the teaching assistants in their class team, all educators liaising closely with colleagues from other disciplines, and all professionals developing strong connections with families (see Chapter 6). The UK's Office for Standards in Education, Children's Services and Skills (Ofsted 2010: 65) note that there is 'better accountability from different aspects of provision when providers had a mixed team of professionals from different disciplines'.

These collaborative partnerships rely on a relationship-based approach. This chapter introduces a selection of case studies which show the different ways educators, families and specialists from other disciplines can work together to overcome children's learning barriers and increase their engagement for learning.

Recognizing teaching assistants and their skills

There is an increasing emphasis on up-skilling the teaching assistant workforce, as more schools try to find sustainable ways of educating increasingly complex children and developing the whole staff knowledge base that will enable them to do so. The contribution of teaching assistants at all levels is crucial in supporting children with CLDD, and in expecting them to support these children effectively, schools need to give detailed consideration to their training needs.

Many of the schools in the CLDD Project valued the knowledge, skills and experience of teaching assistants highly. One teacher described her school's approach:

> We all [teachers and teaching assistants] do exactly the same – such as formulating individual plans. TAs give opinions to teachers for these plans. We do work as a team. TAs know what works and what doesn't . . . they have new ideas. Our management is very forward thinking, and therefore encourages TAs to develop.
>
> (UK SEN trial school)

Teaching assistant involvement alongside teachers in the CLDD Project, both participating in and, in some cases, managing the project in their schools, was a success. In the project exit interviews, a number of schools remarked upon the increased classroom participation and impact of teaching assistants through their use of the Engagement for Learning Framework. They found that teaching assistants could see how they might contribute meaningfully to a child's learning journey, and begin to take a more proactive role. One teacher noted that having the structure they needed through the engagement resources gave teaching assistants greater autonomy.

In recent years, schools have independently been developing creative ways of working with teaching assistants, and Barrs Court School was an early pioneer as the following case study illustrates.

Case study: specialist teaching assistants

Barrs Court School in Hereford, UK, trains specialist teaching assistants to support the work of visiting professionals from different disciplines across the school. Each teaching assistant works closely with, and receives training from, these specialist professionals in their specific knowledge/practice area – for example, speech and language therapy, occupational therapy, sensory integration or post-school transition, etc. These specialist teaching assistants support children during withdrawal sessions, act as an information conduit between the class teacher and specialist professionals and support ongoing therapeutic input for children through class-based, small group or withdrawal sessions.

In addition to their classroom role, the specialist teaching assistants also have a tutoring role in the school's mandatory, two-year training course for teaching assistants. This has been a significant benefit to the school, and in recognition, their job title was changed from 'specialist teaching assistant' to 'training instructor' to reflect their workforce training responsibilities. The (then) headteacher, Richard Aird, also arranged access for the post holders to a Certificate in Education qualification in adult education, in addition to specific qualifications such as 'Picture Exchange Communication System (PECS) Tutor'.

(Fergusson and Carpenter 2010)

There is also a growing trend towards supporting excellent teaching assistants to become teachers. The Salt Review (DCSF 2010) identifies them as a 'rich potential source of teachers'. New Bridge School, Oldham corroborates this:

Case study: New Bridge School, Oldham

At New Bridge, we recognize that effective, high quality and individualized staff development is vital to meeting the school's professional development agenda, realizing future goals and ambitions, and contributing to the development of a responsive and supportive staff.

Our flexible training routes information planner (TRIP) ... has supported colleagues into qualified teacher status from the initial positions of classroom support assistants and higher level teaching assistants. This 'grow your own' model not only offers colleagues the opportunities to develop their skills, but makes economic sense for the school and is less risky than using more traditional employment routes.

(Fergusson and Carpenter 2010: 3)

Collaborating with colleagues

Often educators are unaware of the value that information they hold about a child with CLDD will have for another colleague. Typically educators struggle to find time to share successful strategies with colleagues. However, these strategies, if more widely known, can have a tremendous impact on children's learning potential throughout their school career and beyond. It is therefore important that everyone is aware of others' successes in working with children with CLDD.

Case study: Ivan

Ivan is a 12-year-old boy who has a range of needs arising from his complex diagnoses of Behavioural, Emotional and Social Difficulties (BESD), Attention Deficit and Hyperactivity Disorder (ADHD), Receptive Language Delay and Dyslexic Profile. He attends a day school for children with BESD. Getting Ivan to stay in class is a problem, and he has been regularly excluded from school for damaging school property. The aim of the CLDD Project intervention was to re-engage him in his lessons.

During a reflective discussion with teaching colleagues about Ivan's strengths and difficulties, his Spanish teacher described the success of a computer-based task for the class, recalling that, in contrast with other lessons, Ivan '*was not stressed*' and '*was not looking to leave the lesson*' and remained engaged '*for most of the lesson.*' Through subsequently introducing a computer-based task at the beginning of Spanish lessons, and going through the lesson plan with him beforehand, Ivan's engagement score in Spanish had jumped from 2 to 24 out of a possible 28. This initial activity by-passed Ivan's auditory difficulties, enabling him to stay in class, and to remain calm and ready to engage in learning. He was then supported to rejoin the class group activity at a suitable stage during the lesson. Based on this discovery, Ivan's English teacher realized that starting lessons with a computer-based task which did not require oral explanation might also resolve Ivan's issues at the beginning of her lessons.

When this intervention was put in place during English lessons, Ivan showed a similar level of improvement. Ivan fully engaged in the initial computer task but, on request, willingly stopped the computer task and followed the teacher's instructions to join the main lesson. In each case, after doing so, he was focused, participated in the activities and asked and answered questions relevantly, even when others in the class were disruptive. He increased in confidence, even taking part in activities he had refused before, such as reading aloud in class. The intervention was introduced with equal success in other classes, such as Maths.

(Carpenter et al. 2011)

Involving specialist advisors

Children with CLDD have needs that challenge the knowledge and experience of educators in schools. Many (but by no means all) have high-level health, social and educational needs associated with their conditions, and no single profession is equipped to deal with this diverse array of children's needs. The ability to draw upon specialist advice is a crucial resource for every educator working with children with complex needs, and should be much more widely accessible than it currently is. Educators do not always know what it is they do not know in respect of psychology and therapies, and how this may impact the child's ability to learn.

Advisers from other disciplines, with their specialist foci, can identify barriers to learning for a child that are invisible to generalist educators. They can advise on changes – sometimes very small – that will extend the educational possibilities for a child. They may suggest reading and professional contacts to support educators in meeting the child's needs, and will know the most effective routes to obtain specialist equipment.

As Lacey states (2001: 35): 'Collaborative teamwork is a complex concept'. There may be a wide range of professionals from education, health and social care involved to provide the necessary assessments, treatments, interventions, education and support (Boddy et al. 2006). When multi- and trans-disciplinary teams work well together, they provide enriched support for the child and their family.

Case study: Supporting vision development

Tom is a very happy six-year-old boy, who communicates by smiling and laughing. Tom's severe physical difficulties (postural and visual) create huge barriers to learning for him, both social and educational.

He was born with quadriplegic cerebral palsy, and also has severe vision impairment and epilepsy among other medical and physical difficulties. Tom is therefore dependent on adults for all daily living activities, and is involved with a retinue of specialist professionals including a speech and language therapist, physiotherapist, occupational therapist and a qualified teacher of the vision impaired (QTVI) – aside from numerous medical professionals.

Tom's severe learning disabilities have resulted in delayed receptive and expressive language skills, and delayed social interaction skills, and Tom's class team struggled to engage him in learning. Initially, they decided to increase Tom's social interactions with staff, using sensory experiences as a medium. As Tom's communication was at the pre-intentional stage, the class team wanted to see if he would respond consistently to the introduction and then withdrawal of a sensory experience he enjoyed so that they could respond to this as if it were a communication of his desire for 'more'. They used fans with coloured flashing lights to provide sensory stimulation.

However, the approach was not successful and the school were unsure how to move forward. They requested a consultation with the CLDD Project's specialist VI consultant. She observed Tom during one of the interactive floor sessions. Tom's responses to the sensory stimulus were inconclusive, and she noted:

> Tom looks randomly at the flashing fan but then blinks and turns his head away and then back again. Is it the feeling of the fan he enjoys or the coloured lights? What structural purpose is the fan/light serving for Tom [in terms of his learning]?

As the class team also felt Tom's responses to the sensory stimuli were inconsistent, the VI consultant advised them to swap their chosen task and desired learning outcome for others that had greater clarity around a learning purpose and outcome. She suggested building on Tom's emerging visuo-perceptual skills from a developmental perspective.

Developmentally, humans first learn to visually process and distinguish between black and white, so these are the best colours to introduce when encouraging a child to recognize colour, shape and form. The advisor introduced two clear, defined, bold, black shapes on a white background – in this case, two black mesh fabric squares taped on opposite corners of a piece of A4 white card.

As Tom was out of his wheelchair on a mat, resting on his side with his head on the floor, she placed the card vertically 30–50 cm away from him. (Tom's physical disabilities meant that he was able to raise his head only momentarily.) Gradually he became more aware of the images. He slowly started to look for longer periods of time at the white and black page. His eyes moved both up and down the page and across from left to right. It was interesting to see how long Tom could retain attention. After 20 minutes the VI consultant moved the paper! Throughout this entire time, Tom had been totally engaged – looking, tracking and fixing on the page and shapes. She advised the class team to introduce further coloured shapes or objects of reference slowly one at a time and with reference to vision developmental progression. (Based on this, yellow would have been the next colour to introduce.)

The graph in Figure 7.1 indicates Tom's gradual progression towards his learning target over the course of three sessions.

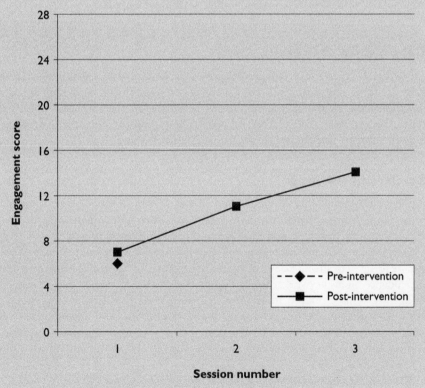

Figure 7.1 Tom's Engagement Scales (June–July 2010)

Facilitating a transdisciplinary focus

In transdisciplinary practice (Lacey 2001) professionals work closely together with the aim of delivering a holistic, child-centred intervention. Pagliano (1999: 120) defines this approach: 'In a transdisciplinary team the roles are not fixed. . . . The boundaries between disciplines are deliberately blurred to employ a "targeted eclectic flexibility".'

Transdisciplinary working at its best can take away insular working practices and incompatible targets for children. It allows professionals to work together, prioritizing and rationalizing their support in a way that enhances the child's quality of life and that of their family.

King et al. (2009), based on work by Foley (1990), identify three essential operational features of transdisciplinary practice:

- Simultaneous assessment of the child
- Intensive, ongoing interaction between the professionals involved – enabling them to 'pool and exchange information, knowledge, and skills, and work together cooperatively' (King et al. 2009: 213)
- Role release – professionals working in the transdisciplinary team enskill one another to help deliver other professional aspects of an intervention under the specialist's supervision.

The following case study illustrates how therapists and educators supported a transdisciplinary intervention to meet a range of children's needs.

Case study: Breaking away

David, aged 9, has a very complex diagnosis including spastic quadriplegic cerebral palsy, dystonic posturing, epilepsy, cortical vision impairment, microcephaly, global developmental delay and severe learning difficulties. He receives input from physiotherapy, occupational therapy, speech and language therapy, hydrotherapy, rebound therapy sessions, music therapy and finally nursing.

Barriers to learning

David is a delightful and engaging young man with a big personality and a great sense of humour. A major barrier to his learning are his complex medical needs, which frequently cause him pain, and leave him tired and unable to engage.

David is very sociable among people he knows. His understanding is very good, and he forms very strong bonds with people he likes. However, this led to an extreme dependence on his keyworker to the detriment of his independence and learning. He frequently refused highly motivating activities, even lunch, if he did not have her full attention. He also refused to use alternative and augmentative communication methods without her support. David's keyworker tended to guess his choices and decisions, thus taking away the need for him to communicate using a formal method.

Based on this issue, David's class-based engagement target was chosen to be: 'To engage with a range of people in a range of settings'. To support this target, the physiotherapist, music therapist and speech and language therapist collaborated on a transdisciplinary, complementary programme in parallel with the class engagement initiative. The approach designed was 'Music, movement and words', which the therapists felt were key elements for enabling David to communicate with confidence.

Transdisciplinary working

In strengthening David's communication (using head-switch vocalization, eye-pointing/gaze and facial expression) with a range of different people, the speech and language therapist, music therapist and physiotherapist worked together in a transdisciplinary way. David was very motivated by singing, so the school's speech and language therapist asked the music therapist to become involved in a transdisciplinary intervention. In order to facilitate his communication and interaction, David also needed support to position his body so that he was able to communicate more freely. The physiotherapist therefore agreed to join the collaborative sessions. With the three therapists supporting David, his keyworker was not needed in the session, therefore separating him from reliance upon her.

In working with David, the three therapists had complementary aims.

The music therapist wanted to explore with David ways of expressing himself through vocalization to music in ways he had not been able to do before, to extend the length of time he was focused and engaged, and to establish a connection between cause and effect.

Music therapy provided the motivation for David to communicate. To use eye-pointing/gaze to best effect, the speech and language therapist needed him to be in the best possible physical position. She aimed to increase his confidence in communicating away from his keyworker, and help him establish control/choice in therapy sessions.

The physiotherapist, in addition to providing the optimum position for David's communication and interaction, was interested to see what positions she could establish for him so he had maximum functionality. Music and making choices also provided a motivator for him to move, thus addressing some other physiotherapy targets.

The therapists' aims are summarized in Table 7.1.

'Music, movement and words' facilitated David's singing, body vocabulary and positioning in one activity. The benefits of this combined intervention for David were increased independence from his keyworker, growing confidence in communicating and enjoyment of the session. During these times, he achieved sustained, motivated and confident communication with a range of adults. For the three therapists, transdisciplinary practice enabled them to transcend the disciplinary boundaries which lock us into fixed roles and responsibilities.

Using body awareness activities and positioning to understand relevant vocabulary, David is now communicating confidently independently of his keyworker.

(Adapted from Parkhouse and Tillotson 2010)

Table 7.1 Therapeutic aims for David

Therapist	Formal therapeutic aims
Music therapist	• To engage David musically by mirroring his vocal sounds • To extend David's time of focus and engagement • To become aware of cause and effect • To allow David to communicate through music and provide the space for him to acknowledge, release and explore often previously unexpressed feelings.
Speech and language therapist	• To re-establish structured communication skills in a motivating context • To enable David to gain ideal positioning for communication • To establish a means of communication by supporting David to gain confidence in communicating independently of his teaching assistant • To enable David to link vocabulary development with body awareness activities • To empower David to take part in and feel in control of sustained interaction episodes.
Physiotherapist	• To position David optimally to maximize his communication and interaction • To observe what functional positions are beneficial for David during activities

As a result of their collaboration using the Engagement for Learning Framework, Charlotte Parkhouse and Claire Tillotson, working at Riverside School in Kent, developed the Diamond Model of Transdisciplinary Working (see Figure 7.2) which reflected the structure of the process they had gone through in working with David.

Transdisciplinary working in the CLDD Project

In the course of the CLDD Research Project, we identified existing areas of promising practice for children with CLDD in project schools. St Nicholas school in Canterbury was involved in the development phase of the CLDD Engagement for Learning Framework. They had developed a transdisciplinary approach for supporting the learning of their most complex children.

Case study: Working together for better outcomes

St Nicholas is a community day special school whose child population has a wide range of learning disabilities, including severe learning difficulties, profound learning difficulties, complex learning difficulties, autism and sensory impairments. In 2007, the school developed a transdisciplinary 'Shared goals' initiative so that professionals working with the most complex children, their families and carers, could work together to create a holistic and supportive approach to the child's development and learning. Six planning meetings per child during the year are attended by all adults involved to assess, review, plan and adapt approaches.

The key benefits of the approach to children are:

- interlinking goals from different disciplines with a common aim and clear direction/strategies;
- transdisciplinary working – therapists get regular information about the child's progress even if they cannot physically be with/work with the child;
- teaching staff at the school get a clear programme of how best to work with the child to optimize their individual learning and functional skills development;
- a focus on functional skills, 'real skills that matter', that will make a real impact on the child's life; and
- ability to show achievement.

This approach generates high-quality, reliable child progress. It is a truly shared approach with the child at the centre.

(St Nicholas School 2008; Fergusson and Carpenter 2010)

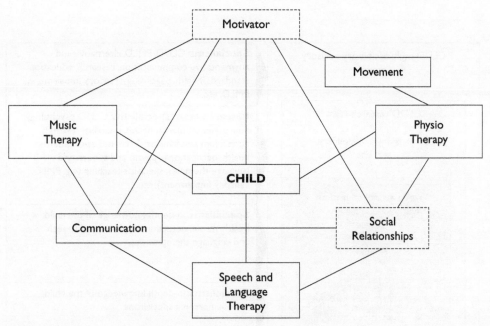

Figure 7.2 The Diamond Model of Transdisciplinary Working

Source: Parkhouse and Tillotson 2010

Collaborating through inquiry: schools and researchers

With the increasing emphasis on inquiry and development in schools, and the need to create an evidence-base to support practice, the schools in the CLDD Project were enthusiastic about the inquiry perspective of their contribution. One of the key tenets of the project was the involvement of educators – teachers, teaching assistants and school-based therapists and psychologists – as practitioner researchers. However, few schools or educators had been previously involved in research, and initially they were more than a little overwhelmed by the idea.

The CLDD Project director, Professor Barry Carpenter, therefore developed the model of inquiry support for schools illustrated in Figure 7.3.

The model linked a research assistant with lead practitioner researchers at a number of schools, and the research assistant became their first point of contact when they wanted to address questions or issues about their inquiry. The lead practitioner researchers themselves were often acting as the within-school link for a number of other educators at their school who were also involved with the project, so the research assistant also acted as a backstop for any questions they had not been able to answer for others in their school.

As well as their own specialist areas, the research assistants were able to draw on the support of high-level specialist professionals who had agreed to be part of a multidisciplinary advisory group. If schools came to the research assistants with questions above their level of expertise, they could seek advice from the advisors who had a range of specialisms.

Post-project, some schools have since gone some way to replicating this advisory model for themselves by creating links with Higher Education Institutions, often with the reciprocal benefits of offering student placement opportunities for the HEI's Education or Psychology Departments.

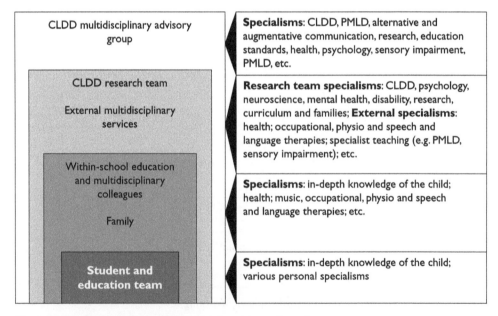

Figure 7.3 Model of multidisciplinary inquiry support for educators

In addition to having access to specialists who can act in an advisory capacity, schools also needed to build their internal collaboration networks to support the development of evidence-based inquiry in their schools. The case studies in two New Zealand schools involved in the CLDD Project demonstrate how this can be achieved.

Case study: School One

School One is a small rural town special school of approximately 133 children ranging in age from 5–21 years. The school's senior leadership team were very committed to taking engagement for learning forward for the children in the school and supported the staff involved, providing additional resources when necessary. This commitment was essential to the success of the project.

The engagement for learning (CLDD; Carpenter et al. 2011) project at the school was managed by the school's music therapist, who had an interest in the engagement process, and an International CLDD Project advisor now teaching at the school. Together with two teachers and other therapists, they created a collaborative transdisciplinary team to support engagement for learning within the school, initially trialling it with two children.

This multidisciplinary collaboration was extremely powerful as by developing a small group each term, who focused on a set group of children, teachers and therapists could focus on their nominated child, develop creative, shared, innovative ideas and trial the engagement for learning resources very effectively.

Regular weekly meetings were set where teachers would bring their video clips and the team would view and collaborate on 'next steps' and any 'barriers to learning'. Parents of all the children involved were also provided with the opportunity to share in the journey. Video clips and photos were regularly sent home for them to view and they had an open invitation to attend meetings. New Zealand embraces the concept of 'whānau support' – whānau being the extended family; anyone who would like to be involved in the child's journey who has the endorsement of the family/whānau can indeed be involved.

Crucial learning information gained as a result of using the Engagement for Learning Framework was used to support each participating child's Individual Education Plan (IEP) review; another forum where parents, teachers and therapists meet and collaborate on the best ways forward for the child.

The implementation of the Engagement for Learning Framework was so successful within this school that, having been trialled in one class at the school, the project was then extended to three other classes.

Another form of collaboration was used at a High School Satellite where there were four classes for 40 children with varying complexities of learning needs. The four teachers and the associated staff all had the opportunity to learn about the engagement for learning approach for one term so that they understood the project. The satellite then identified a small group to carry out an initial trial of the engagement for learning initiative comprising two teachers working with two nominated children from their classes, and involving the children's associated therapists and teaching assistants.

Interestingly, as all staff had initially been inducted, many continued to contribute feedback to the class teacher on how the focus children were 'engaging' during the school day. This information was invaluable given the frequent, subject-associated change of classes.

Again, weekly staff meetings were held for those formally involved in the engagement for learning project. Across the school, teachers and therapists not yet involved with classes doing the engagement for learning programme were not excluded. Any staff member was welcome to join the weekly meetings. Natural collaboration started to take place with informal meetings and discussions and raised excitement about the approach around the school. Other satellites and teachers/therapists started to request future involvement.

Case study: School Two

School Two is a larger city special school whose population has a high proportion of Pacifica and Māori children. There are nine classes on site and a range of satellites across primary, intermediate and secondary levels.

Again a similar process of 'informed collaboration' described above was key to the successful embedding of the engagement for learning process, involving as before whole-school induction, teaching assistant and therapist involvement, and weekly meetings. In this school the large staff group split up into multiple collaborative working teams, each including 3–4 teachers and the therapists who worked with the child.

The Advisor also met with the teams on a regular basis to share ideas and hear feedback. When teams met – especially when the successes started to become more apparent, staff could see the benefits of the collaboration. Therapists too – who initially were not as directly involved – requested to join the meetings for children they worked with.

Conclusion

The Engagement for Learning Framework was designed to be a collaborative tool, both in bringing together education colleagues and in maximizing multidisciplinary input and the opportunities for specialist advice. Educators not only formed stronger working relationships within their own schools, but were able to share difficulties and solutions with schools supporting children with CLDD across the four UK countries and internationally with schools in Australia, Ireland, New Zealand and the USA. Teachers who thought they had a child with a 'rare' complex profile found colleagues at other schools dealing with very similar learners and learning styles. Together they were able to pioneer ways forward.

Through being involved in the engagement for learning process, schools discovered that often educators and families did not realize the educational value of the information they held about a child. One headteacher reflected:

The [CLDD] project has been useful for Meera because it has given a focus for pulling together knowledge from a range of different people, including people who would not usually contribute. They did not realize the importance to everyone else of the little things they knew about her. They now realize that 'That thing that I noticed' is important for us all to know and to share. Having the Engagement Profile and Scale has focused people's knowledge.

When educators work with professionals from other disciplines to achieve true, respectful partnership, together they can achieve insights that would not be possible working alone. These relationships lead to significant steps forward in learning engagement for many children. Schools shared snippets of their success stories of their children's engagement journeys during the end-of-project interviews. One teacher remarked:

Even a change to seating can make a difference. Laurie's awareness and anticipation is really low. We asked the OT [occupational therapist] to look at her and she suggested a foot rest. It made a difference to Laurie's attention – she even started to look for the chair with the foot rest.

The Engagement for Learning Framework creates a common framework and terminology within which professionals from a range of disciplines can work effectively together. Professor Michael Brown, a nurse consultant, and one of the project advisors observed: 'This transdisciplinary interactive approach to Engagement is evolving a common shared language and understanding that is applicable to all disciplines.'

Charlotte Parkhouse, Speech and Langauge Therapist at Riverside School, describes the benefits that this shared language has had among the therapists at Riverside School, Bromley:

Practitioners have found that the 'language of engagement' from the Engagement Profile provides the vocabulary for a effective professional dialogue among multi-agency professionals. Therefore, teachers, teaching assistants and therapists have at their fingertips a terminology to describe their pupils' responses that they can share. Progress in communication and movement skills for the most complex of learners is dependent on the opportunity for these skills to be embedded within motivating and meaningful activities. For example, when a pupil with PMLD needs to be positioned in a pacer, their physiotherapist will be concerned about giving that pupil a purpose to move independently within this supportive equipment, otherwise the pupil's tolerance of the equipment may be low. Likewise, the speech and language therapist may be concerned about this pupil's ability to show that they can initiate interaction with objects for extended periods of time and, therefore, will want to provide enticing multi-sensory stimuli that the pupil will want to move towards independently. The Engagement Profile Indicators provide the perfect vehicle for these professionals to come together to discuss how to create 'Initiation' opportunities. For example, by placing an enticing switch to operate an electric fan slightly out of reach, this gives the opportunity for the pupil to both move in their pacer as well as to independently control and interact with their environment. The shared language of the Engagement Profile makes these therapists realise the great extent that their targets are interwoven at a functional level and, therefore, can be jointly recorded.

Therapists also tapped into the potential of the Engagement Profile and Scale to chart the progress of the children they worked with. One therapist in an international school who took the lead educator role commented:

I . . . was thrilled to be in a position to quantify a very qualitative aspect of our students' learning. I also enjoyed the organic process the project took as we moved through it and that we ended up somewhere different to where we thought we would (as the process is student centred and not dictated by us).

While maintaining a clear focus on learning for children with CLDD, the Engagement for Learning Framework has the flexibility to accommodate transdisciplinary approaches to working with children towards a common learning goal. It enables all to evidence their contribution towards children's engagement for learning and to chart their progress collaboratively.

References

Boddy, J., Potts, P. and Statham, J. (2006) *Models of Good Practice in Joined-up Assessment: Working for children with 'significant and complex needs'*, London: Thomas Coram Research Unit, University of London. [Online at: www.education.gov.uk/publications/eOrderingDownload/RW79.pdf; accessed: 27.07.11.]

Carpenter, B., Egerton, J., Brooks, T., Cockbill, B., Fotheringham, J. and Rawson, H. (2011) *The Complex Learning Difficulties and Disabilities Research Project: Developing pathways to personalised learning*, London: SSAT.

DCSF (Department for Children, Schools and Families) (2010) *Salt Review: Independent review of teacher supply for pupils with severe, profound and multiple learning difficulties (SLD and PMLD)*, Annesley: DCSF Publications.

Fergusson, A. and Carpenter, B. (2010) *Professional Learning and Building a Wider Workforce* (Complex needs series), London: SSAT.

Foley, G.M. (1990) 'Portrait of the arena evaluation: assessment in the transdisciplinary approach'. In E. Biggs and D. Teti (eds) *Interdisciplinary Assessment of Infants: A guide for early intervention professionals*. Baltimore, MD: Paul H. Brookes, pp. 271–286.

King, G., Tucker, M., Desserud, S. and Shillington, M. (2009) 'The application of a transdisciplinary model for early intervention services', *Infants & Young Children*, 22(3): 211–223.

Lacey, P. (2001) *Support Partnerships: Collaboration in action*, London: David Fulton.

Ofsted (2010) *The Special Educational Needs and Disability Review: A statement is not enough*, Manchester: Ofsted. [Online at: www.ofsted.gov.uk/news/statement-not-enough-ofsted-review-of-special-educational-needs-and-disability-0; accessed: 26.08.12.]

Pagliano, P. (1999) *Multisensory Environments*, London: David Fulton.

Parkhouse, C. and Tillotson, C. (2010) 'Music therapy, speech and language therapy and physiotherapy with children with complex learning difficulties and disabilities'. Presentation to the SSAT/DfE Complex Learning Difficulties and Disabilities Interim Research Conference, University of Wolverhampton (30 November).

St Nicholas School (2008) 'Working together for better outcomes', *Special Children*, (June/July): 40–44.

Chapter 8

Mental health and children with Complex Learning Difficulties and Disabilities

A ticking time bomb

Introduction

There is international concern about the mental health status of young people. Troedsson (2005) states: 'It is a time bomb that is ticking and, without the right action now, millions of our children growing up will feel the effect'. It is estimated that by 2020, depression will be the most prevalent childhood disorder (Pretis and Dimova 2008). In the UK, the Good Childhood Report (Children's Society 2012) found that around one in 11 children in the UK are not happy with their lives. The British Medical Association (2006) reported a rise in the prevalence of mental health problems of all children (with and without disabilities) from one in 10 to two in 10. The Mental Health Foundation (2007) suggests that 20 per cent of children have a mental health problem in any given year, and about 10 per cent at any one time.

For children with learning disabilities, the figures are still more bleak. Having SEN is the greatest predictor of deterioration in the mental health for children (DfE 2011). Over one-third (36 per cent) of children with a learning disability have mental health needs, and are 'over six times more likely to have a diagnosable psychiatric disorder than their peers who do not have a learning disability ... [and] significantly more likely to have multiple disorders' (Emerson and Hatton 2007: 14).

At least a third of those with a mild learning disability will have mental health problems that are diagnosable, which, if not addressed will cause underachievement and significantly impair their quality of life (Bernard and Turk 2009). Those with an IQ of below 50 have a one in two chance of experiencing mental health/behavioural difficulties (Pote and Goodban 2007). ASD is a major risk factor for underlying and co-existing mental health difficulty (Ghaziuddin 2005), and seven in ten will experience at least one mental health issue (Dossetor et al. 2011). Too often we attribute their anxiety to being a core feature of their ASD, rather than an additional impairment, which needs to be assessed and diagnosed separately. For children with Fetal Alcohol Spectrum Disorders (FASD), the prevalence of mental health problems rises to nine in ten (NYS FASD Interagency Workgroup 2008). Among children with PMLD, Rose and colleagues (2009) note that often mental health difficulties are overlooked or changes in their behaviour are misinterpreted. They also note the 'co-occurring' nature of mental health needs, a fact which resonated frequently in this study.

Children with learning disabilities demonstrate the complete spectrum of mental health problems with higher prevalence than found in those without learning disabilities (Bernard and Turk 2009; Hardy et al. 2006 2010; Hollins and Curran 1996). For example:

- Schizophrenia – 3 per cent of people with learning disabilities (three times higher than the general population)
- Depression – 1.3–3.7 per cent at any one time (twice as high as the general population)
- Generalized anxiety disorder is equally common or higher among people with learning disabilities
- Bipolar disorder prevalence is higher in the learning disability population.

Hardy and colleagues (2010, 2011) provide useful descriptions of the most common problems including how they might appear in people with severe learning disabilities.

Children with learning disabilities not only have a right to positive mental health and emotional well-being (Carpenter 2004; Foundation for People with Learning Disabilities 2002), but also, as Carpenter (2009: 1) observes:

> What we are failing to recognize is that underpinning success and achievement for any student of any ability is the quality of their mental health. As the United Nations Convention on the Rights of the Child, Article 24, states: 'Health is the basis for a good quality of life and mental health is of overriding importance in this.'

Defining mental health and ill-health

There is often confusion among educators about the different terms relating to mental health and mental ill-health terms, so for clarity 'mental health', 'mental health problems', 'mental health disorders' and 'mental illness' are defined below.

Mental health and emotional well-being

There are many ways of describing mental health. The UK's Department of Health (2011) describes it as 'more than the absence or management of mental health problems' and as foundational well-being and effective functioning. Friedli (2009: 52) highlights the Health Education Authority (1997: 7) definition of mental health as: 'emotional and spiritual resilience which enables us to enjoy life and survive pain, disappointment and sadness.'

Well-being can be emotional, psychological and social (Adi et al. 2007; National Institute for Health and Clinical Excellence description (NICE) 2008). The National CAMHS Support Service (2011) describes emotional well-being as 'A positive state of mind and body, feeling safe and able to cope, with a sense of connection with people, communities and the wider environment'; Dossetor et al. (2011) and *Count Us In* (Foundation for People with Learning Disabilities 2002), the 2002 Mental Health Foundation report on the mental health of people with learning disabilities identifies different aspects of well-being including: self-esteem, optimism, a sense of mastery and coherence; the ability to initiate, develop and sustain mutually satisfying personal relationships; and the ability to cope with adversities, a belief in our own worth and the dignity and worth of others.

Mental ill-health

Mental health problems are a very broad range of emotional and behavioural difficulties which may cause concern or distress (National Assembly for Wales 2001; Sedgewick et al.

2005). They are common and often present as an extreme form of everyday emotions. Mental disorders and illnesses also fall under the umbrella term of 'mental problems' but they have a clinically recognized set of symptoms (Hackett and Bromley n.d.; Sedgewick et al. 2005). However, there is blurring between the categories and the distinction can be hard to make even for mental health professionals.

They can be defined as follows (National Assembly for Wales 2001):

- *Mental health problems* may be reflected in difficulties and/or disabilities in the realm of personal relationships, psychological development, the capacity for play and learning, development of concepts of right and wrong, and in distress and maladaptive behaviour. They may arise from any number or combination of congenital, constitutional, environmental, family or illness factors. 'Mental health problems' describes a very broad range of emotional or behavioural difficulties that may cause concern or distress. They are relatively common, may or may not be transient but encompass 'mental disorders', which are more severe and/or persistent.
- *Mental disorders* are those problems that meet the requirements of ICD 10, an internationally recognized classification system for disorder. The distinction between a mental problem and a mental disorder is not exact but turns on the severity, persistence, effects and combination of features found.
- In a small proportion of cases of mental disorders, the term *mental illness* might be used. Usually, it is reserved for the most severe cases. For example, more severe cases of depressive illness, psychotic disorders and severe cases of anorexia nervosa could be described in this way.

Emotional well-being/mental health issues within the CLDD Project's 'development phase' group

In the light of the shocking statistics on mental health among people with learning disabilities, and the potential impact on children's engagement for learning, the CLDD team wanted to gain an insight into the emotional well-being and mental health of the 59 children in 12 special schools involved in the development phase of the engagement for learning resources. From children's school files and initial interviews carried out with their educators, families and therapists, the CLDD research team gained an overview of concerns about the children's emotional well-being/mental health (EWB/MH). Although the findings cannot be applied to other child populations, they indicate a worrying level of educator concern for the EWB/MH for the children involved in the project, and the need to explore this further.

Using information from documents and interviews, the children were categorized into four groups:

- children with mental health issues who received support from mental health professionals (e.g. CAMHS, the educational psychologist or a counsellor);
- children with mental health issues who did not receive support from a mental health professional, but whose behaviours caused concern to educators and were attributed to mental health issues;
- children whose behaviours caused educators concerns about their emotional well-being;
- children whose mental health caused educators no concern.

Table 8.1 Comparison of educators' EWB/MH concerns expressed about children by phase and gender

Children (n=28)	Primary and below	Secondary
Boys	8 (57%; n=14)	15 (65%; n=23)
Girls	1 (33%; n=3)	4 (36%; n=11)

Summary of within-participant group mental health findings

Of the 59 children (43 boys and 16 girls) in the 'development phase' group, EWB/MH information was available for 51. For over half of these (28), educators had logged concern about their EWB/MH. Within this relatively small group of children with CLDD, educators were twice as likely to express EWB/MH concerns about boys than girls both in primary and secondary phases (see Table 8.1).

The 28 children who caused educators EWB/MH-related concern were categorized into the three remaining groups:

- There were nine children who had an identified EWB/MH concern and who were seeing a mental health professional (clinical psychologist (3),[1] psychotherapist (2), CAMHS professional (2), counsellor (2)). Of these, all but two (a primary-aged boy and a secondary-aged girl) were secondary-aged boys.
- There were six children about whom there were serious mental health concerns, but who were not seeing a mental health professional. All were boys – two of primary age and four of secondary age.
- Educators were concerned about 13 further children whose emotional well-being difficulties were affecting their ability to learn and were not being adequately addressed. These concerns included: depressed mood for 50 per cent or more of the time; excessive sleeping (most of the school day); very low self-esteem; a possible victim of rape.

With children with CLDD, it may be difficult to differentiate between EWB/MH issues that are associated with their conditions, and those which are not (Fergusson et al. 2008). Nonetheless, within the development phase group of children with CLDD, over half were causing concern due to EWB/MH.

Specific concerns were categorized into the areas listed below (drawn from SNASA (Kroll et al. 1999) and HoNOSCA (Gowers et al. 1999) categories). This list was not compiled as part of a systematic investigation into the EWB/MH difficulties within the project children, and therefore there may be relevant conditions that were not mentioned in relation to individual children. However, it does give an indication of educators' main concerns across this participant group. The number of children identified as having a particular issue is represented by the bracketed number.

- Aggression (13)
- Social relationship issues (11)
- Sleep issues (8)
- Family issues (7)
- Anxiety (6)
- Oppositional/disruptive (3)
- Sexualized language and behaviour (3)
- Self-esteem issues (3)
- Over-dependency (2)
- Cultural/racial difficulties (1)

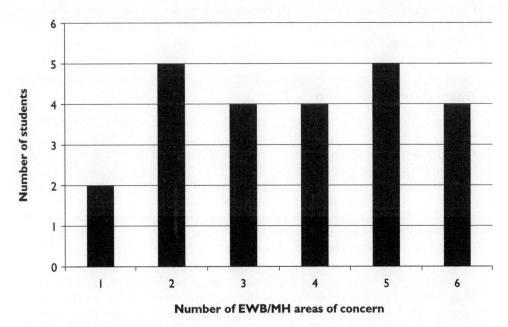

Figure 8.1 Count frequency of EWB/MH areas of concern per student where identified (n=24)

- Deliberate self-harm (6)
- Depressed mood (5)
- Anger (4)
- Hallucinations/delusions/bizarre behaviour (4)
- Hyperactivity/attention issues (3)

- Drug or alcohol misuse (1)
- Eating disorder (1)
- Obsessive compulsive symptoms (1)
- School attendance issues (1)

Each child had difficulties in between one and six EWB/MH areas, and the count frequency of EWB/MH concerns per child is represented in Figure 8.1.

Mental health in trial phase school children with CLDD

While specific information about children's mental health was not collected during the trial school phase, anecdotally schools were concerned about children's mental health issues. One mainstream school said during their exit interview that mental health issues, together with ADHD and autism, were the three main child difficulties in their school.

Where mental health issues exist, these must be identified, prioritized and addressed. Allen et al. (2008: 4) warn: 'Behavioural and emotional difficulties in people with intellectual disabilities are often only addressed when they have become fully established in a person's behavioural repertoire, present for many years, and therefore likely to be more resistant to effective intervention.'

A school from the CLDD Project's development phase observed: 'With K there are medical and mental health issues that need dealing with. . . . It's not about how to motivate him; it is a medical issue that needs to be dealt with.'

The case study below from the CLDD Project illustrates a similar situation in which the mental health needs of a child with CLDD are being addressed, but continue to overshadow his ability to engage with learning.

Case study: Stephen

Stephen is 11 years old and currently attends a mainstream secondary school. He transitioned from primary school with a statement to support his learning needs due to complications with speech and language communication and behavioural, emotional social development needs. His parents are currently pursuing referral routes to investigate the possibility that he falls within the Autistic Spectrum.

Stephen became involved in the CLDD Project due to his behavioural outbursts and difficulties in engaging within the curriculum. He is currently working below age-related National Curriculum norms for Maths and Literacy, but the support he is provided with allows for appropriate educational strategies to be put into place. His behavioural outbursts can, however, disrupt this learning support.

There is a growing concern for Stephen's emotional well-being as he becomes less motivated by learning and interacting within his environment. These concerns are heightened by verbal outbursts from Stephen, including suicide threats and comments about his own mental state. Stephen also engages in self-injurious behaviours including scratching his arms and legs. The difficulties his mental health poses are becoming increasingly hard to manage within this inclusive setting.

The school is working with Child and Adolescent Mental Health Services (CAMHS) together with speech and language therapists (SALTs) to investigate Stephen's issues and appropriately support him. The school is also implementing strategies which have been shown to benefit children's mental health – increasing the amount of exercise he can access, involving him in peer mentoring and giving him time with trained staff to allow him to discuss his difficulties.

It is hoped that addressing Stephen's mental health issues with CAMHS in collaboration with the SALTs will enable him to focus on learning once again. This will allow the school to use the Engagement Profile and Scale so appropriate strategies can be put into place to re-engage Stephen in school life and reduce his vulnerability to mental health issues in the future.

Despite this bleak overview of EWB/MH issues for many children in the CLDD Project, there were unlooked-for positive outcomes in the area of emotional well-being linked to the Project. This was particularly striking among the small mainstream school participant group (12 schools – six primary and six secondary; 24 children). During their final interview, educators were asked in relation to their use of the engagement for learning resources '[to] Describe the most successful outcome for each of the children in the project' and 'Is there anything else you would like to say about the project?' All 12 schools (100 per cent) in the mainstream phase commented on children's improved emotional well-being in response to one or both of these: nine mentioned improved relationships between the children and their staff, peers or family; eight commented generally on improvements in the children's well-being; and two, on children's increased self-esteem. In special schools there were fewer

EWB/MH-focused comments, with 29 (68 per cent) UK trial schools and five (33 per cent) international trial schools mentioning a positive impact on the emotional well-being of the children involved.

The powerful positive impact of engagement in learning on children's emotional well-being is illustrated by the following quotes from the CLDD Project:

> L has gone from exclusion to attending lessons and asking for extra work . . . [She] said yesterday, 'I used to tell my mum I hated this school. I don't tell her that now.'
>
> (Teacher, Mainstream secondary school)

> M is a different child. . . . I think he was so frustrated [because he was not engaged at school] he just let it all out at home. I was scratched and hurt . . . We've none of that now.
>
> (Parent of a child attending a special school)

EWB/MH – the challenge

The challenge for educators is to lift children from vulnerability to positions of resilience. In collaboration with mental health professionals, it is important to identify and put in place school-based interventions that can alleviate the impact of mental health problems.

When children are feeling emotionally vulnerable, their emotional turmoil may affect their ability to focus on, understand and begin a task. Coughlan et al. (2012) suggest that educators can support children by helping them to acknowledge their feelings about their class work, structure it by breaking it down into a sequence of small steps and build in strategies for asking for help. Carpenter (2010; see also Coughlan et al. 2010, 2012) describes how one secondary mainstream academy accommodated a young girl's periodic mental health issues:

Case study: Bethany

Fourteen-year-old Bethany has a diagnosis of anorexia nervosa, obsessive compulsive disorder and depression for which she sees a child psychiatrist. Due to her poor concentration, teaching staff differentiate lessons to increase her engagement in the curriculum. Learning mentors provide her with emotional and practical support. When Bethany's behaviour significantly affects the learning of other children, she is offered time in the Student Support base where she receives direct support and a personalized learning programme until she can cope once again with classroom dynamics. The pace of lesson delivery can be adjusted to allow for her erratic mood swings and lack of concentration. By adjusting her educational setting, and intensifying specialist support for short periods when needed, Bethany is able to remain included in the academy.

Although most schools have programmes in place to support the emotional well-being and emotional/social literacy of children with learning disabilities, research suggests that educators are less confident about responding to mental health difficulties (Byers et al. 2008; NASS (National Association of Independent Schools and Non-Maintained Special

Schools) 2007). 'Mental health is still poorly defined as an issue for staff in many of the schools. This results in confusion with regards to policy development and the co-ordination of response and services' (ibid.: 14).

All staff need sufficient knowledge, training and support to:

- promote psychological well-being;
- identify early indicators of mental health problems/disorders;
- provide positive support towards children's recovery from severe mental health problems/disorders.

(Forster and Grundy 2008; Sedgewick et al. 2005)

Without it, educators may not:

- understand how the work that they do within school supports mental health;
- pick up on cues that a child needs support from a mental health professional;
- have foundational knowledge about causes and interpretations in mental health;
- deliver effective interventions;
- develop professional skills and understanding beyond their own discipline.

(Byers et al. 2008; NASS 2007)

Seeing the warning signs

Picking up on the early warning signs and symptoms of underlying mental health problems is critical (Coughlan 2010). It is important that the people who know the child best and work and live with them are aware of any signs and symptoms and changes in how a child behaves, feels, communicates and goes about their daily life (Bernard and Turk 2009; Fergusson et al. 2008; Forster and Grundy 2008; Hardy et al. 2010). Educators need to:

- build a picture of what 'normal' functioning for the child is, including all their idiosyncratic behaviours that are normal in the context of the individual's learning disabilities, life experiences and culture – this avoids the danger of 'diagnostic overshadowing';
- maintain awareness of the mental health of children at risk by systematically observing and assessing changes in behaviour (e.g. through making and monitoring observations, daily behaviour records, video evidence, liaising with colleagues and families and comparing behaviours across different environments;
- be aware of and respond to uncharacteristic behaviour changes for that child, such as unusual or bizarre behaviours (e.g. aggression or self-harm; anxious, obsessive or compulsive behaviours; sexualized behaviours), physical changes (e.g. abnormal weight loss or gain; incontinence); loss of skills (e.g. communication, personal care); health difficulties (e.g. pain) with no apparent cause.

Mental health concerns should be triggered if these signs shown become long-term (e.g. longer than two weeks) and are generalized across different environments (e.g. school, home, respite, community). Extreme behaviours (e.g. self-harm, running away or not wanting to go on living) need urgent professional help. Close contact between parents and educators is important to provide support (Mind 2010).

This series of questions will help educators reflect on their concerns about a child's mental health (Fox 2012; Hardy et al. 2010). Consider:

1 why you are worried;
2 the behaviour(s) causing the problem;
3 when it started;
4 when it happens (e.g. continuously, at a particular time of day, etc.); observe carefully;
5 whom it affects – how, when and where;
6 how it impacts the child's everyday life;
7 what might have triggered it (e.g. divorce/illness);
8 the child's present and past risk and protective factors for mental health difficulties:

   • which risk factors can be decreased?
   • which protective factors can be increased?

9   strengths in the child, family, community, school that can be built on;
10 what is the worst thing that could happen? Is specific mental health professional support needed?

Risk and protective factors

To support the mental health of children with learning disabilities effectively, it is important to know the risk factors which make mental ill-health more likely (e.g. poverty, parental ill-health, etc.) and the protective factors which increase a child's resilience so the impact of risk factors is lessened (Allen et al. 2008).

Some schools screen all incoming children for risk factors and problem behaviours which might predict mental ill-health so that preventative actions and early interventions can be put in place before problems appear. The Pupil Attitudes to Self and School (PASS), the Strengths and Difficulties Questionnaire (SDQ) and the Developmental Behaviour Checklist have been used to screen children with mild learning difficulties for emotional and behavioural disturbances (Storey and Statham 2006). For children with PMLD, there is a lack of diagnostic tools to diagnose mental health difficulties, and mental health problems are often masked by complex health needs (Fergusson et al. 2008).

Developing protective factors for children with learning disabilities

When developing protective factors in children with CLDD, there are three fundamental building blocks of resilience (Gilligan, in Fox 2012):

1 a secure base, whereby a child feels a sense of belonging and security;
2 good self-esteem, that is, an internal sense of worth and competence;
3 a sense of self-efficacy, that is, a sense of mastery and control, along with an accurate understanding of personal strengths and limitations.

To support children's EWB/MH, schools and other educational organizations need to establish a clearly articulated ethos and a whole-school approach to EWB/MH (Atkinson and Hornby 2002) underpinned by principles of:

- **early intervention** in mental health problems and disorders for children with learning disabilities and their families from the time of diagnosis of a learning disability;
- **promotion** of emotional well-being;
- **prevention** of mental health problems through interventions.

(Carpenter and Morgan 2003; Dossetor et al. 2009)

This may include:

Policy and curriculum

- A well-established programme in personal and social education and citizenship
- An active sex education policy and programmes for personal care, personal relationships and sex education
- Physical health programmes (e.g. regular exercise)
- Clear opposition to injustice and discrimination across the school (e.g. anti-bullying and anti-abuse policies)
- A policy on EWB/MH which identifies within-school criteria for identifying children who have an intellectual disability and mental health problems, and procedures for support and referral of children.

A school community which sustains mental health

- Caring, empathic teachers and support staff who have genuine interest in and concern for children's learning and well-being
- Effective EWB/MH professional development opportunities for staff
- A holistic, transdisciplinary approach to mental health, together with health, psychology and therapies professionals
- Sustained family involvement and support (including provision of appropriate information, skills teaching, emotional support, etc.)
- A 'Well-being Team' to promote emotional well-being in all children and build emotional resilience in those with CLDD
- Availability of additional pastoral supports, including advocacy/communication, counselling (including loss, trauma and bereavement), 'circles of support', targeted prevention and early intervention programmes/strategies
- Specific activities designed to promote strong relationships with peers, teachers and the school
- Shared decision-making with children and families.

Fostering self-efficacy

- Fostering a sense of aspiration, achievement, developing emotional awareness and providing emotional support
- Empowering children to play a central role in their future planning.

(Carpenter and Morgan 2003; Carpenter et al. 2011;
Coughlan et al. 2012; Dossetor et al. 2011; Foundation for People with
Learning Disabilities 2002; Holdsworth and Blanchard 2006)

Programmes and strategies to support the mental health of children with learning disabilities

Suggested approaches to supporting the mental health of children with learning disabilities should focus on developing self-regulation, increasing motivation, enhancing empathy, improving social skills and developing children's self-awareness. Coughlan et al. (2012) give detailed guidance on this in a section entitled 'The right learning environment'. Carpenter (2010; Carpenter et al. 2010) also describes adaptations which have been made in both mainstream and special schools to support the mental health of children with complex learning needs which allow them to achieve.

Pastoral approaches which can support mental health include (Alexander 2005):

- buddy systems;
- circle time;
- circle of friends;
- emotional literacy;
- ground rules (group agreement);
- inclusiveness;
- working to processing preferences (e.g. visual, auditory and kinaesthetic?);
- paired learning;
- peer support;
- school councils;
- social support/development groups;
- pastoral mentoring;
- whole-school approach.

Case study: Nurture groups

Abbey Hill is a secondary school for children with complex needs. Many have mental health issues, including attachment disorder, anxiety and high stress levels. Nurture groups are one of a range of interventions offered to children identified as vulnerable through an attitudinal survey. Environmental activity groups withdraw children from parts of their academic timetable to participate within an enterprise context. The children determine the organization and their roles in activities such as growing and selling produce, bee management, etc. Other children need smaller group settings, with high staff:child ratios, that build trust and a sense of emotional security through intensive interactional techniques. Moving from a learning environment which they find stressful into a therapeutic one builds confidence and self-esteem.

Clare Devine, Headteacher (Carpenter et al. 2010)

Most existing programmes are appropriate for children with mild to moderate learning disabilities. Dossetor et al. (2011) introduce a wide range of available resources. Dossetor also publishes a CHW School link – a newsletter offering guidance on supporting children with mental health needs (www.schoollink.chw.edu.au/newsletter/).

The NASS (2007) survey found that some schools had trialled mainstream resources but found them inadequate for their population of children with learning disabilities. Only two schools were using Social and Emotional Aspects of Learning (SEAL) (DfE 2010), while a minority of schools used commercially produced schemes such as Zippy's Friends (Partnership for Children 2003) or Listen to Me (NASS 2007). These resources may need considerable modification for most children with learning disabilities. Similarly, there is little available for those with severe and profound learning disabilities.

'Friends for Life' may provide an alternative. It is the only programme of its kind endorsed by the World Health Organization as 'appear[ing] to be efficacious across the entire spectrum, as a universal prevention program, as a targeted prevention program and as a treatment' (Waddell et al. 2004: 17). Research evidence suggests that children who have taken part in the programme experience reduced anxiety and depression, increased coping skills and self-esteem, with improvements maintained up to six years after the completion of the programme. Details of an adapted programme for children with learning disabilities is available on the Foundation for People with Learning Disabilities website (www. learningdisabilities.org.uk/our-work/health-well-being/friends-for-life/).

It is important, before buying programmes, for educators to identify which skills the programmes address and check out their suitability for their child group (Dossetor et al. 2011). Young Minds (www.youngminds.org.uk/training_services), the UK's leading charity committed to improving the emotional well-being and mental health of children, also provides guidance to children, families and professionals.

Conclusion

It appears from research literature and the CLDD Project evidence that mental health problems may be the most pervasive and co-occurring need to compound and complicate the special educational needs and disabilities of children with CLDD. We have to investigate this ticking time bomb. Together with the Centre for Mental Health and other mental health organizations (2012) we need to recognize that 'Mental health is everyone's business' and that 'good mental health and resilience are fundamental to our physical health, our relationships, our education, our training, our work and to achieving our potential.'

As Atkinson and Hornby (2002: 3) have recognized, 'Teachers are uniquely placed to influence the mental health of children and young people.' The CLDD Project developed the briefing packs on mental health and attachment (see Appendix B), and the SSAT's mental health Complex Needs series booklet (Carpenter et al. 2010), to support schools.

Bear in mind this guidance on responding to possible signs of mental ill-health in a child (Association for Real Change 2009; Bernard and Turk 2009):

• Acknowledge the issue, and do not ignore or dismiss it; other colleagues might not have noticed. Early intervention improves a child's chances of full recovery and can change their future for the better.
• Keep a written record of the signs, your concerns and the time/context/date including any causes or events which precipitated the behaviour (who was involved, where), what the behaviour was, what happened as a result (ABC forms – Antecedents/Behaviour/ Consequences). Is there anything reinforcing the behaviour? Is the function attention-seeking, avoidance, escape?
• Assess the risk of harm for the child or others.

- Consider other possible causes of the behaviours than a mental health problem (e.g. the child's developmental stage, a condition such as ASD or epilepsy, pain or physical ill-health, sensory impairments, experiences of anxiety or loss due to change or transition).
- Talk to line managers, colleagues and the child's family about your concerns.
- Refer the child to a medical professional if appropriate.
- Gather evidence and information the medical professional might need to make a diagnosis.
- Keep colleagues who need to know, the child and their family appropriately informed.
- Support the child to keep mentally well, and provide self-help strategies.

Note

1 Bracketed numbers indicate numbers of children.

References

Adi, Y., Kiloran, A., Janmohamed, K. and Stewart-Brown, S. (2007) *Systematic Review of the Effectiveness of Interventions to Promote Mental Wellbeing in Primary Schools: Report 1: Universal approaches which do not focus on violence or bullying*, Coventry: University of Warwick.

Alexander, T. (2005) *A Bright Future for All: Promoting mental health in education*, London: Mental Health Foundation.

Allen, D., Langthorne, P., Tonge, B., Emerson, E., McGill, P., Dosen, A., Kennedy, C. and Fletcher, R. (2008) 'Towards the prevention of behavioural and emotional difficulties in people with intellectual disabilities'. A position paper on behalf of the Special Interest Research Group on Challenging Behaviour and Mental Health of the International Association for the Scientific Study of Intellectual Disabilities. [Online at: www.kent.ac.uk/tizard/documents/prevention.pdf; accessed: 04.10.12.]

Association for Real Change (2009) *Clear Thoughts: Checklists, wordbanks, images*, Chesterfield: ARC.

Atkinson, M. and Hornby, G. (2002) *Mental Health Handbook for Schools*, London: RoutledgeFalmer.

Bernard, S. and Turk, J. (2009) *Developing Mental Health Services for Children and Adolescents with Learning Disabilities*, London: RCPysch Publications

British Medical Association (2006) *Child and Adolescent Mental Health – A guide for healthcare professionals*. [Online at www.bma.org.uk/health_promotion_ethics/child_health/ Childadolescentmentalhealth.jsp?page=4; accessed: 04.03.11.]

Byers, R., Davies, J., Fergusson, A. and Marvin, C. (2008) *What about Us: Promoting emotional well-being and inclusion by working with young people with learning difficulties in schools and colleges*, London: Foundation for People with Learning Difficulties.

Carpenter, B. (2004) 'The mental health needs of young people with profound and multiple learning disabilities', *PMLD-Link*, 16(1): 9–12.

Carpenter, B. (2009) 'Mental health: the new dimension in the curriculum for children and young people with special educational needs' (A discussion paper). [Online at: http://v.clickspecialednz. com/wp-content/uploads/MentalHealth-New-Dimension-in-the-Curriculum-for-Children-a. pdf; accessed: 24.06.14.]

Carpenter, B. (2010) 'Navigators of learning', *Special!*, (March): 22–23.

Carpenter, B. and Morgan, H. (2003) 'Count us in', *British Journal of Special Education*, 30(4): 202–206.

Carpenter, B., Coughlan, B. and Fotheringham, J. (2010) *Mental Health and Emotional Well-being*, London: SSAT.

Carpenter, B., Egerton, J., Brooks, T., Cockbill, B., Fotheringham, J. and Rawson, H. (2011) 'The complex learning difficulties and disabilities research project: developing meaningful pathways to personalised learning' (project report). London: SSAT. [Online at: http://complexld.ssatrust.org.uk/project-information.html; accessed: 21.03.12.]

Centre for Mental Health, Department of Health, Mind, NHS Confederation Mental Health Network, Rethink Mental Illness, Turning Point (2012) *No Health without Mental Health: Implementation framework*, London: HM Government.

Children's Society (2012) *The Good Childhood Report: A review of our children's wellbeing*, London: Children's Society.

Coughlan, B.J. (2010) *Critical Issues in the Emotional Wellbeing of Students with Special Educational Needs*, London: SSAT.

Coughlan, B.J., Carpenter, B. and Fotheringham, J. (2010) *Mental Health and Emotional Well-Being: The new dimension in the curriculum for children and young people with special educational needs*, London: SSAT.

Coughlan, B.J., Rae, T. and Fotheringham, J. (2012) 'Emotional well-being and mental health: 12. The right learning environment', in Teaching Agency (2012) *Teaching Materials for Teachers of Learners with Severe, Profound and Complex Learning Disabilities*, London: Department for Education. [Online at: www.education.gov.uk/complexneeds/modules/Module-3.4-Emotional-well-being-and-mental-health/All/m12p070b.html; accessed: 04.10.12.]

Department of Health (2011) *No Health without Mental Health: A cross-government mental health outcomes strategy for people of all ages*, London: Department of Health.

DfE (Department for Education) (2010) 'Social and emotional aspects of learning (SEAL) programme in secondary schools: national evaluation'. [Online at: www.education.gov.uk/publications/eOrderingDownload/DFE-RR049.pdf; accessed: 28.09.14.]

DfE (Department for Education) (2011) *Support and Aspiration: A new approach to special educational needs and disability – a consultation*, Norwich: The Stationery Office.

Dossetor, D., Caruana, J., Saleh, H. and Goltzoff, H. (2009) *Leading the Way in Mental Health and Intellectual Disability: A focus on the needs of children and adolescents in schools for specific purposes in NSW*, Sydney: The Children's Hospital at Westmead.

Dossetor, D., White, D. and Whatson, L. (eds) (2011) *Mental Health of Children and Adolescents with Intellectual and Developmental Disabilities: A framework for professional practice*, Melbourne: IP Communications.

Emerson, E. and Hatton, C. (2007) *The Mental Health of Children and Adolescents with Learning Disabilities in Britain*, London: Foundation for People with Learning Disabilities/Lancaster University.

Fergusson, A., Howley, M. and Rose, R. (2008) 'Responding to the mental health needs of young people with profound and multiple learning disabilities and autistic spectrum disorders: issues and challenges', *Mental Health and Learning Disabilities Research and Practice*, 5, 240–251.

Forster, K. and Grundy, D. (2008) *Candle: CAMHS and new directions in learning disability and ethnicity – A resource for frontline staff, their supervisors/managers and trainers*, Chesterfield: Association for Real Change.

Foundation for People with Learning Disabilities (2002) *Count Us In: The report of the committee of inquiry into meeting the mental health needs of young people with learning disabilities*, London: Mental Health Foundation.

Fox, J. (2012) 'Building resilience'. [Online at: www.childcentredpractice.co.uk/Websites/ccp1/files/Content/1553772/Use%20of%20the%20Risk%20and%20resilience%20matrix%20when%20planning%20for%20children.doc; accessed: 24.06.14.]

Friedli, L. (2009) 'Future directions in mental health promotion and public mental health'. In I. Norman and I. Ryrie (eds) *The Art and Science of Mental Health Nursing: A textbook of principles and practice* (2nd edn), Maidenhead: Open University Press, pp. 43–61.

Ghaziuddin, M. (2005) *Mental Health Aspects of Autism and Asperger Syndrome*, London: Jessica Kingsley Publishers.

Gowers, S.G., Harrington, R.C., Whitton, A., Lelliott, P., Beevor, A., Wing, J. and Jezzard, R. (1999) 'Brief scale for measuring the outcomes of emotional and behavioural disorders in children: Health of the nation outcome scales for children and adolescents', *The British Journal of Psychiatry*, 174, 413–416.

Hackett, L. and Bromley, J. (n.d.) 'Child and Adolescent Mental Health Services: Psychiatric disorders in Learning disability' (Powerpoint presentation). Manchester: CAMHS.

Hardy, S., Kramer, R., Holt, G., Woodward, P., Chaplin, E. (2006) *Supporting Complex Needs: A practical guide for support staff working with people with a learning disability who have mental health problems*, London: Turning Point/Estia Centre.

Hardy, S., Chaplin, E. and Woodward, P. (2010) *Mental Health Nursing of Adults with Learning Disabilities*, London: Royal College of Nursing.

Hardy, S., Woodward, P., Woolard, P. and Tait, T. (2011) *Meeting the Health Needs of People with Learning Disabilities: RCN guidance for nursing staff*, London: Royal College of Nursing.

Health Education Authority (1997) *Mental Health Promotion: a quality framework*, London: HEA.

Holdsworth, R. and Blanchard, M. (2006) 'Unheard voices: themes emerging from studies of the views about school engagement of young people with high support needs in the area of mental health', *Australian Journal of Guidance and Counselling*, 16(1), 14–28.

Hollins, S. and Curran, J. (1996) *Understanding Depression in People with Learning Disabilities*, Brighton: Pavilion.

Kroll, L.,Woodham, A., Rothwell, J., et al. (1999) 'Reliability of the Salford Needs Assessment Schedule for Adolescents', *Psychological Medicine*, 29, 891– 902.

Mental Health Foundation (2007) *The Fundamental Facts: The latest facts and figures on mental health*, London: Mental Health Foundation.

Mind (2010) 'Children, young people and mental health' (factsheet) [Available from www.mind.org.uk].

NASS (National Association of Independent Schools and Non-Maintained Special Schools) (2007) *Making Sense of Mental Health: The emotional wellbeing of children and young people with complex needs in schools*, York: National Association of Independent Special Schools.

National Assembly for Wales (2001) *Child and Adolescent Mental Health Services: Everybody's Business – a strategy document*, Cardiff: National Assembly for Wales.

National CAMHS Support Service (2011) *Better Mental Health Outcomes for Children and Young People: A resource directory for commissioners*, London: NHS.

National Institute for Health and Clinical Excellence (2008) *Promoting Children's Social and Emotional Wellbeing in Primary Education*, London: NICE. [Online at: www.nice.org.uk/nicemedia/pdf/PH012Guidance.pdf; accessed 28.09.14.]

NYS FASD Interagency Workgroup (2008) *Take Another Look: A guide on fetal alcohol spectrum disorders for school psychologists and counsellors*, New York, NY: Council on Children and Families.

Partnership for Children (2003) *Zippy's Friends*, Kingston upon Thames: Partnership for Children.

Pote, H. and Goodban, D. (2007) *A Mental Health Care Pathway for Children and Young People with Learning Disabilities: A resource plan for service planners and practitioners*, London: CAMHS Publications.

Pretis, M. and Dimova, A. (2008) 'Vulnerable children of mentally ill parents: towards evidence-based support for improving resilience', *Support for Learning*, 23(3): 152–159.

Rose, R., Howley, M., Fergusson, A. and Jament, J. (2009) 'Mental health and special educational needs: exploring a complex relationship', *British Journal of Special Education*, 36(1): 3–8.

Sedgewick, J., Jones, N. and Turner, P. (2005) *Short Child and Adolescent Mental Health Programme (SCAMHP)*, York: Care Services Improvement Partnership/Selby and York NHS/University of York.

Storey, P. and Statham, J. (2006) *Mental Health Services for Children and Young People with Learning Disabilities (Research Briefing)*, London: Thomas Coram Research Unit.

Troedsson, H. (2005) 'Mental health of children and adolescents'. Paper presented at WHO European Ministerial Conference on Mental Health, 'Facing the Challenges, Building Solutions', Helsinki, Finland (12–15 January).

Waddell, C., Godderis, R., Hua, J., McEwan, K. and Wong, W. (2004) *Preventing and Treating Anxiety Disorders in Children and Youth*, Vancouver: University of British Columbia, Children's Mental Health Policy Research Program.

Chapter 9

Inquiry gives you wings

School-based inquiry and engaging children with Complex Learning Difficulties and Disabilities

The current emphasis on practitioner inquiry (DfE (Department for Education) 2014; NCSL (National College for School Leadership) 2012) is an indicator of the complexities educators face in their day-to-day practice. There comes a time when every educator's experience runs out. If they are not to be caught out, they need to have strategies that will take them into teaching's unknown and enable them to pioneer pathways into learning for children with CLDD. As Byers et al. (2008: 76) write: 'Staff need flexibility in determining appropriate and imaginative approaches to teaching and learning when they are working with young people with learning difficulties, disabilities and/or special educational needs.'

With an inquiry approach as part of their professional repertoire (see Figure 9.1), educators have that way forward. As one CLDD Project class teacher observed of the inquiry approach, 'It's given us the skills and the confidence . . . to tackle the problem.'

Inquiry is a dynamic not just of the classroom domain but of the education system. Just as the teacher seeks ways to teach the child with a rare syndrome, the likes of whom they

Figure 9.1 The practice-to-research spiral

Source: Adapted from Carpenter 2012

have never seen before, so do other education professionals at other levels in the service seek to evolve coherent pedagogical frameworks that articulate what quality teaching and learning means for this new generation of children. For example, we know much about how to teach children with autism or Down's syndrome. Research has recently shown us more about how a child born prematurely may learn and what some of the affective teaching and learning processes may be for these children. But this is a crude pedagogy compared to the rich, diverse, tried-and-tested pedagogies which educators apply to the two former groups of children. There is no escaping that pedagogy for complex, twenty-first-century learners will be evolved through, and maintained and informed by, the dynamic process of inquiry. As Carpenter (2010: 3) writes: 'Schools need to become pedagogical think-tanks – nurturing, shaping and framing approaches that are dynamic and innovative, and that transform these children into active participants in learning.'

University academics also recognize the importance of educator inquiry. Michael J. Guralnick (2004), Professor of Psychology and Pediatrics at the University of Washington, has stated: 'We now know so much about childhood disability that we must move to second generation research. This must be practitioner led and evidence based.'

It is only educators working face-to-face with these children who can, through a process of inquiry, fine-tune and adjust academic research findings to create sustainable support for real-world learners in real-world classrooms.

Why formalize inquiry?

What is the advantage of putting inquiry within a formal framework? Science has demonstrated how unreliable human minds can be. All of us, not only those who struggle with memory, confabulate – that is, unconsciously, and with no intent to deceive, we create false memories which justify our opinions, decisions and actions (Phillips 2006). The appeal of intuition and anecdote is strong. Often educators, schools and even governments hold beliefs about interventions that fly in the face of existing scientific evidence – for example, some interventions (e.g. Brain Gym) are widely believed to be beneficial, but there is no empirical evidence that supports this (Howard-Jones 2014); yet some interventions for which there is strong evidence of a positive impact (e.g. in specific situations, not applying sanctions in response to challenging behaviour; LaVigna and Willis 2002) are often rejected because they are counter-intuitive.

Through subjecting educational approaches to formal inquiry, educators can establish their value to children, and reduce the risk of false beliefs corrupting teaching and compromising children's learning opportunities. Such practice makes a significant contribution to the current educational trend for evidence-based intervention (DfE 2014). As Cleaver et al. (2014: 4) write: 'The challenge for us all is . . . moving from assumption, supposition and non-informed opinion, to a more evidence-based approach that includes information gathering, analysis, conclusion drawing and decision-making.

Benefits of inquiry

Inquiry is the cutting edge of practice innovation. The process is familiar and central to most educators' classroom practice – identifying children's learning barriers, implementing interventions to overcome them, reviewing the success of outcomes, and then, if need be, further modifying or adapting interventions to improve children's learning. This everyday practice is, in fact, the basis of the 'Action Research Spiral' (Kemmis 1982). However, for many teachers, the process is intuitive, broadly applied and largely informal.

Making inquiry formal is a relatively small step, but as a result its value and power increases exponentially. It allows educators to create order, manage and take initiative within new or challenging teaching and learning situations that do not have straightforward solutions. This is often the case with children who have CLDD. Formalized inquiry generates evidence which will support innovation and sustain that practice. For example, one CLDD Project headteacher was persuaded, based on systematically presented evidence from one class team, to change the whole school's educational approach with children with profound and multiple learning disabilities (PMLD).

Formalized inquiry is a focused and strategic process. It cuts through the cloud of teaching and learning concerns that compete for educators' attention. It has identified priorities, a clear evidence base, and consistent aims, objectives, targets, approaches and contexts. Interventions are systematically introduced, and evidence of their impact collected in a planned, systematic way. This information is analysed deductively to guide the next teaching and learning steps. All steps are recorded to create a clear evidence-base of what works (and does not work) for children, and to justify educators' decisions and next actions. Educators share findings with each other so that they continue to benefit children across their whole educational experience, and record them in children's files to support their learning into adult life and beyond. Within the CLDD Project, this process was supported by the Accessible Research Cycle (Jones et al. 2012; see Figure 9.3).

Complex learners have many needs vying with one another for educator attention. With many educators involved, including families, each with their own priorities and practice ideas, responses can be conflicting, inconsistent and un-co-ordinated. Taking a collaborative inquiry approach, as advocated in the previous chapters, to engaging children with CLDD in learning unifies and democratizes a school's response to learner need. Everyone can become an agent of change.

Taking an inquiry approach centres the child and their learning need. Most educators want only the best for children, and their attachment to their adopted practices and approaches usually stems from the belief that these are, indeed, best for the children. An inquiry approach, a collaborative professional team, and an agreed priority of possible interventions to meet the child's learning needs gives everyone involved, from teaching assistants to therapists, an opportunity to put forward solutions for overcoming barriers to learning.

Interventions are implemented over a defined inquiry period. If the evidence collected proves an intervention is successful for the child then it is adopted and takes precedence. Everyone is happy; a solution which benefits the child has been found. However, if the intervention is unsuccessful or only moderately successful, the inquiry approach means that educators are not committed to such an intervention indefinitely. Ideas offered by other educators can then be trialled as adaptions or alternative solutions. Having the child at the heart of inquiry, knowing that there will be proof of an intervention's success or failure and knowing that the inquiry approach builds in the flexibility for change if needed allows an education team to commit to a common goal and a consistent approach for the benefit of the child. The inquiry approach thus encourages clear prioritization, a team focus, a workable time frame and consistency.

This democratization through formalized inquiry works at school level also. Practitioners can provide measured, evidence-based responses to school leadership initiatives, increasing appropriateness and impact within classrooms. Inquiry can be the vehicle for trialling good practice across the school, spreading and embedding expertise, and extending the potential of new resources, as well as providing opportunity for professional challenge and up-skilling.

Finally, it is an unparalleled form of holistic professional development that deepens educator knowledge and understanding, extends and fine-tunes practice and thinking skills, uniting them conceptually while building specialism in the educator's chosen area of inquiry and embedding them in practice. As a result of taking part in the CLDD Project, 88 per cent of the 77 schools who trialled the final Engagement for Learning Framework described positive changes to their educators' professional ethos, and 91 per cent identified positive practice benefits. Similarly, the General Teaching Council for England et al. research (2010), which asked similar questions of teachers involved in inquiry, found that of 21 teachers whose pedagogic knowledge and skills were measured at the beginning and end of their involvement in research, 19 (90 per cent) showed improvement in pedagogic knowledge and skills. Handscomb and MacBeath (2008: 1) also conclude: 'Engagement with research encourages practitioners to question, explore and develop their practice, making a significant contribution to improved teaching and learning.'

Embracing inquiry

It is important that the inquiry processes are robust – that they have integrity and are rigorous, well-planned, carefully executed, accurately reported, transparent and ethically identified (Porter and Lacey 2005). The schools-based CLDD Project used three inquiry tools to guide and support educators in investigating personalized learning pathways for children with CLDD:

- the Action Research Spiral (Kemmis 1982);
- the Accessible Research Cycle (Jones et al. 2012);
- the Inquiry Framework for Learning (Carpenter *et al.* 2011).

These tools value the inquiry dimension of every teacher's activity and support educators to structure and articulate their inquiry, giving it a voice that will be a powerful mechanism in learning and school improvement.

Action Research Spiral

The Engagement for Learning Framework is designed for use with individual children with CLDD using an action research approach. Action research is carried out by practitioners within dynamic work-based situations. It provides educators with a means of solving everyday problems in schools to improve both children's learning and teacher effectiveness (Norton 2001).

Action research has well-documented success in schools due to its capacity for framing innovations, its emphasis on trialling approaches and its ability to support interpretation within a specific context (General Teaching Council for England et al. 2010; Shaddock 2006). Within the action research approach, educators can collect and draw on evidence from a range of complementary sources to support action and strengthen findings. These sources may, for example, include documentary evidence, questionnaires (e.g. from children, families, educators, multidisciplinary colleagues), participant and non-participant

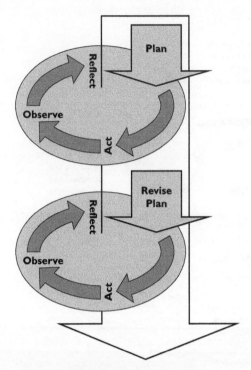

Figure 9.2 The Action Research Spiral
Source: Kemmis 1982

observations (perhaps supported by selective video capture), assessment, dated notes from inquiry journals, etc.

The Action Research Spiral is characterized by an initial 'reconnaissance' when the educator evaluates the learning situation and context, and prioritizes a 'problem' (e.g. a child's barrier to learning). Having identified a target outcome for their action research, educators carry out multiple cycles of (1) planning an intervention, (2) implementing it, (3) observing the outcomes and (4) reviewing it, before further adapting it and repeating the cycle (Kemmis and McTaggart 2008; Mertler 2013; Roberts-Holmes 2011). This continues until the educator is satisfied with the outcome. The process is illustrated in Figure 9.2.

Educators using action research for the first time should seek advice from informed colleagues, read a reputable introduction to the approach (e.g. Mertler 2013; Roberts-Holmes 2011) and practice (i.e. 'pilot') the approach before embarking on a full-scale investigation.

The Accessible Research Cycle

The Action Research Spiral should be set within the context of an inquiry framework such as the Accessible Research Cycle (ARC; Jones et al. 2012). The purpose of the ARC is to provide a framework that encourages practitioners to plan and reflect on the different stages of formal inquiry. The ARC uses the clear, familiar language of the classroom

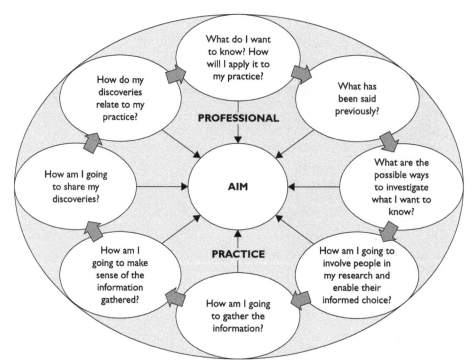

Figure 9.3 Accessible Research Cycle (ARC). An ARC template is provided in Appendix E for educators who would like to use it to plan their own inquiry.

Source: Jones et al. 2012

(see Figure 9.3), demonstrating, in the words of Mary Whitehead, executive headteacher at Halstow Primary School, that inquiry 'is not distant from practice but its lifeblood. It's what excellent teachers do.'

The following sections will review the stages of the ARC. Chapters 2 to 8 of this book provide the guidance needed to plan an engagement for learning inquiry project based on the ARC, supplemented by the information below. To find out how other educators have used the ARC for different inquiry projects, read *Creating Meaningful Inquiry in Inclusive Classrooms* (Jones et al. 2012).

What do I want to know?

The answer to this question will be a second question – one that can jump-start the inquiry process. Many such questions are the basis of staffroom discussions; for example, 'Have you got any ideas about. . .?', 'How do you manage when. . .?', 'What do you know about. . .?', 'How do you make that work?'. However, many of the solutions shared in staffrooms are anecdotal rather than evidence-based.

Transforming staffroom questions into inquiry questions means that educators can test possible solutions in a systematic way, creating an evidence-base that becomes a firm foundation for practice. As such, it has the potential to influence how a child is taught, or how educators practice, long after they have moved to another class or school.

The question that quickens an educator's interest should be the one to drive their inquiry. The process of inquiry, until educators become familiar with it, does need a significant investment of time and energy. It will be enthusiasm that will carry them through – either as a result of personal interest or a whole-school focus. This CLDD school had a clearly articulated, whole-school incentive for becoming involved in inquiry:

> We wanted our school to be part of the CLDD research project because we recognised that there were some students who always made us ask 'What else can we do?', 'What can we do to motivate them?', and 'How can we tap into their abilities?'
>
> (Carpenter et al. 2011: 36)

It is important that the inquiry question does not over-reach resources (e.g. time, people, etc.). Refer back to Chapter 4 for guidance on how to focus and scale down inquiry questions. Educators may find it useful to discuss their ideas with line managers to try to bring their inquiry in line with school improvement or development plan priorities. This will raise the project's school-wide interest and impact, and may open up possibilities for additional time or resource allocation.

What has been said previously?

It is important that any inquiry is based on and justified by reliable evidence. Chapters 1 to 3 will provide educators with much of the background information on engagement for learning, and the CLDD Project Briefing Packs (see Appendix B) will provide useful background about some co-existing conditions, but educators will need to carry out some further investigations into the learning needs of the children involved.

Case study: a shared vision

Beaucroft Foundation Special School in Dorset educates 150 children with moderate learning difficulties. The increase in staff numbers – from 24 in 1997 to over 60 in 2010 – is evidence of their students' increasingly complex needs. Although judged outstanding by Ofsted, Beaucroft continually reviews its curriculum and pedagogy, and seeks collaboration with other schools. The headteacher, Paul McGill, says:

> It is vital to have an open mind to change, to be prepared to look closely at current practice. The 21st century special school will be significantly different to the present one to meet the needs of the children and their families.

In response to its new generation of learners, the school is shaping a 'fusion' curriculum based upon its specialism plan. . . . Using a 'task and finish' approach, seven staff groups – with foci of communication, community, culture, well-being, economics, physical development and global development – discuss, recommend and implement necessary changes.

> (Carpenter 2010: 3)

However, educators do not have time to sit for hours in libraries so it is important to capitalize on the information and resources easily available. For example, educators (including families and colleagues in both teaching and other disciplines) who have experience and expertise in the area of inquiry may be able to share knowledge and recommend key reading; specialist charities may be able to offer advice; a group of colleagues may be willing to each read an article and then meet to discuss findings, opinions and inquiry options.

What are the possible ways to investigate what I know?

Educators already collect huge amounts of useful information about children's learning through reading specialist reports on file, observing, assessing and monitoring. Particularly in the case of children with CLDD, they need to recognize the potential value of this and their own practice-based knowledge, and link it into the process of inquiry through rigorous, consistent recording.

Using the action research approach, described above, Chapter 4, backed up by Appendices A–E, provides a framework for inquiry into engagement for learning for children with CLDD. If finding a way into inquiry seems difficult, explore the Inquiry Framework for Learning (see Appendix C).

If educators are considering alternative inquiry approaches that are outside the scope of this book – for example, evaluations, surveys, etc. – a useful first step is to talk with research-experienced colleagues either within their schools and/or a local university education department. Organizations such as the National Foundation for Educational Research (NFER) and the British Educational Research Association (BERA) may also provide useful starting points.

How am I going to involve people in my research and enable their informed choice?

This section draws attention to inquiry ethics. It is always good practice, as advocated in the UK's new Special Educational Needs Code of Practice (DfE 2014) to involve families and children as far as possible within school initiatives and to keep them fully informed. However, schools have a responsibility to deliver the most effective and up-to-date curriculum to their children, and in most cases (apart from, for example, religious and sex education), this is at the discretion of the school. Therefore, in cases where inquiry falls within the school's day-to-day remit, to ask parents for their consent for involving their children would be pointless; a refusal would run counter to a school's obligation to deliver the most effective and appropriate curriculum.

However, the moment the inquiry moves outside the school's remit – for example, requesting families to share personal information; sharing information with school staff not usually party to this; sharing inquiry outcomes beyond the school; developing additional, alternative or non-school curriculum interventions for specific children as part of an inquiry process; taking videos and photographs; etc. – it must become a matter for parent/guardian consent, child assent and additional school approval, freely given and without coercion. The consent needs to be based on full information about the inquiry, its process and its implications in a format that parents/guardians and children can understand.

Appendix F includes a copy of the letters of permission used in the CLDD Project, and a copy of the 'Project information sheet for families' as examples of information which can be shared. However, for parents, children and others with communication difficulties, the information will need to be personalized so that their consent/assent is meaningful. For example, the information might be in a different format (e.g. Plain English, symbolled). An educator or, better still, an advocate unconnected with the inquiry such as a social worker, may visit a family with literacy difficulties to explain the inquiry, as well as their rights in relation to the inquiry (e.g. access to information collected about their child; to confidentiality; to refuse consent/assent; to withdraw from the inquiry without prejudice; etc.). In addition to parent/guardian consent, children should be additionally asked for their assent. Again, for some, the information will need to be personalized. The 'What about us?' project website also shows a symbolled 'Permission proforma for students' (www.whataboutus.org.uk/make_a_difference/to_start/check_this_out.html). For a child with severe or complex learning difficulties, behaviour on each inquiry occasion may be used to indicate assent/dissent. For a child with PMLD, educators might gauge their assent/dissent to being filmed on each occasion by interpreting their behaviour when shown a video of themselves, with a negative response resulting in withdrawal of filming.

Further information about ethics and involving others in inquiry can be found in the most up-to-date copy of the British Educational Research Association's *Ethical Guidelines for Educational Research* (available from www.bera.ac.uk) and the National Children's Bureau's Guidelines for *Research with Children and Young People* (currently online at www.ncb.org.uk/what-we-do/research/involving-children-and-young-people-in-research and the NFER: www.nfer.ac.uk).

How am I going to gather the information?/How am I going to make sense of the information gathered?

The answers to these questions are governed by the original decisions that educators take at the start of their inquiry concerning the question or questions they want to answer. This will dictate the type of inquiry methods they use, the evidence they decide to collect, the way they choose to collect it and how they analyse it.

It is crucial for educators to make sure the evidence they are collecting (a) will help them answer their inquiry question, (b) is not affected by issues other than the one they are investigating and (c) that other people interpreting their evidence will come to the same conclusions.

If their project is based on the Engagement for Learning Framework, the answer to these questions can be found in Chapters 4 and 5. For examples of other ways of carrying out inquiry, refer to *Creating Meaningful Inquiry in Inclusive Classrooms* (Jones et al. 2012), *Inquiring in the Classroom* (Mitchell and Pearson 2012) and texts with a similar focus. Educators should also discuss inquiry options with research-experienced colleagues, local university education departments and/or educational research charities. The NFER, for example, has some useful downloadable research 'Tool-kit' information sheets (search 'tool-kit' at www.nfer.ac.uk/publications/pre/) as well as two related *Research Toolkit* publications (Lawson 2008, 2011).

How am I going to share my discoveries?/How do my discoveries relate to my practice?

We need to develop communities of practice and inquiry within and beyond the school (Handscomb and MacBeath 2008). Once an inquiry has been completed, the outcomes need to be shared, whether or not the outcomes were positive or negative. However successful the inquiry, if it does not have an impact on practice, everyone's time and effort will have been wasted – and an opportunity to make a real change for children will have been missed.

Colleagues, both internally and externally, need to be aware of what works in schools and classrooms. Expertise may have developed in one classroom, but when that teacher or teaching assistant leaves or a young person transitions to their next class, transformative knowledge may be lost unless it is recorded and shared.

All educators have a responsibility to maximize life chances for children by giving them best-chance opportunities to succeed at school and in their future life. This is a goal worthy of sharing 'trade secrets'. In so doing, educators ensure approaches that work for a child or children are generalized to other learning areas, and can inspire change beyond their own classrooms and schools.

Discoveries can be shared one-to-one by talking with families and colleagues, but also through presenting at a child's review or a staff meeting, sending an 'inquiry update' to senior leadership and governors' meetings, writing a short article for a professional magazine, or presenting at professional workshops or conferences.

Inquiry Framework for Learning

The Inquiry Framework for Learning is a content-free, web-based tool designed to support educators in exploring and developing personalized learning pathways for children with CLDD. It encourages multidisciplinary involvement and transdisciplinary team working. It was created in the development phase of the CLDD Project based upon the questions educators asked about children's learning barriers which led to transformative findings. The Framework consists of engagement for learning-focused questions structured around 12 areas of inquiry:

- engagement for learning;
- communication and interaction;
- identify, self-advocacy and independence;
- behaviour for learning;
- sensory perception and processing;
- health and physical well-being;
- teaching and learning;
- emotional well-being and mental health;
- motor skills;
- improving life chances;
- social skills;
- environment.

With unique learners, it is often those adults who live and work most closely with the child who hold the answer to their learning engagement, but it is easy for educators to become overwhelmed by all the issues. An SEN school involved in the development phase of the CLDD Project describes the benefits: 'the Inquiry Framework is a really good place to start. You're not just thinking about that particular lesson or content, but the bigger picture like environment, family situations, medical conditions.'

Educators can use the questions in the areas to prompt focused discussion with families and colleagues (teaching and multidisciplinary). Often the Inquiry Framework questions are familiar, but written down they provide prompts to areas which can be overlooked in the press of an educator's working day.

Case study: Leo

When I first looked at [the Inquiry Framework for Learning] there was so much to take in, but it is well worth taking the time to look through it. We focused on key areas for Leo [emotional issues, learning, environment, relationships] using the audit sheet.

We first profiled Leo's difficulties using the question, 'What are the sticking points or difficulties for this student?' Then, in the 'Engagement for learning' area of the Inquiry framework for learning we took one key question – 'In what circumstances is the student most receptive to learning?' Through the process of using the engagement profiles to guide observations of Leo's learning journey, we were able to identify key points that helped to answer [this] . . .

We . . . used this information to set targets for Leo, and also addressed a few of the other key questions, such as 'What are the student's priority areas for development?' and 'How can this [the circumstances in which Leo is most receptive to learning] be built into the student's curriculum in a way that will engage him?'

(Carpenter et al. 2011: 36)

The Inquiry framework for learning thus proposes pathways for inquiry into children's learning. It supports educators to map the processes they go through in exploring and developing personalized learning pathways for children. It also gives educators a means of demonstrating and justifying the lengthy but very valuable inquiry process which is an integral part of creating a child's personalized learning pathway. These solution-finding discussions can be recorded and kept as part of the engagement for learning evidence for each child. A CLDD Project trial school teacher described its impact on staff.

The [Inquiry Framework questions] frame discussion and generate ideas. It showed staff what knowledge they have and what they are already doing. It showed TAs' wealth of information and knowledge. It's empowering for TAs to contribute and be recognised and go on the learning journey.

Further information about using the Inquiry Framework for Learning can be found in Appendix C.

Must-have advice for would-be inquirers

As a result of the CLDD Project, the core team, together with the schools and educators involved in inquiry, many for the first time, developed 'Must have advice for would-be inquirers', both senior leaders and class-based educators. This is the advice:

Involve an inquiry partner or critical friend

Having a colleague or colleagues involved means that educators do not have to go into their project alone. There are others alongside them, whether fully involved or as 'inquiry associates' with whom they can discuss ideas, review plans and trouble-shoot or from whom they can just gain support during the tough times. These colleagues, especially if they are at one remove from the inquiry, may be able to look at the inquiry with new eyes – spotting errors and anomalies, bringing another perspective or being able to corroborate observations and analysis.

When more than one colleague is involved in the same kind of inquiry, there is potential for even deeper support, through joint or complementary trialling of strategies, joint planning and reflection, dividing up inquiry tasks that can be shared, etc. (General Teaching Council for England et al. 2010).

Remember these tips from CLDD Project school educators:

- 'Don't be over ambitious. . . . It is a learn-as-you-go process.'
- 'Don't be over ambitious; keep it small – one child, one task at a time.'
- 'Introduce modifications singly so you can see what works. It is so tempting to try lots of things at once when you've decided what might help.'
- 'Work in a team and speak with other people. . . . When you do something on your own, there are only your ideas. Working in teams helps.'
- 'We tried to meet every week, and, although it didn't happen every week, it meant we could share practice, and that motivated us and helped us to think more.'

Additionally:

- From the very beginning, be sure you know what you're doing, and, ask if not. It is not worth gambling three months of careful inquiry on an early misunderstanding that could have been put right.
- If you are struggling with practical difficulties or concerns, share the issue with your line manager immediately; issues rarely disappear on their own.
- Start the inquiry as soon as possible, and collect evidence regularly (e.g. weekly or twice weekly). Make an evidence collection schedule and stick to it. You cannot cram all your evidence collecting into the last week of your inquiry project; the results will be meaningless. By collecting and reviewing evidence regularly, you can take early action on difficulties.
- Recording inquiry evidence clearly, accurately and validly is essential. Such evidence will not only support effective learning and teaching, but will also prevent unsuccessful approaches being revisited.
- Date all the evidence you collect – notes, photos, videos, etc.; without a date, evidence is meaningless.
- Complete observation records at the time. However good your memory, other events will overtake you, and crucial details will be lost.
- Don't forget to baseline – that is, collect pre-intervention evidence – you will need these results to compare with later ones to demonstrate change.

Building a sustainable inquiry culture in schools

Inquiry is continuing professional development (CPD) for the twenty-first century (DfE 2014; National College for School Leadership 2012). School-based inquiry, particularly if educators are new to the process, requires prioritization and resourcing not only by educators, but also by senior leadership teams. Just as the school would invest time, personnel, resources and money through training, cover and support for more traditional CPD for teachers involved in new pedagogical approaches, practitioners involved in inquiry need similar support. When educator inquiry is aligned with school development/improvement plans, the necessary training, resource allocation and support becomes possible.

General Teaching Council for England et al. (2010) found that when educators became involved in educational inquiry, it enhanced their professional growth, their confidence, their motivation and their skills, as well as fostering closer educator/child learning relationships. A deputy head from one of the CLDD Project trial schools commented on the engagement for learning inquiry:

> I can honestly say it has inspired me and changed my way of thinking about teaching and learning – it has given a very practical way forward with our most complex pupils and has helped with empowering staff. It has given us a way to go forward with our questions and thoughts that we didn't have before.

Developing and sustaining an inquiry culture

Schools need to work gradually towards establishing a culture in which educators are supported to carry out school-based inquiry – through school leadership recognition; opportunities to share findings with colleagues, senior leaders and families; school development aligned special interest groups; support networks (e.g. a staff library, guidance from identified educators with research experience, links with local universities); links with CPD; school policy and guidance (Carpenter 2007; Carpenter and Egerton 2007). Inquiry should also become a feature of school development and improvement planning. Without this strategic embedding, inquiry will remain classroom-bound and its benefits will be short-term.

It may start with one or two educators carrying out inquiry as part of a National Vocational Qualification or Master's degree, but when nurtured over time it can become a power house that improves learning for children, drives school and educator improvement, builds relationships between schools and opens up opportunities for collaborative working with universities, education-invested organizations and external funders (Carpenter 2007). Leach (2014: 79) notes: 'Creating a culture of inquiry and research practice may not be quick or easy but any small step towards encouraging teachers to embark in research will lead to positive change.'

School leaders can support educators towards inquiry success by:

- creating priority – supporting links between inquiry and school development; senior leaders communicating that 'inquiry counts' by recognizing educators' inquiry achievements;
- introducing inquiry support for educators – for example, pairing less confident educators with more confident educators; allocating time to research-qualified senior leaders to support educators in inquiry;

- establishing a recognized line of accountability for inquiry;
- honouring educators' time commitment for joint working, discussion and recording through school-level support (O'Connor et al. 2006).

When beginning to introduce whole-school inquiry projects, remember that educators will more readily commit to inquiry projects which are child or family centred, have a clear positive practice impact and are whole-school relevant. Small trials or 'pilot projects' involving one or two classes pique the interest of other educators and create a sense of importance for the classes involved. Grainger and Flavell (2005) found: 'it is amazing when trialling new ways of working, how many others come on board as they see the results of the joint labours on the children affected.'

Pick staff who are enthusiastic to take them forward; they will create a positive vibe around the initiatives. People like to feel a part of something larger, and feel they are contributing to a 'hot topic'. They enjoy speculating and commenting on it (positive or negative!).

In schools, inquiry creates capacity for change, and the opportunity for educators to contribute to change, at all levels. It encourages staff progression and provides them with a way of moving forward with leading edge of education. It strengthens their awareness and use of the evidence-based supporting practice. It facilitates development of specialist areas, knowledge transfer within and among schools, and school team building.

Conclusion

Twenty-first-century learners require educators to find new ways of leading learning, and, in response, we need to 'implement innovative ways of working that can meet the needs of our 21st century schools' (Fergusson and Carpenter 2010: 3). Educators cannot be expected to know all the answers, but, as described above, schools have the building blocks for inquiry well within their grasp. As Morgan (2014: 3) writes: 'what matters is having a means of finding out what works for our children and having a model within which we can experiment with new ideas, building our knowledge base and consequently our confidence in what we do.'

Using inquiry, educators are not held hostage by a lack of knowledge. It gives them a way forward into teaching children with CLDD so they can:

- adapt what they know, systematically and deductively;
- find out, trial and personalize learning solutions; and
- build capacity by sharing what they have learned.

It may take time for some educators to be comfortable in situations where they do not have the answers. However, the real strength comes from knowing the questions to ask about children's learning, and having a solution-finding framework for taking action. One school principal who took part in the CLDD Project commented: 'I used inquiry as a method of engaging the staff. . . . Initially, they wanted answers, but by the end they were more comfortable with it being an inquiry. It enabled them to explore more.'

When educators take this focus, it enables them to take into account children's progress not only in respect of learning outcomes, but also in respect of the learning process within which the learning successes of *all* learners can be 'noticed' (Watkins 2011) and validated.

As Meehan (2013) states: 'Every child has a different learning style and pace. Each child is unique, not only capable of learning but also capable of succeeding.'

It is this tenet that keeps educators searching for ways to support even the most 'hard to reach' child into learning. In the words of a CLDD Project special school principal: '[We] have to acknowledge that [we] don't have the answers. Contexts and children have changed dramatically. We need a 'finding-out' culture in schools.'

In doing this, educators and schools need to step beyond traditional boundaries into a new pedagogy in which 'They take what might seem to others to be risks, knowing that in education the biggest risk is not to take one!' (Watkins 2011: 37).

References

Byers, R., Davies, J., Fergusson, A. and Marvin, C. (2008) *What about Us?: Promoting emotional well-being and inclusion by working with young people with learning difficulties in schools and colleges*, London: Foundation for People with Learning Disabilities/University of Cambridge. [Online at: www.whataboutus.org.uk/whataboutus_report.pdf; accessed 22.07.14.]

Carpenter, B. (2007) 'Developing the role of schools as research organisations', *British Journal of Special Education*, 34(2): 67–76.

Carpenter, B. (2010) *A Vision for the 21st Century Special School* (Complex Needs Series 1), London: SSAT.

Carpenter, B. and Egerton, J. (eds) (2007) *New Horizons: Evidence-based practice in action*, Clent, Worcestershire: Sunfield Publications.

Carpenter, B., Rose, S., Rawson, H. and Egerton, J. (2011) 'The rules of engagement', *SEN Magazine*, 54: 34–37.

Cleaver, E., Lintern, M. and McLinden, M. (2014) *Teaching and Learning in Higher Education: Disciplinary approaches to educational enquiry*, London: Sage.

DfE (Department for Education) (2014) *Special Educational Needs (SEN) Code of Practice for 0 to 25 years: Statutory guidance for organisations which work with and support children and young people with special educational needs or disabilities*, London: DfE.

Fergusson, A. and Carpenter, B. (2010) *Professional Learning and Building a Wider Workforce*, London: SSAT.

General Teaching Council for England/Curee/Learning Skills and Improvement Service (2010) *Report of Professional Practitioner Use of Research Review: Practitioner engagement in and/or with research*, London: GTC. [Online at: www.curee-paccts.com/files/publication/1297423037/Practitioner%20Use%20of%20Research%20Review.pdf; accessed: 22.10.12.]

Grainger, J. and Flavell, L. (2005) 'Multi-disciplinary working within an inclusive system to serve the needs of the individual'. Paper presented to the Inclusive and Supportive Education Congress (ISEC) International Special Education Conference, 'Inclusion: Celebrating Diversity?', Glasgow, Scotland (1–4 August). [Online at: www.isec2005.org.uk/isec/abstracts/papers_f/flavell_l.html; accessed: 22.07.14.]

Guralnick, M. (2004) 'Early Intervention for children with intellectual disabilities: current knowledge and future prospects.' Keynote address to the 12th IASSID World Congress, Montpellier, France (June).

Handscomb, G. and MacBeath, J. (2008) 'CPD through teacher enquiry and research', *Learning and Teaching Update*. [Online at: www.teachingexpertise.com/articles/cpd-through-teacher-enquiry-and-research-3684; accessed: 22.10.12.]

Howard-Jones, P. (2014) *Neuroscience and Education: A review of educational interventions and approaches informed by neuroscience*, London: Education Endowment Foundation.

Jones, P., Whitehurst, T. and Egerton, J. (eds) (2012) *Creating Meaningful Inquiry in Inclusive Classrooms*, London: Routledge.

Kemmis, S. (1982) *The Action Research Planner*, Victoria: Deakin University Press.

Kemmis, S. and McTaggart (2008) 'Participatory action research: communicative action and the public sphere'. In N.K. Denzin and Y.S. Lincoln (eds) *Strategies of Qualitative Inquiry* (3rd edn), Thousand Oaks, CA: Sage, pp. 271–330.

LaVigna, G.W., and Willis, T.J. (2002) 'Counter-intuitive strategies for crisis management within a non-aversive framework'. In D. Allen (ed.) *Ethical Approaches to Physical Interventions*, Plymouth, UK: British Institute of Learning Disabilities (BILD), pp. 89–103.

Lawson, A. (2008) *Research Toolkit – Volume 1: The how-to guide from practical research for education*, Slough: National Foundation for Educational Research.

Lawson, A. (2011) *Research Toolkit – Volume 2: The how-to guide from practical research for education*, Slough: National Foundation for Educational Research.

Leach, S. (2014) 'Jumpers, lip-balm and music: the management of engagement'. In Innovation Teaching School (ed.) *Developing a Finding Out Culture: Teachers evidencing interventions and impact*, Farnham: Innovation Teaching School, pp. 73–79.

Meehan, R.J. (2013) *Teacher's Journey: The road less travelled*. [Online at: http://prezi.com/_lwbkctu3mcr/a-teachers-journey-chapter-6/; accessed: 18.07.14.]

Mertler, C.A. (2013) *Action Research: Improving schools and empowering educators*, London: Sage.

Mitchell, N. and Pearson, J. (2012) *Inquiring in the Classroom: Asking the questions that matter about teaching and learning*, London: Continuum.

Morgan, D. (2014) 'Developing a finding-out culture'. In Innovation Teaching School (ed.) *Developing a Finding Out Culture: Teachers evidencing interventions and impact*, Farnham: Innovation Teaching School, p. 3.

NCSL (National College for School Leadership) (2012) *How Teaching Schools Are Already Starting to Make a Difference*, London: NCSL.

Norton, L.S. (2001) 'Researching your teaching: the case for action research', *Psychology Learning and Teaching*, 1(1): 21–27.

O'Connor, K.A., Greene, H.C. and Anderson, P.J. (2006) 'Action research: a tool for improving teacher quality and classroom practice'. Paper presented to the Paper Discussion Session of the 2006 Annual Meeting of the American Educational Research Association (AERA), San Francisco, CA (7 April). [Online at: http://files.eric.ed.gov/fulltext/ED494955.pdf; accessed: 28.09.14.]

Phillips, H. (2006) 'Mind fiction: why your brain tells tall tales', *New Scientist*, 2572: 32–36.

Porter, J. and Lacey, P. (2005) *Researching Learning Difficulties*, London: Paul Chapman.

Roberts-Holmes, G. (2011) *Doing Your Early Years Research Project: A step by step guide* (2nd edn), London: Sage.

Shaddock, T. (2006) *Researching Effective Teaching and Learning Practices for Students with Learning Difficulties and Disabilities in the Australian Capital Territory: Final Research Report*, Barton, ACT: Commonwealth of Australia.

Watkins, C. (2011) *Learning: A sense-maker's guide*, London: Association of Teachers and Lecturers.

Chapter 10

Visioning the future
Schools taking forward the Engagement for Learning Framework

As UNICEF (2001) emphasizes, 'All children deserve the opportunity to learn in ways that make the most of their strengths and help them overcome their weaknesses'. Children with CLDD need educators, as leaders of learning, to support them in their 'building-up of narrative about learning' (Watkins 2011: 37) that will travel with them into their future. Watkins (2011: 38) describes leaders of learning as those who:

- notice learning;
- focus on the way people make sense of their experiences;
- seek to improve learning by slowing down the pace;
- focus on the quality thinking;
- drive improvement through indicators of quality learning experiences;
- talk publicly about learning; and
- promote inquiry into learning.

These are qualities of the educators and schools who use the Engagement for Learning Framework. While Watkins describes mainstream learners as 'being taught', gradually taking over responsibility for 'individual sense-making', 'building knowledge' in association with others and recognizing links to new contexts, for most children with CLDD, educators will need to look for ways to bridge that learning and understanding for them.

Since the CLDD Project began in 2010, many schools have continued to work with the Engagement for Learning Framework resources and other schools have started to use them. This final chapter describes how schools have used evidence-based inquiry processes to extend the CLDD Engagement for Learning Framework to meet the needs of their unique contexts and populations of learners. It includes examples of the continuing work schools and educators are carrying out in engaging their children with CLDD.

Using the Engagement for Learning Framework to develop high expectations of pupils with CLDD

Julia James, Headteacher, Bedelsford School, Kingston-upon-Thames

Bedelsford is a foundation school for children aged 2–16 years with physical disabilities and complex health needs. Our pupils' cognitive abilities cover a wide range with 30 per cent having moderate learning difficulties and a further 30 per cent with PMLD.

I had used the Engagement for Learning Framework in both the development and trial phases of the CLDD Project in different schools. At Bedelsford, we began using the resources following recognition of the increasingly complex learning needs of our pupils. Following training received from the CLDD Project research team, each class team identified a focus pupil for whom a specific area of learning was proving challenging.

Six focus pupils were selected and, with iPads, were each videoed taking part in an activity in which they engaged highly as a basis for completing their individual Engagement Profile. Staff teams then completed these collaboratively during our weekly after-school training sessions.

Teams were also encouraged to look at the CLDD Briefing Packs relevant to a particular diagnosis (see Appendix B) and also to begin to use relevant Inquiry Framework for Learning questions (see Appendix C). This was a positive and revealing stage of the process as the Inquiry Framework supported staff to realize how much they collectively already knew about a pupil as well as to question and discuss areas they could explore or trial further.

We used Engagement Scales to carry out pre-intervention observations, and then to record the level of pupils' engagement for learning after each individual adaptation. Once successful interventions had been found, staff returned to using simplified sheets to record progress.

Of the six pupils who started in our initial pilot, one pupil left the school, one pupil dropped out of the pilot and four pupils increased their engagement and progressed in their identified area. Early outcomes and the particular engagement and learning achievements of the four pupils were encouraging:

1   One pupil developed the ability to use her iPad for early writing activities after it was discovered that she needed a yellow background and a darkened area of the classroom to use it successfully.
2   A tactile selective pupil developed the ability to use his hands more functionally to support dressing.
3   A pupil made significant progress in identifying then consistently choosing a preferred stimuli.
4   A pupil with PMLD who had previously cried when taken outside began to show consistent anticipation and 'like' responses to movement and sounds in his environment (e.g. the accessible swing and birds singing on his iPad and outside).

Five staff who were very motivated in using the engagement for learning materials formed a team with a senior leader to support rolling the approach out for identified pupils across the school. This core staff team has also worked with the online 'Training Materials for Teachers of Severe, Profound and Complex Learners' to train other local special and mainstream schools. They hope to get the materials university-accredited.

In summary, while it may seem that progress using the materials for more children has been slower than we would have wanted, our whole staff team is now involved in questioning how we can better enable our very complex pupils to engage and learn. Everybody is familiar with the engagement for learning approach and thinking about the principles, and we are steadily developing our expertise in using the tools when appropriate. We are working towards the concepts and materials becoming an embedded and integral part of the way we work at Bedelsford.

We are challenging previous expectations for pupil engagement and using the materials as a catalyst for change to find ways to enable even our most profoundly disabled pupils to engage, learn and become more intentional communicators who can enjoy and achieve an improved quality of life.

Using a case study 'starter' for whole-school Engagement Profile and Scale induction

Becki Wright, Key Stage 2 teacher and research co-ordinator, Manor Mead School, Shepperton

Manor Mead School wanted to use the Engagement Profile and Scale to focus on improving the engagement in learning of children with complex needs. Before introducing the approach to the whole-school staff, the project lead teacher and a member of the school's senior leadership team (it cannot be stated highly enough how important it is to have the full support of the leadership team for such a project) went through the process together to see how it would work and what adaptions may need to be made. This also meant they could learn from their initial mistakes in order to support other teachers who would be completing their own 'case studies'.

Once this had been completed, the project lead teacher delivered an introductory talk to the teachers in the school to explain and outline the project. This included a background of the involvement with the research project, the aim for the school, what should be completed and when, video footage of the first case study child (a baseline and an intervention video) to show the impact and examples of the paperwork completed.

The first job was to inspire staff to invest their time into completing profiles, baselines and interventions, which is something the video case study was extremely good for – it gave a real purpose and clear evidence of the impact of using the approach along with the evidence collected using the Engagement Profile and the final analysis which takes the form of a graph.

Case study: 'J'

J is a mobile and active 8-year-old boy with PMLD. He also has a severe vision impairment, a history of frequent epileptic seizures and is exceptionally tactile defensive. (He needs an occupational therapy programme to address this.) The aim for J was to improve his engagement during shared literacy text work and exploration of related props, which has always been quite a challenge for him.

The project lead teacher, working together with a colleague, analysed what J found most motivating to complete the Engagement Profile. Using the Engagement Scale, they then recorded baseline observations and engagement scores for the shared literacy text work for which he had very low engagement (see Figure 10.2). Over a two-month period, they trialled changes to their teaching approach, one at a time, recording and analysing each on further Engagement Scales to discover the impact of each on his learning.

The second intervention (29.03.13; see Figure 10.2) had a remarkable impact. The teachers decided to change J's learning position by taking him out of his supportive chair and sitting him in front of an adult with his back to them. This gave him physical reassurance and meant that any hand-over-hand support could be at his level from either side rather than from above (see Figure 10.1).

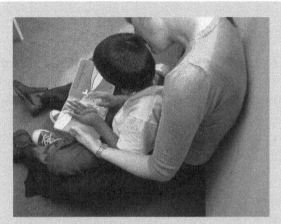

Figure 10.1 Photograph of the positioning intervention for J

The impact of this was immediate, as the graph in Figure 10.2 demonstrates. The video clips throughout the period show a more relaxed boy who becomes increasingly prepared to reach out and touch to explore tactile pages in a book – a first for him to do independently. He appears happy, often looking up to the adult and laughing, and uses his own initiative in trying to activate the prop.

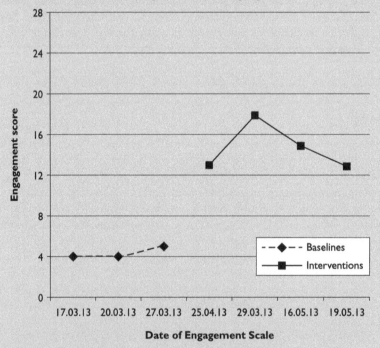

Figure 10.2 J's engagement scores (intervention period: 17 March– 19 May 2013) demonstrating the leap between his baseline Engagement Scales (pre-intervention) and his second intervention engagement score (29.03.13).

A later intervention was to carry out the reading of the book in two stages; one where the focus was solely on listening and then the second time on touching and exploring. Again the impact of this was clear both in the way the child turned to listen to the adult and in the tolerance of touching and exploring the book and prop. (17 March–19 May 2013) demonstrating the leap between his baseline Engagement Scales (pre-intervention) and his second intervention engagement score (29.03.13).

The importance of these findings for this boy's learning cannot be over-estimated. Most importantly they supported J to be a more confident and relaxed learner even when he found tasks challenging. It helped to give him a wider range of learning experiences and to develop his exploration skills (e.g. reaching out to touch and explore) which were once a huge barrier to his learning.

The power of an introductory case study when introducing a new approach, especially from a child known to school staff, helped educators to understand the value of the new intervention and to be inspired by its potential impact for children.

Moving forward with the engagement for learning resources

Jane Thistlethwaite, International CLDD Consultant and Director, Positive Path International

The CLDD Engagement for Learning Framework tools have been used now in a number of New Zealand special schools over the past four years. They have enabled educators to ascertain objectively 'what, how, where, when and with whom' the student is most or least engaged. Over time, schools have evolved new perspectives on the engagement for learning process.

Rather than relying on task completion alone as the indicator of engagement, educators have become more adept at recognizing how the environment, people and things around a child's learning areas can impact on how they engage. They also reflect more deeply on their own practice, challenging themselves as to why, when and how they may or may not be contributing to student engagement and disengagement.

As educators have become more familiar with the Engagement for Learning Framework resources, they have decoded each of the seven Engagement Indicators more effectively and specifically. This has enhanced their accuracy in assessing a child's engagement over time and in demonstrating how a child is making gains in all Engagement Indicator areas. They have begun to see the engagement areas in which the student is 'hooked in', and those areas that require more support to facilitate deeper engagement. For example, a student who shows curiosity when working out in a garden, but does not initiate at all, may need to be encouraged by the strategic placement of high-preference items (e.g. a preferred coloured bucket with high-interest items in it) that might lure them to initiate and be curious of other new or unknown garden items strategically placed in the bucket.

As a facilitator of the engagement process, I find the following terms useful when talking with educators about engagement:

Incidental engagement: those things we would never have predicted or noticed a student engaging with until we stopped to 'look' and 'observe' actually 'what' really interests the student about their world. I encourage teachers to weave these incidental things, environments, even people or traits into the student's 'engagement diet'.

Functional engagement: I use this term to assist educators in a better understanding of engagement for learning. Some educators confuse happiness with engagement, assuming that when children are happy, they must automatically be engaged. However, we are looking for engagement for learning, when children have fully sustained engagement across all seven Engagement Indicator areas – being fully aware, initiating, being curious, investigating, being persistent, anticipating and discovering.

Engagement diet: I use this phrase to describe the 'kit' of things, places, people and activities that a student most readily engages with and can be used to enhance their learning. Over time this diet becomes more extensive as the student learns to trust new things and begins to engage more deeply in the different Engagement Indicator areas.

Engagement passport: Engagement passports – in which educators note how, when and where students are positively engaging across the seven indicator areas – are becoming popular in some schools. These are particularly beneficial when students are transitioning within and between schools and for families. Different formats include a pocket book that is always with the student or a readily accessible A4 or A3 page for educators to refer to as needed (see Appendix G).

Implementing the Engagement for Learning Framework: challenges and successes

Neil Jourdan, Music Therapist/Dean of Engagement, Parkside School, Pukekohe, New Zealand

Since Parkside School's initial involvement in the CLDD Engagement for Learning Project during 2010, we have trained and inducted almost 60 staff members – including teachers, Teacher Aides, transdisciplinary specialists, school leaders and release teachers – in using the Engagement Profile and Scale. Twenty-four focus students with CLDD have participated in the engagement for learning inquiry process.

As we have become increasingly familiar with the Engagement Profile and Scale, we have streamlined its implementation and recording, while remaining true to the original CLDD Project process. This has allowed more teachers and students to become involved. A number of factors have made this possible, most significantly:

- full support from the Parkside School leadership team and the Board of Trustees
- ongoing critical review of the engagement for learning programme (e.g. through formal surveys and informal collaborative team discussions)
- the appointment of a Dean of Engagement to support and co-ordinate the programme training, the teachers involved, the evidence collection and analysis process, collaborative team meetings and programme reviews
- the identification of a Lead Engagement Teacher, an experienced user of the Engagement Profile and Scale, to support other educators and the Dean of Engagement
- access to an international CLDD consultant/trainer
- twice termly 'Community of Practice' meetings of staff involved to address and discuss their needs around implementation
- a weekly 45-minute meeting, with a focus on evidence collection and analysis, attended by as many staff involved with students in the programme as possible
- training and inclusion of Teacher Aides in the programme

- ongoing training and induction of new school staff into the approach
- full involvement throughout the engagement for learning process (including interpreting evidence) of the school's transdisciplinary team (e.g. Speech and Language Therapist, Occupational Therapist, Physiotherapist, Music Therapist)
- involvement and inclusion of families in preliminary profiling (e.g. contributing their own ideas and video clips of their child engaged in learning) and viewing school video clips.

Initially there were some concerns around the effective introduction of the Engagement Profile and Scale across the school as educators were already under pressure with their existing workloads. We worked to implement them in a way that would: keep the workload for educators to a minimum; streamline the related observations and video review process; and maintain a collaborative, transdisciplinary team approach.

Strategies put in place in order to achieve this included:

- piloting the engagement for learning programme with those teachers who were enthusiastic about the Engagement Profile and Scale first;
- training small groups of staff as opposed to the entire staff body;
- providing a clear timeline and description of the programme tasks for staff participating;
- providing significant professional support from colleagues as detailed above;
- limiting the number of students involved in the programme to two per term so that the team approach could be maintained.

Four years of implementing the engagement for learning programme have led to an increasingly 'user friendly' model. It takes place over a school year (four terms), supported by twice-termly Community of Practice meetings. The first meeting of the term (week 2 or 3) is dedicated to training and to discussion of what is expected from educators. Possible administrative challenges are also discussed. During the second meeting (week 8), educators are invited to share their successes, discuss challenges and reflect on the past term. (It may also include further professional development on using the resources.) In addition to educators involved in the programme, all school staff are invited and welcome to attend these meetings which provide them with the opportunity to learn more about the programme, and to contribute to the group discussions.

Engagement for learning programme task timeline

Term 1: Selecting and profiling the focus student

- Participating students are identified collaboratively
- Fully informed consent from parents/guardians for student participation is requested (see Chapter 9)
- Student information: parents/guardians and professionals are requested to complete an Initial Student Information Form and a short questionnaire about the student
- Engagement Profile completion: all educators, parents/guardians and transdisciplinary colleagues contribute to an A3 copy of the Engagement Profile template which is available in the classroom by jotting significant observations under the relevant Engagement Indicator. For example, the music teacher might notice the focus student

consistently showing a high degree of 'Anticipation' during a specific song; a release teacher may notice that the student is very 'Persistent' when playing with play dough
- CLDD Briefing Packs (see Appendix B): educators are encouraged to read any Briefing Packs or other relevant information relevant to their focus students' needs.

Terms 2 and 3: Gathering video footage, analysis and the inquiry process

Collaborative video analysis (model currently being trialled): Teachers load the relevant video clip onto a laptop and allocate 10–15 minutes' independent viewing time each week for each Teacher Aide involved. The Aide watches the clip and jots down their observations, ideas and engagement scores on a preliminary engagement record form. The teacher then uses this to inform their own video analysis when completing the Engagement Scale with other relevant professionals, and when possible parents/guardians, usually during lunch or after school. This resolves Teacher Aides' time limitations due to after-school commitments.

Inquiry Framework for Learning (see Appendix C): Teachers are encouraged to access the Inquiry Framework to assist their inquiry and provide them with leads for investigation.

Term 4: Collating and disseminating the findings

Engagement Profile and Scale Report: In the final term, the teachers review all their Engagement Profile and Scale evidence, complete the engagement graph (for instructions, see http://complexld.ssatrust.org.uk/project-resources/engagement-profile-scale.html), and compile the Engagement Profile and Scale Final Report (for the template, see Appendix H).

Engagement passport: In addition to the final report, an engagement passport is written for the child. This was developed in response to a family's request to share the Engagement Profile findings with other carers (see Appendix G for an example).

Using the Engagement Profile and Scale to support skill transfer

Alexis George (Engagement Lead), Portfield School, Haverfordwest, Wales

At Portfield School, we have used the Engagement Profile for several years with students with PMLD. We have not adapted the Profile greatly as we feel that it suits our learners' needs very well and, through the use of the Engagement Indicators, educators working with the child are able to consider the child's learning style.

There is a great deal of experience in teaching children with complex needs at Portfield School. While over time we are able to teach a range of skills to children with PMLD, there was a consensus that we found it far more difficult to teach children to transfer a skill.

We have found it very useful to look initially at how a child engages in relation to the Engagement Indicators as described in earlier chapters (see Chapters 4 and 5). However, to support skill transfer, we may take a task or activity based on the Routes for Learning Skills (http://wales.gov.uk/; Welsh Assembly Government 2006) for which the child we are working with is now scoring in the zone of 'mostly and fully sustained' on the Engagement Scale. The child will therefore be comfortable with the skills involved and will have demonstrated the task readily over several sessions. We then begin to work on the child's ability to transfer the skills associated with the task by changing activity variables.

For example, we might start by changing where the adult and learner are sitting during the very familiar activity. We may then move on to varying how the resources that the child is already familiar with are presented at the table; we may begin introducing more background noise or changing the adult working with the child. The key factor is that we repeat the session in its new format many times after each individual change, giving the child opportunities to practise the familiar task within the new context and become comfortable with it once more. We continue to score the student throughout using the Engagement Scale and only change the next variable in the activity when they are scoring again at the 'mostly or fully sustained' level of engagement.

The Engagement Profile and Scale enables us to work with children on transferring skills to new and different situations focusing on meaningful engagement by the learner. This provides an excellent child-led way of extending learning for children with profound and multiple needs.

Supporting observations linked to child emotional well-being

Ruth Durdle, Specialist Teacher, and Michelle Hodge, Looked After Children Co-ordinator, New Rush Hall School, Ilford

New Rush Hall School (NRHS) is a school for children with behavioural, emotional and social difficulties (BESD), and has been involved in school-based inquiry for the last six years. Since being a CLDD Project development school in 2010, NRHS has continued to use the Engagement Profile and Scale to develop and monitor changes in engagement with over 20 individual children working at Key Stages 1–4.

As a BESD school, it is crucial that teachers and learning support assistants can notice the often subtle behaviours that indicate a child's emotional well-being, unease or distress. Engagement inquiries have often focused upon:

- transition times within and outside of school;
- children's fear of the unknown and developing resilience to take risks;
- students who express their emotional needs passively rather than overtly.

Carrying out research when studying with the Tavistock Institute in London, Michelle found that adults often did not notice the signs of children becoming alternately 'engaged for learning' and disengaged before, during and after lessons. As a result, some children were working only periodically and not consistently depending on the circumstances. She found that we could discover a lot about a child's availability to learn, even before activities had begun, by observing their physical expressions, movements and body language.

As a result, Michelle developed two checklists of behaviours to direct educators' attention to key mannerisms indicating children's emotional and learning readiness. We found that fine-tuning these observations gives educators great insight into children's perceptions and availability to learn; for example, subject matter can evoke negative feelings. The checklists are used alongside the Engagement Scale and support educators in making their observations effective so that their choice of 'next action' strategies is appropriate.

One student, who has now left NRHS, gained immensely from the use of the Engagement Scale observation together with the checklists. Having both medical and non-medical needs, including global delay, medical staff did not expect him to learn to read before he started school. He was excluded from mainstream school on his first day. Using the Engagement Profile and Scale together with the checklists, different strategies were trialled and modified to strengthen his ability to learn, including:

- using humour, singing or expressing emotions as poetry at the start of one-to-one sessions to enable him to settle;
- encouraging him to own his own learning and say what he 'did not get' so that his work could be reframed and/or broken down into smaller chunks when needed.

At the end of Year 11, he left NRHS with GCSEs in the core subjects and a range of other qualifications. He was awarded a national 'Engage in Their Futures' achievement award for his educational and emotional progress during his 11 years at school.

In conclusion, the CLDD Project engagement for learning resources was originally introduced as a pilot to support children with Fetal Alcohol Spectrum Disorders (FASD) and complex difficulties from disengagement into learning. By using the Engagement Scale and the supplementary checklists, educators' observations have increased in relevance and meaning, and greatly improved the well-being and advancement of the children involved.

Using the Engagement Profile and Scale to demonstrate achievement in a child-led, relationship-based communication intervention

Claire Truman, Research Co-ordinator and Special Needs Teacher, Freemantles School, Mayfield Green

In the following case study, the school used the Engagement Profile and Scale to demonstrate a child's achievement and progress during a programme of Intensive Interaction (Nind and Hewett 2006), which is focused on a developing child-led interactive relationship with an adult rather than on development of specific skills.

Case study: Blaine

Blaine is a five-year-old boy with autism. When he joined our day school for children with autism, aged four, he found it difficult to tolerate social interaction of any kind. He did not make eye contact with other people and would scream when adults approached him. If he was sitting on the carpet and someone came to sit alongside him he would move away and would not tolerate any touch. Staff in Blaine's class hoped that a programme of Intensive Interaction, which had been used successfully with other students in the school in the past, would help Blaine engage more fully with other people in social situations.

Sara, the lead assistant in Blaine's class, worked one-to-one with him using the Intensive Interaction model to develop his social skills. Sara made use of as many social opportunities as possible, so that spending time together became part of Blaine's daily routine. Sara would take time to respond to and imitate Blaine's actions and behaviours. Over the course of several sessions as Blaine became more aware of Sara's imitation and participation he began to give her eye contact and pause for her to copy him, allowing for turn-taking. Sara continued to use Intensive Interaction

Table 10.1 A summary of Blaine's Engagement Scales (1 March 2012–25 January 2013)

Date	Engagement score	Description
01.03.2012	5	Blaine is mainly on his own agenda (e.g. opening and shutting doors). When an adult comes towards him he anticipates that they will stop him opening and shutting the doors and he screams. His attention is very fleeting and there is no eye contact with other people. There was a very short response to being tickled (he laughed) but it was not sustained and there was no eye contact. (Source: Teacher Observation Notes)
xx.09.2012	17	Blaine initiates the singing of Humpty Dumpty and leaves regular pauses when he looks at Sara, anticipating that she will copy his singing and actions. He reaches out to touch Sara's hand several times and gives her a hug. Blaine persists with this interaction for six minutes before turning away. (Source: video)
16.11.2012	18	Blaine initiates the 'roll me up' game with another child. Sara steps back to allow the interaction between the children to continue without adult intervention. He sings 'roll me up' as he lies down on the mat several times and persists with the game for six minutes before walking away. (Source: video)
25.01.2013	25	Blaine plays for 36 sustained minutes. He initiates several games including a tickling game and a caterpillar game. He comments on Sara's caterpillar and invites her to join him in the play tunnel. He gives directions, maintains eye contact and shares attention and laughter with Sara. (Source: video)

with Blaine daily and saw his social skills develop to the point where he was able to initiate and sustain 36 minutes of intensive turn taking games with Sara in the soft play room, including tickling games, swapping and sharing toys and singing songs.

All the staff were delighted with Blaine's progress but found it difficult to share this success with other professionals. They needed a quantifiable way to demonstrate and celebrate Blaine's amazing achievements, and that was when we began to use the Engagement Profile and Scale to provide a clear measure of Blaine's engagement in social interaction. Sara had video and written records of her work with Blaine, and together we analysed those using the Engagement Scale (see Table 10.1 and Figure 10.3).

After almost a year's worth of Intensive Interaction, Blaine has developed into a sociable young boy. Sara describes the way in which he is 'now spontaneously and independently seeking out interaction using all of his communication skills. He is using and understanding eye contact and vocally communicating with adults and peers. He seems keen and has a willingness to interact and be social.'

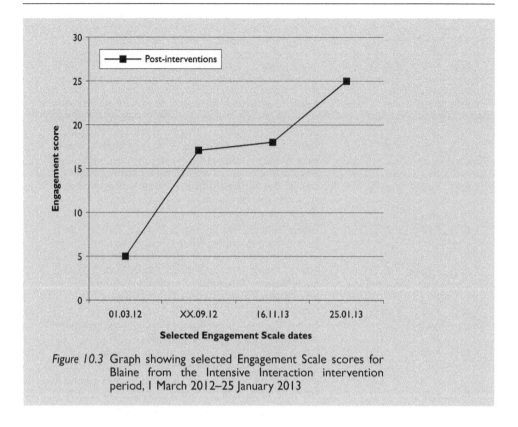

Figure 10.3 Graph showing selected Engagement Scale scores for Blaine from the Intensive Interaction intervention period, 1 March 2012–25 January 2013

Seeing Blaine blossom like this has enthused staff, and Sara is now using her experience to train a team of assistants to deliver Intensive Interaction with students in their classes. As part of this training we are using the Engagement Profile and Scale to monitor the students' progress from the outset so that we can measure the impact of the intervention as it is being used.

Evidencing the impact of a specific intervention in different learning areas using the Engagement Profile and Scale

School and contributor details withheld on request to protect the child's identity

School Three applies the engagement for learning resources across a range of approaches including Activate, Floortime, TEACCH and Sherborne Developmental Movement, which are delivered consistently through a timetabled programme. These approaches complement each other holistically; the CLDD engagement for learning resources enables the staff to measure and gain essential information on how individual children engage in these activities and how best to personalize their learning pathways. In the following case study, the engagement resources show the impact of Developmental, Individual-Difference, Relationship-based model (DIR®/Floortime) (Greenspan and Wider 2009) on engagement for learning in other areas.

Case study: Tim

Tim is a three-year-old boy who lives with his foster parents, and attends a local nursery for children who have a physical disability and additional needs. His SEN statement lists the cause of his learning difficulties as significant global developmental delay with significant sensory needs – probably a result of complex medical/health, physical, speech/language/communication and social/emotional/behavioural needs. He also displays traits commonly associated with autistic spectrum disorders. He was separated from his birth mother at an early age, and had little experience of nurturing and interaction with others until he was placed with his present foster parents at the age of two years. Consequently, he became distressed when held or hugged. He has hyper-mobile joints which frequently lead to dislocation of his knees.

At his local nursery, Tim was able to sit unsupported on the floor, and could crawl and climb with physical support. The nursery had a number of provision objectives for Tim, and an important aim was for him to develop meaningful communication and interaction with staff and peers at the nursery. However, he showed little interest in people or his nursery environment. He appeared to be distressed most of his time in nursery, and consequently staff struggled to communicate and interact effectively with him. He was very sensory-orientated and would only engage in activities that give him the sensory feedback he craved. If activities lacked some form of sensory feedback, Tim would self-harm by dislocating his knees despite the obvious pain this caused him. Tim was also at risk of self-injury due to his sensory craving; for example, packing food or non-food items such as small stones solidly under his top lip to gain deep pressure.

The adults working with Tim needed to find out what motivated him so they could engage him in interaction and communication. By observing Tim in nursery activities, staff found that he was most engaged during sensory story-telling sessions, when the story-teller would link sensory experiences to a simple story. Although he did not appear to understand the story, Tim became animated when the story-teller interacted with him using a water spray or when she swung a rattle toy near him. Tim's high engagement behaviours in this activity were recorded on his Engagement Profile illustrating how he behaved when he was showing awareness, curiosity, investigation, etc. Having this record of high engagement behaviours for Tim allowed all educators to recognize the level of engagement that he could potentially show in other activities/lessons, and recognize features from his high engagement activities that could be transferred to other activities to increase his engagement in them.

Trampoline and Art sessions were low engagement activities for Tim. The nursery staff wanted him to be able to enjoy and engage with them. However, he would begin to cry as soon as he saw the resources. Sometimes he would then continue to cry for two hours. Initial interventions led to some increase in his engagement in these activities, but staff were at a loss as to how to move forward. The nursery decided to implement DIR®/Floortime with Tim, and features that engaged Tim from his Engagement Profile – materials which made unique sounds – were included in his DIR®/Floortime sessions.

DIR®/Floortime is a form of play therapy which meets children where they are and builds upon their strengths and abilities through interacting and creating a warm relationship. It challenges them to develop as individuals irrespective of any learning difficulty. DIR®/Floortime is used to excite a child's interests, draw them to connect to a key adult, and to challenge them to be creative, curious and spontaneous – all of which move them forward intellectually and emotionally. (As children get older, DIR®/Floortime morphs into an exciting, back-and-forth time of exploring the child's ideas.) This approach is particularly complementary to the Engagement Profile and Scale as it looks at what motivates the child and how to use their strengths to move forward in learning.

Using the Engagement Profile and Scale (see Chapter 4), the evidence collected by Tim's staff from the Art and Trampoline sessions following the introduction of DIR®/Floortime seems to indicate that a significant improvement in Tim's engagement with interacting with others and in learning dated from the introduction of DIR®/Floortime sessions into his curriculum (see Figures 10.4 and 10.5); his engagement in the sessions increased significantly.

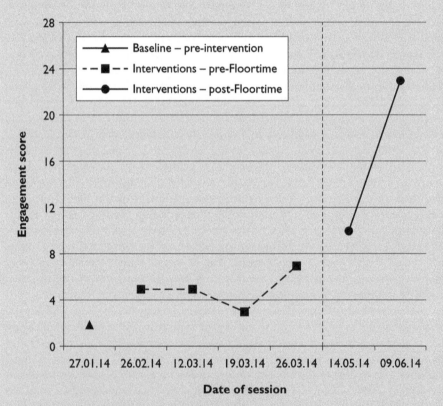

Figure 10.4 Graph showing Tim's engagement scores for Art (intervention period: 17 January–9 June 2014). The vertical dotted line indicates the introduction of DIR®/Floortime sessions into Tim's curriculum (28 April 2014).

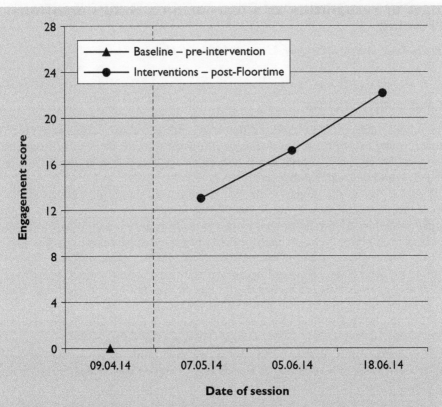

Figure 10.5 Graph showing Tim's engagement scores for Trampolining (intervention period: 9 April–18 June 2014). The vertical dotted line indicates the introduction of DIR®/Floortime sessions into Tim's curriculum (28 April 2014).

Following the DIR®/Floortime intervention, Tim became more settled in nursery. Staff began to understand how to communicate and interact with him, and he enjoyed short bursts of interaction with them. His level of self-harm reduced significantly. His foster parents also mentioned a change in Tim's behaviour at home – they felt he was becoming less stressed and more inquisitive.

Although the evidence is not robust enough to prove that the introduction of DIR®/Floortime sessions into Tim's curriculum was the cause of the notable increase in his engagement with adults and peers during Art and Trampoline sessions, there is some indication that this may be so. The school intends to carry out future evidence collection with other children to investigate the possible impact of DIR®/Floortime further.

Impact of recognition as a learner on a child's emotional well-being

Dr Phyllis Jones, Associate Professor, University of South Florida

Case study: Julius

Julius is an eight-year-old little boy with a huge smile and equally large heart. He is, now, a young boy with a sense of humour who loves to tease, manipulate situations and play. He has been formally diagnosed with a Pallister-Killian Syndrome, a rare genetic syndrome, and is ambulatory.

Prior to using the Engagement Profile and Scale, and the reason for its implementation, Julius was introverted and refused to let anyone within close proximity of him. He would either remove himself from an area and/or begin crying and shaking his body back and forth in refusal when asked to participate in a classroom activity. He would engage in self-stimulating behaviour by engaging in play with his saliva. Once this began, he would become so engrossed within it that even walking became dangerous. His teacher felt as though she was not able to reach him and desperately wanted to figure out how to meet his needs.

Through the Engagement Profile and Scale, a series of collaborative video analyses was conducted by educators on four-minute video clips that portrayed Julius engaging independently within an area of his choice. We soon found patterns, schemas and objects that Julius was attracted to. His affinity for certain colours and his desire to self-direct his activities were duly noted.

Upon determining this, strengths and interventions were discussed and introduced into his low engagement learning activities. Using colour overlays and by allowing Julius to initiate activities, he began to participate in classroom-based lessons that were once a struggle even to begin.

Using Julius' preferences, we extended our investigation using the Engagement Profile and Scale. We began to focus on communication, giving him even more control over his environment. As the school began to take account of who Julius was as a learner, his behaviours started to change both in the classroom and at home. He became far more independent in many areas. His learning progressed rapidly and by the end of the year he began to use computer programs on an ActivBoard within a group setting with a smile, intent and gumption. He also began to interact with familiar and unfamiliar adults.

Engagement = learning: an insight into implementing the Engagement for Learning Framework

Leanne Curreli, Classroom Assistant, Woodlands School, Leatherhead

Woodlands is a school for children and young people with SLD, PMLD and ASD aged 2–19 years. The Engagement Profile and Scale was introduced at Woodlands as a tool for inclusion and for assessment to gather information about new children entering the school and those facing significant barriers in their learning.

The school has now adopted the Engagement for Learning Framework long-term, through their five-year development plan, but before they did this, they trialled the approach on a small scale in the Early Years Foundation Stage (EYFS). This allowed them to address implementation questions and issues which arose in the early stages.

Class teams were trained in how to use the Engagement Profile and Scale. However, after less than a month, the staff were struggling with implementation. After some consideration a meeting was called to discuss the opportunities and challenges of the 'engagement for learning' project. After listening to questions from the staff, it became clear that for the project to be successful three major issues needed to be addressed by senior leadership:

1   Staff needed to know not only what they needed to do but *why* they needed to do it.
2   Staff needed to feel that they would benefit personally and professionally from the project.
3   Staff needed to know that the school were deeply invested in the project and prepared to support them accordingly.

In response, the senior leadership team called a meeting to answer all of the class team's questions and demonstrate sincere investment in the project both practically in terms of resources and in guidance. Through the senior leadership's commitment to the engagement for learning approach, clear guidelines, roles and expectations were developed to give a solid basis for implementation. They dedicated half (45 minutes per week) of each participating classroom assistant's non-contact time to the project. The project leader in class was paid extra hours to plan and deliver the project, and cover was organized when possible for her to complete paperwork on behalf of the team.

The Project Leader clarified aspects of delivery with the EYFS team:

- Two teaching assistants were involved with the project for every child, so they could share ideas and responsibilities and support each other.
- The engagement investigation should be in line with normal curriculum or individual education plan targets. (The engagement for learning investigation was not extra work but an essential part of ongoing work.)
- The length of the Engagement Scale observations on each child should be tailored to the child's attention span and also the length of time available to record.
- The time taken to record evidence was reduced by ensuring staff viewed the video clip of each intervention only once using a strict 'pause, point, play' video analysis protocol (i.e. watching a minute of video, pausing it, recording any relevant evidence and repeating the process until the end of the clip; no second view permitted!).
- iPads, positioned near the child's activity space, were used to capture short video clips for analysis (the 'camera reverse' option was used to check positioning) so an additional person to video was not needed.
- If staff felt uncomfortable being in the video, the camera was positioned to capture the child's actions alone.
- All Engagement Scales were completed electronically and stored on the intranet in an access-restricted folder. This evidence was used to support teaching and learning for the child.
- Family liaison supported the two-way exchange of useful information to support the engagement for learning investigation.

- The project leader would answer questions or questions were raised at the weekly meeting of participating staff.

The main findings from the end-of-project questionnaire demonstrated how the staff team felt about the project and how it was managed after the changes were made:

- There was whole-team agreement that personal and professional reflection and practice had improved during the project. The team also reported feeling listened to and valued, and therefore felt that they had made a valid contribution in shaping the project.
- Every member of the team thought they would continue to use the Engagement for Learning Framework and noted a significant positive difference in how it was managed following the changes described above.
- Finally, weekly meetings for the team to discuss any aspects of the project, share evidence, motivate staff and implement future interventions were considered the most valuable way of extending and embedding excellent practice. This outcome was noted particularly by staff because it improved practice to a level that helped every child in the class, whether they had been involved with the Framework or not.

Following the pilot, the school decided to embed the Engagement for Learning Framework long-term. Realistically they found it was better to stop interventions after five weeks to give staff a chance to naturally implement the effective ones.

Conclusion

Through the Engagement for Learning Framework, the CLDD Project aimed to provide educators with the means to develop sustainable and personalized learning pathways for children with CLDD. By setting up a structure through which educators begin by discovering how individual children *do* learn – carrying out observations, talking with involved adults and, when possible, talking with the children with CLDD themselves. In this way, the children are given a voice (even if they cannot articulate this themselves) in establishing 'the way I can learn' as educators begin to customize their teaching from the student's perspective through determining effective pedagogical approaches that match children's learning abilities, strengths and interests. One assistant headteacher commented:

> The [Engagement for Learning] tools have already had a positive impact on pupil voice for person-centred annual review and on our focus for learning during lesson observations. . . . One of the most significant uses is that these pupils with CLDD now have a very positive profile that can be one of the first things people get to know about them – giving them a voice and a tool for people to focus on their abilities and positives rather than their complexities!

Engagement can be described as the liberation of intrinsic motivation. Therefore we must ask, 'How do we release that motivation?', 'How do we increase the participation of the child?'. Engagement for learning empowers, makes stronger and moves the child from a position of vulnerability to resilience. Asking the question, 'How do we unlock their curiosity?' will in itself enable educators to take children with CLDD with them on their journey of inquiry as learners.

References

Greenspan, S. and Wider, S. (2009) *Engaging Autism: Using the Floortime Approach to help children relate, communicate, and think*, Cambridge, MA: Da Capo Lifelong Books.

Nind, M. and Hewett, D. (2006) *Access to Communication: Developing the basics of communication for people who have severe learning disabilities through Intensive Interaction* (2nd edn), London: David Fulton.

UNICEF (2001) 'Many pathways of learning'. In UNICEF (2001) 'The learner'. [Online at: www.unicef.org/teachers/learner/; accessed: 20.07.14.]

Watkins, C. (2011) *Learning: A sense-maker's guide*, London: Association of Teachers and Lecturers.

Welsh Assembly Government (2006) *Routes for Learning Assessment Booklet: Assessment materials for learners with profound learning difficulties and additional disabilities*, Cardiff: Qualifications and Curriculum Group, Department for Education.

Instructions on completing the Engagement Ladders

(http://complexld.ssatrust.org.uk/project-resources/engagement-profile-scale.html).

The Engagement Ladders are used to identify which children will most benefit from working with the Engagement for Learning Framework and the low-engagement areas/subjects will be most useful to focus on (see Figure A.1).

Ladder 1 – Whole Class Ladder: identifying children who will most benefit

Look at the various levels of engagement down the left hand side of the ladder, and reflect where each child in your class is on the ladder in terms of their general engagement for learning across their learning environments. (This can be inside or outside the classroom.)

Write the children's names in the 'Student Names' column at the level you feel is appropriate.

Ladder 2 – Individual Student Ladder: deciding where to focus interventions with an individual child

Select a child from Ladder 1. You will need to work on engagement for learning with children at the lower levels first, preferably a child who is 'Partly engaged', has 'Emerging/fleeting' engagement or is demonstrating 'No focus' in learning.

If you are using the Engagement for Learning Framework for the first time, we advise that you do not choose to work with a child who is completely disengaged ('No focus') as this will be your most challenging child. Choose a child from those who are 'Partly engaged' or have 'Emerging/fleeting' engagement. It will help to become familiar with the process and the paperwork before working with very challenging children.

Write your selected child's name and the date at the top of the Engagement Ladder document.

On Ladder 2

Complete an overview of the selected child's engagement across their learning areas (e.g. lessons, activities, subjects or tasks) by writing the name of individual areas at the appropriate engagement level.

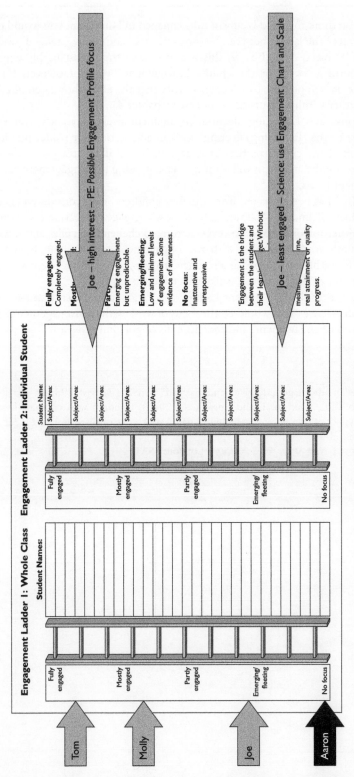

Figure A.1 An illustration of the process of selecting a child who will benefit from working with the Engagement Profile and Scale

For example, if you think the child is almost fully engaged in Numeracy, you would place them towards the top of the ladder between 'Mostly engaged' and 'Fully engaged', writing 'Numeracy' in the 'Subject/Area' box. *If* this is also one of their most highly engaged activities it *could* form a focus for the child's Engagement Profile. However, for the Engagement Profile, it is important to select an activity that the child shows genuine high engagement in whether within or outside school (see Chapter 4).

If the child demonstrates 'Emerging/fleeting' engagement levels in Literacy, you would write 'Literacy' next to the 'Emerging/fleeting' section, and so on. The ladder provides a visual representation of the child's pattern of engagement and illustrates where they are least engaged. These are the areas you will want to focus on using the Engagement Scale to raise their engagement levels.

In Figure A.1, 'Joe' has been selected from the four children being considered (Ladder 1: Whole Class Ladder). Tom and Molly are at least mostly engaged in learning, so you will want staff time to either Joe or Aaron. However, Aaron is a challenging child, and it would be better to wait until you are familiar with the Engagement for Learning Framework before using it to address his needs. Joe has a real need to improve his levels of engagement, and, for a first time user of the resources, is likely to be more responsive.

From the completed 'Individual Student Ladder' for Joe, it can be seen that he is only fleetingly engaged in Science. This would be the focus of work with the Engagement Scales to try to raise his level of engagement, and therefore his opportunity to learn.

References

Carpenter, B. (2010) 'Disadvantaged, deprived and disabled', *Special Children*, 193: 42–45.

Carpenter, B., Cockbill, B., Egerton, J. and English, J. (2010) 'Children with complex learning difficulties and disabilities: developing meaningful pathways to personalised learning', *The SLD Experience*, Autumn: 3–10.

Hargreaves, D. (2006) *A New Shape for Schooling?*, London: SSAT.

Appendix B

Complex Learning Difficulties and Disabilities Briefing Packs

(http://complexld.ssatrust.org.uk/project-resources/cldd-briefing-packs.html)

The CLDD Briefing Packs are an information resource to support educators in developing interventions to support children's engagement for learning. They identify the main learning barriers, learning needs and key teaching strategies associated with specific conditions which often co-exist in children with CLDD, such as autism, sensory impairment, etc.

The ten Briefing Packs focus on learning implications in the following areas:

1 Fetal Alcohol Spectrum Disorders (FASD)
2 Attachment
3 Premature birth
4 Rare chromosome disorders
5 Attention deficit hyperactivity disorder (ADHD)
6 Sensory impairment
7 Fragile-X syndrome
8 Mental health
9 Autism
10 Effects of drug use and smoking during pregnancy.

Each Briefing Pack contains three sections:

1 a 4–6-page 'briefing sheet' to give class leaders an overview of the condition and guidance on teaching and learning strategies; this will provide the class teacher with enough background on the learning implications for a child with this condition to enable them to prepare initial teaching and learning strategies (e.g. for a child coming into their class);
2 a 1–2-page classroom support sheet to equip an educator providing unexpected, short-term support to a child with the condition; the sheet provides a 'must have', quick-access list of strategies for working immediately with the child;
3 a 6–10-page information sheet that provides more in-depth information about the condition, together with guidance on further reading and other resources, for the educator who has a greater level of need for or interest in more detailed information about the condition.

Due to the frequent overlap of conditions in CLDD, one pack alone may not provide adequate information about supporting a child. Therefore the briefing sheets should be only a starting point for practitioners working with a child, until a personalized learning pathway can be established for that child. It is important to be aware of the unique learning needs of children with CLDD.

Sharing the information from the CLDD Briefing Packs with families and professionals from other disciplines as well as educators will enable a greater insight into the challenges experienced by learners. It is important that the appropriate professionals are consulted about integrated targets and interventions around issues such as positioning, sensory integration and arousal levels, health and medication.

Schools involved in the CLDD Project used the Briefing Packs in a variety of ways to support continuing professional development, staff induction and families' information needs. One mainstream school teacher wrote:

> I have shared the sheets with a spectrum of professionals from student teachers, TAs, teachers and professionals in that area, but they have been relevant to all of them. With three types [of sheet], the packs are useful for all types of staff no matter what their level of knowledge.

Appendix C

The Inquiry Framework
for Learning

(http://complexld.ssatrust.org.uk/project-resources/inquiry-framework-for-learning.
html)

Some children with CLDD come to a point in their educational lives where their educators
stop asking questions about how to engage them – because they are plain out of questions!
They have asked all the questions they can think of about how the child may learn; they
have posed possible solutions, but none have worked.

However, for the vast majority of children with CLDD there are learning solutions; it is
a case of asking ourselves, and crucially others (e.g. families, multidisciplinary colleagues,
the child themselves if possible), the question or questions which unlock the information
we need. The Inquiry Framework for Learning is an online resource designed to support
this.

The Inquiry Framework for Learning is organized in two sections:

1   Preliminary profile
2   Inquiry areas.

The 'Preliminary profile', if fully completed, will result in a foundation document for the
educator's learning inquiry which draws together information from a range of adults who
know the child well.

The 12 'Inquiry areas' (see Figure C.1) suggest pathways for inquiry into the learning of
children with CLDD through 'starter questions' for systematic reflection and discussion by
staff. Educators may find either the questions are helpful in themselves or that they stimulate
creative debate and solution finding.

A mouse-click to access an individual inquiry area will reveal that each area is prefaced by
a set of headings that act as short cuts to related question sets. Figure C.2 shows one of the
multiple question sets below the list of headings. The question sets may have several frames
and are designed so that educators can scroll or navigate the frames within the set. Educators
can create a list of their questions of interest by checking the boxes beside the questions,
and then clicking on the grey 'Click here to save and present your selected questions' bar
below the question set.

The Inquiry Framework for Learning also has links to 'progress' and 'audit' forms on the
inquiry area selection page that give educators a means of recording, demonstrating and
justifying their valuable and sometimes time-consuming inquiry process. This process is an
integral part of creating a child's personalized learning pathway; if the lines of inquiry are

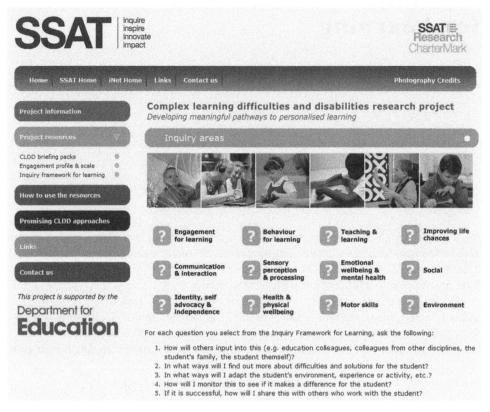

Figure C.1 The 12 inquiry areas of the Inquiry Framework for Learning

not successful, educators will have evidence of what they have tried, and what does not work.

The Inquiry Framework for Learning evolved from exploratory questions asked by educators involved in the CLDD Project which led to the development of successful strategies in engaging children with CLDD in learning. The Inquiry Framework for Learning resources capture problem solving, fix attention and channel focus. Further guidance on how to use the Inquiry Framework for Learning can be found at the website listed above.

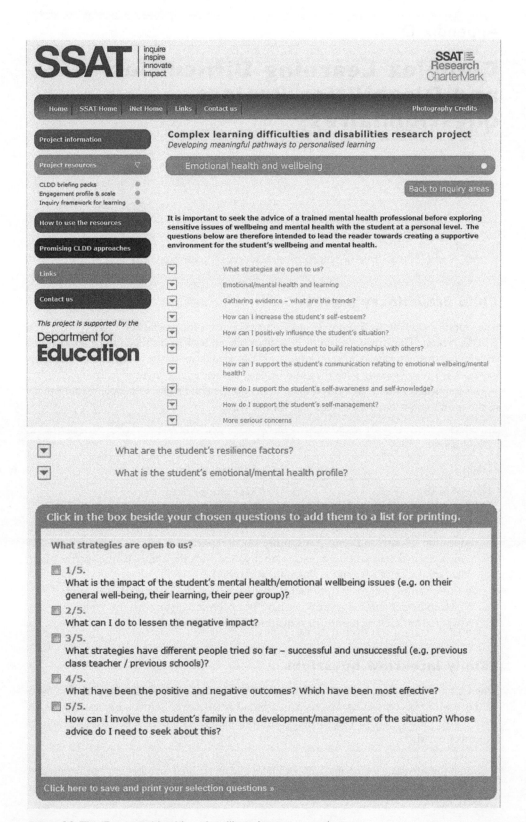

Figure C.2 The 'Emotional health and wellbeing' inquiry area layout

Complex Learning Difficulties and Disabilities Project questionnaires

(http://complexld.ssatrust.org.uk/project-resources/preliminary-profiling.html)

Child preliminary profile

The questions below were used to gain an initial learning profile for each child in the CLDD Project. The answers given by educators related back to detailed information about the child in their education files and educators' knowledge about the child. The information gained was key in working with the child to deepen their engagement in learning.

It is important to date all written documents on the child's file, so people reading them in the future know when they were true for the child.

Child name:	School name:
Date:	Completed by:
Date of birth:	Year group/class:

1   What are the child's identified conditions/needs (as articulated in statements of SEN, Education, Health and Care Plans, professional reports, etc.)
2   Which professionals and/or agencies are involved with the child on an ongoing basis?
3   What are the child's strengths (learning and others)?
4   Are there any strategies or approaches that have been successful with this child?
5   Which strategies and/or approaches have not been successful with this child?
6   What are the 'sticking points' or difficulties for this child?

Family interview questions

When establishing a baseline profile for a child, it is important to gather information from all those who know the child well to gain a broad perspective. Below are questions which were used in the CLDD Project when consulting family members. They were chosen so educators could:

•   Gain the parents'/guardians' view of their child as a valued member of their family, and
•   Find out what parents/guardians felt about how their child learned at home and at school.

The bulleted points underneath the main questions are prompts for the interviewer and should be phrased in a way that is tactful and does not suggest a specific answer.

CONFIDENTIAL

Child name:	School name:
Date:	Completed by:
Date of birth:	Year group/class:

1 How would you describe [*child's name*] to me?
2 On a good day, how does s/he relax at home?
3 [*If not covered above*] What makes [*child's name*] most happy? Or what does s/he enjoy most?
4 [*If not covered above*] What does [*child's name*] least like?
5 Parents are their child's first teacher, helping them to learn things at home. What ways did you find were best for helping [*child's name*] to learn?

   • *When younger/now*

6 At home, when does [*child's name*] concentrate/focus/get involved the most? What kinds of things do you do to help him/her to focus more?
7 What do you think/feel about how [*child's name*] is learning in school at the moment?

   • *Is there anything that you would like to see added or changed in school to help [child's name]?*

8 What experiences during [*child's name*]'s schooling particularly stand out for you?

   • *Positive/negative*

9 What are your main hopes for [*child's name*]'s education?

   • *Short/medium term; future outcomes*

10 What have been your happiest or favourite moments so far with [*child's name*]?

Professional interview questions

An interdisciplinary perspective may come from any professionals or external agencies that are involved with the child. They may include: nurses and medical professionals, therapists (e.g. occupational, speech and language, art, physio), child and adolescent mental health professionals, educational psychologists, social workers, and so on. It generally refers to any specialist involved with the child aside from educators and family members.

   Below are questions which were used in the CLDD Project when consulting other professionals. They were chosen to:

• Gain professional perspectives about their contribution to the child's education as part of an interdisciplinary or trans-disciplinary team;

- Invite professionals to share their views about the most effective way to work with the child and their class team.

CONFIDENTIAL

Child name:	School name:
Date:	Completed by:
Date of birth:	Year group/class:

1   Please briefly describe the background of your involvement with [*child's name*].
2   Describe how you currently work with the school in meeting [*child's name*]'s needs? What do you feel/think about this way of working?
3   What opportunities do you have to meet/work with parents, teaching staff and other professionals to discuss [*child's name*]'s needs, targets and strategies?

- *What are the barriers to this?*
- *How do you think this could be achieved sustainably/effectively?*

4   From your professional perspective, what are the key areas of need for [*child's name*]?
5   How do you think [*child's name*]'s needs might impact on his/her learning in the classroom?

- *From your professional perspective, what needs to be in place to help [*child's name*] in the learning context?*

6   What are your current key targets for [*child's name*], if any?
7   What targets for [*child's name*] are shared with his/her teaching staff/family?

- *How did you do this?*
- *How do you ensure consistency of approach?*

8   What strategies do you use to encourage [*child's name*] to engage with you?

- *Which are the most successful?*

Appendix E

Accessible Research Cycle template

The Accessible Research Cycle (Jones et al. 2012) is described in Chapter 9. This template (Figure E.1) can be photocopied and enlarged for educators to complete.

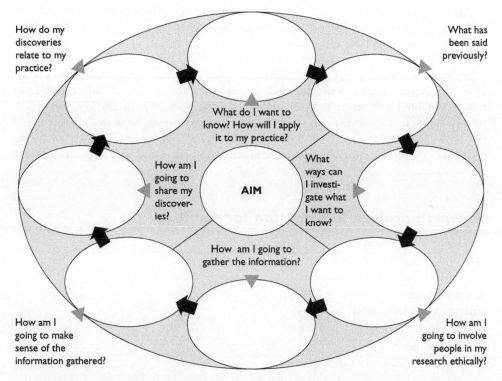

How do my discoveries relate to my practice?

What has been said previously?

What do I want to know? How will I apply it to my practice?

How am I going to share my discoveries?

AIM

What ways can I investigate what I want to know?

How am I going to gather the information?

How am I going to make sense of the information gathered?

How am I going to involve people in my research ethically?

Figure E.1 Accessible Research Cycle template for educators involved in school-based inquiry

Source: Adapted from Jones et al. 2012

Reference

Jones, P., Whitehurst, T. and Egerton, J. (eds) (2012) *Creating Meaningful Inquiry in Inclusive Classrooms*, London: Routledge.

Project information and consent form relating to the Complex Learning Difficulties and Disabilities Project

Below are examples of the 'Research information for families' and the 'Parent/guardian consent form' formats used by the CLDD Research Project (November 2009–August 2011). They may act as a guide to the areas that should be covered. Educators will need to customize the information to suit their inquiry project, and may want to create a completely different format. However, whatever the format, the content needs to include broadly the same areas so parents/guardians have full information about the inquiry project, how it will affect them and their child, and their rights.

It is important to remember that some parents with literacy/communication difficulties may need a simpler or different language version, a symbolled version or to have the inquiry implications and their rights explained in a face-to-face conversation, preferably by someone independent of the project so they do not feel pressurized to give consent. Also, in the case of children whose parents are separated, both parents may still have full parental responsibilities and rights and/or maintain contact with their child; tactful inquiries will need to be made to find out if one or both parents should be consulted.

Research project information for families

Name of research project:
[insert inquiry project name]

Research dates:
[Insert appropriate dates]

Research team:
[Names, roles and contact details]

Introduction to the research project and an invitation to take part

This leaflet gives a brief description of the research project, what it will mean for you and your child if you decide to take part. We hope you will find the information you need in the questions and answers below, but please contact us if there is anything else you would like to know.

1. What is the project about?

[Insert a short description of what the project is about. For example: 'We are developing excellent educational practice with children with Complex Learning Difficulties and Disabilities based on personalizing their learning . . .', then describe what you hope the outcome of your project will be.]

2. What do we mean by [insert one or more terms used that families may not understand]?

[For example, to explain 'complex learning difficulties and disabilities' you might write: 'Within our project, a child described as having 'complex learning difficulties and disabilities' has two or more education, health and/or care needs. The child may also have a range of other difficulties (e.g. communication, social, behavioural, physical and/or sensory difficulties). They may use forms of communication other than speech (e.g. signing, symbols, etc.). They will need involvement from two or more support professionals (e.g. social worker, therapist, psychologist, etc.).']

3. If I agree for my child to take part in this project, what would happen?

[Educator name/job title] is leading the project together with [names/job title/organization]. They would work with you and your child to find out . . . [For example: 'which teaching and learning approaches suit them best, and also talk to other professionals working regularly with your child. They would trial different ways of increasing your child's learning.']

4. What are the benefits for your child?

Between [dates], your child would . . . [For example: 'have a range of people looking at different ways to improve their opportunities to learning. The information collected would not only help your child, but also children or young people with Complex Learning Difficulties and Disabilities within and outside our school.']

5. What are the risks?

[Insert text relating to your project. For example: 'Your child may indicate occasionally or regularly that they do not want to work on the project activities. If this happens, and they do not respond to gentle encouragement, their choice will be respected. The person working most regularly with your child will be a teacher from your child's school. Occasionally [name/job title/organization] may meet your child. All people working with your child will have a current Disclosure and Barring Service check. They will abide by your child's school's policies.']

6. What if I do not want my child to take part?

You do not have to give your permission for your child to take part, and may withdraw your permission at any time during the project without prejudice.

7. What happens to the information about my child collected during the project?

All information about your child collected during the project will be confidential to the people listed above and your child's school. Nothing will be disclosed outside the school in any way that will identify you or your child without your consent. All information, whether electronic or physical, will be held securely. Copies of written and recorded information relating to you or your child will be available to you on request.

8. Who else is taking part?

[Describe participant groups in non-specific terms, e.g. numbers, ages, learning difficulties of children, etc., but no names]

9. What if something goes wrong?

You will be free to withdraw your permission for your child to take part at any time.

10. What happens at the end of the project?

At the end of the project, the findings may be shared in a written report. They will also be shared through articles and presentations with:

- families and schools whose young people have taken part;
- other professionals who work with children and young people with [insert appropriate text. For example: 'severe and complex learning difficulties'] and related jobs.

11. What if I have more questions or do not understand something?

You may contact your school or a member of the project team using the information on the front of this leaflet at any time.

12. What happens now if I decide that my child can take part?

You will be asked to sign a statement that you have read, accept and understand the information in this leaflet, and agree to different types of information about your son/ daughter being collected. All personal data will remain confidential within the project team.

13. What happens if I change my mind during the project?

You may withdraw your permission at any time without prejudice.

14. Expenses

There will be no monetary outlay for the child or family. [If this is not the case, insert the appropriate text.]

Letter requesting parent/guardian consent for their child's participation

This request for parent/guardian consent is an example of one format that can be used; educators may prefer their own format, but it should cover the same types of areas. Some tips for increasing the likelihood of parents/guardians responding to the request for consent, include:

- speaking to parents/guardians about the project and letting them know to expect the request – make sure they know they have the right not to give permission without prejudice;
- enclosing a stamped addressed envelope for return of the consent form;
- sending two copies of the consent form so they can keep one;
- setting a 'return by' date, and letting them know that if a reply does not arrive someone will contact them to confirm whether or not they would like their child to take part;
- sending a reminder just before the deadline date to parents/guardians who have not replied.

Example of a letter requesting consent

Dear

[Insert title of project/dates of project]

Our school is involved in . . .

[Insert name of research project, the purpose of the project and likely benefit for children. Include two or three sentences listing any other organizations/people involved and their role and purpose.]

Please find enclosed with this letter an information sheet which will tell you more about the research project, and give the contact details of the project team. The information sheet also describes you and your child's rights concerning participation in this project.

We would like to ask for your permission for your child to be involved in this project. If you agree to your child's participation, the project team will:

[Insert text. For example:

- read information about your child's needs and learning;
- work with your child using an 'engagement approach', which personalizes learning for your child;
- develop learning resources for your child;
- observe your child during the school day;
- seek you and your child's views or preferences; and
- collect information related to your child's learning.]

The project team will at all times operate within school policies, and have the well-being of your child at the heart of all activities. Everyone on the project team who has contact with your child will have a current Disclosure and Barring Service check.

Any information which identifies your child will be kept confidential to the project team and school, and only [people's job titles/organizations], and the school will have access to it. If the project team wish to use it outside the project (e.g. as part of an article or presentation) they will ask for your permission before doing so. Information identifying your child will be anonymized and kept securely. You have the right to see any of the information relating to him or her.

At the end of the project, the outcomes will be available in a project report. The project team will send a copy to you.

If you would like to find out more about the project or have any questions, please contact the project team.

To give your permission, please complete one copy of the form(s) attached and return it to [insert contact name and details]. Please keep the copy(ies) for your records.

With kind regards

[Name, job description, professional contact details]

Example of a consent form for a child's participation
CONSENT FORM FOR YOUR CHILD'S PARTICIPATION IN

[Insert title of project/dates of project]

Once you have read and understood the project information leaflet and this form please complete the following. (If you have further questions contact [insert contact details].):

	Please tick to show your response:	*Yes*	*No*
1	I understand the aims of the research project, and agree that my child can participate.		
2	I have received and understood the information explaining the project.		
3	I understand I may withdraw my child from the project at any time, without prejudice.		
4	I understand that everything that is recorded shall remain confidential to the project, and that nothing will be reported to people outside the project in any way that could identify me or my son/daughter without my permission.		

If you would like to talk to someone further about the project, please tick here   ☐

Child's name . . . .

Address . . . .

I agree to my child taking part in the research project as described in this letter.

Signature . . . . Date . . . .

I am this child's parent/legal guardian . . . .(please sign)

Print name . . . .

Please return this form to your child's school by [date]. Thank you.

Example of a consent form for a child to be photographed or videoed

CONSENT FOR MY CHILD TO BE VIDEO OR PHOTOGRAPHED DURING

[Insert title of project/dates of project]

During the course of the research project, we would like to collect video and still camera evidence to support the project findings around [insert text. For example: 'teaching and learning strategies for your child'.]

This letter is to ask for your permission to video or photograph your child over the course of the inquiry project. Any videos or photographs we take of your child will be held securely in a locked cabinet or in a secure computer filing system.

It will be seen only by the school, the project team and their advisors. If, at a later date, we would like to use your child's photo in a report, article or presentation, we will ask for your permission to do so first.

You may withdraw your permission for your child to be videoed or photographed at any time without prejudice.

If you want to give your permission, please would you sign, date and return one copy of this form to [insert name/job title/contact details], and keep the other for your own reference.

PERMISSION FOR MY CHILD TO BE VIDEO OR PHOTOGRAPHED FOR

[Insert title of project/dates of project]

I give/do not give (please delete unwanted words) my permission for the [insert name of project] team to take still and video camera pictures of my child during the [insert title of project/dates of project].

I understand that:

• any photographic material taken will be held securely;
• only the school, the project team and their advisors will have access to the material;

- I will be asked for my permission if the project team wants to show or print the video/ still images outside this group; and
- I can withdraw my permission at any time without prejudice.

Child's name . . . .

Address. . . . .

Signature. . . . . Date. . . . .

I am this child's legal guardian. . . . . (Please sign)

Print name. . . . .

Please return this form to your child's school by [date]. Thank you.

Engagement passport example from Parkside School, Pukekohe, New Zealand

Engagement passport: Annabelle[1]

Hi, I'm Annabelle and here is some information about me and what helps me engage in learning . . .

I like to move! My favourite activities are spending time on the swing or slide. It is difficult for me to sit still and do a task, and I may wander around the room, spin on a chair or bounce on an exercise ball. This movement (known as vestibular input) helps me self-regulate. Without access to movement I find it difficult to concentrate.

Being able to move while doing a learning task can help me concentrate when I am working. This will help me stay at my desk and provide what I need to self-regulate my behaviour. The best way for me to get this movement is to be seated on a peanut ball (see Figure G.1).

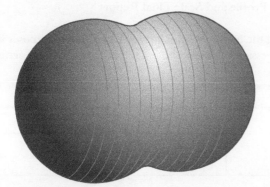

Figure G.1 Peanut ball

---

1 Illustrate with photos of child engaged in relevant activities.

Parkside School's 'Engagement Profile and Scale Final Report' template

This report format is used by Parkside School, Pukekohe, New Zealand to support their educators in writing reports on their child's engagement outcomes.

PARKSIDE SCHOOL
"Homai Te Aroha"
TEACHING PEOPLE WITH SPECIAL NEEDS

Engagement Profile and Scale Final Report

This report is CONFIDENTIAL and the information in it is restricted to the purposes for which it is intended. If you are in possession of this report and it is not for you please return it to Parkside School.

Child's name:	Date of birth:
Date of programme delivery: *(e.g. 'Terms 1 & 2, 2013')*	Date of report:
Report compiled by:	

Team members:

Name(s):	Position/Job description *(e.g. 'Class Teacher')*

Background

The Engagement Profile and Scale Pro-gramme (EPS hereafter) enables us to better understand the learning needs of an individual student. It encourages us to reflect upon, and inquire into, our own practice in order to plan more effectively and create personalized learning pathways. A personalized learning pathway enables the

This standard text is personalized with the child's name and programme details.

student to better engage with their learning (or learning environment) leading to 'deeper learning'.

The process begins by observing and videoing the student engaged in a highly engaging preferred activity (such as water play, music, sensory activities). Following this, the highly engaging activity session is repeated with aspects of it altered. These sessions are videoed and reviewed by a team who complete the Engagement Scale. This review and inquiry process allows us to truly grasp what it is that engages the student and hence informs our practice at a deeper level. The entire process is student-led and often reveals beneficial findings.

<Name> has been involved in the EPS over the past <Insert months/terms> and a total of <Insert number of sessions> sessions were conducted and videoed. These videos were reviewed by a team who undertook an inquiry process and engaged in reflective practice so as to explore potential avenues for personalized learning pathways.

Programme outline

Why did you do the EPS with this student? Which learning activity did you want to raise their engagement in? What was their engagement target? What were their barriers to learning? (NOTE: Remember to write this from a positive perspective as opposed to a deficit one.) What was their high engagement activity (Engagement Profile)? How did you use this to raise the engagement in the low

This section is fully personalized using (then deleting!) the italic prompts.

engagement activity? What did you do in the engagement process? (Provide an overview of the EPS process, you could explain some of the 'next steps' or the process of Teaching as Inquiry.) What was your line of inquiry? (Give some examples of your inquiry questions or 'focus inquiry'.) Feel free to insert some pictures in this section.

Findings

Share some of the WOW moments or results of the EPS sessions. What did you learn about the student's learning pathway?

Insert the EPS graph to demonstrate the impact of the project on the student's learning.

Conclusion

What are the relevant findings resulting from the EPS programme? How will these be incorporated into the students' personalized learning programmes? You could also include some reflections and input from the rest of the team, for example: 'I believe this programme has benefited <Name> *in a number of ways.* He/she *is more communicative,* he/she *is enthusiastic about working, and* he/she *is energetic and willing to do tasks* he/she *doesn't like . . .'* <Name (job title)>*.*

In what way, if any, has being part of the EPS team informed your/your team's/the school's practice (or may in the future) in regards to working with the student?

Schools involved in the original Complex Learning Difficulties and Disabilities Research Project (2009–2011)

Abbey Hill School, Stockton-on-Tees
Alfreton Park School, Derbyshire
All Saints CE School, Weymouth
Allenvale School, Christchurch, New Zealand
Applefields School, York
Arbour Vale School, Slough
Arohanui School, Auckland, New Zealand
Bardwell School, Bicester
Beacon Hill School, Wallsend
Bettridge School, Cheltenham
Blackfriars School, Newcastle under Lyme
Bradfields School, Chatham
The Bridge School, Telford
Brookfields School, Reading
Castle Hill School, Huddersfield
Castle Tower School, Ballymena, Northern Ireland
CDC, Warstones School, Wolverhampton
Chadsgrove School, Bromsgrove
Christchurch CE Primary School, London
Colmers Farm Junior School, Birmingham
Concord School, Bundoora, Australia
Dawn House School, Rainworth
Downs View School, Brighton
Ellen Tinkham School, Exeter
Federation of Rosendale Primary School, London
Firwood School, Bolton
Fitzwaryn School, Wantage
Fosse Way School, Radstock
Garratt Park School, London
Gem Centre, Wolverhampton
George Hastwell School, Barrow-in-Furness
Gilbertstone Primary School, Birmingham
Haberdashers' Aske's Federation, London
Haybridge High School, Hagley
Highfield School, Wakefield

Highfurlong School, Blackpool
Holly Bank School, Mirfield
The Hub, Sanderson's Wynd School, Tranent, Scotland
Ifield School, Gravesend
Jack Tizard School, London
James Rennie School, Carlisle Kilton
Lakeside School, Welwyn Garden City
Lancasterian School, Manchester
LaVoy Exceptional Centre, Tampa, USA
The Manchester Health Academy, Manchester
Mapledown School, London
Marshfields School, Peterborough
Mary Rose School, Southsea
Mayfield School, Whitehaven
Meath School, Ottershaw
Merstone School, Birmingham
The Milestone School, Gloucester
Modbury School, Hope Valley, Australia
New Bridge School, Oldham
New Rush Hall School, Ilford
North Devonshire Personalised Learning Service, Barnstable
North Ridge School, Manchester
North West SILC, Leeds
Oak Field School, Nottingham
Oak Lodge School, East Finchley
Oakfield Park School, Pontefract
Orange Ridge Bullock School, Bradenton, USA
Parkside School, Pukekohe, New Zealand
Patcham House School, Brighton
Patricia Avenue School, Hamilton, New Zealand
Percy Hedley School, Newcastle Upon Tyne
Phoenix Children's Resource Centre, Bromley
Phoenix School, London
Portfield School, Haverfordwest, Wales
Portland College, Sunderland
Priory Woods School, Middlesborough
Riverside School, Orpington
RNIB Rushton School, Coventry
Robin Hood School, Birmingham
Ross High School, Tranent, Scotland
RSA Academy, Tipton
Severndale School, Shrewsbury
Sidney Stringer Academy, Coventry
Sir Charles Parsons School, Newcastle Upon Tyne
Spa School, London
Springhead School, Scarborough
St Gabriel's School, Dooradoyle, Ireland

St Luke's School, Scunthorpe
St Nicholas' School, Canterbury
St Vincent's School, Lisnagry, Ireland
St Vincent's School, Liverpool
Tiverton Primary School, Birmingham
Tiverton School, Exeter
Tor View School, Haslingden
Watergate School, London
West Exeter School, Exeter
West Gate School, Leicester
Westfield School, Bourne End
Wightwick Hall School, Wolverhampton
William Henry Smith School, Brighouse
Wilson School, Auckland, New Zealand
Wolverhampton Special Needs Early Years Service, Wolverhampton

Index

Locators to plans and tables are in *italics*.